The
Lakeland
Terrier

Other books by Seán Frain and published by Swan Hill Press

The Traditional Working Terrier

The Pet Ferret Handbook

The Patterdale Terrier

Fox Control

The
Lakeland
Terrier

SEÁN FRAIN

SWAN·HILL
PRESS

First published in the UK in 2007
by Swan Hill Quiller Press, an imprint of Quiller Publishing Ltd

British Library Cataloguing-in-Publication Data
A catalogue record for this book
is available from the British Library

ISBN 978 1 84689 001 7

Typeset by Phoenix Typesetting, Auldgirth, Dumfriesshire.
Printed in England by Cromwell Press Ltd, Trowbridge, Wiltshire.

Swan Hill Press

An imprint of Quiller Publishing Ltd
Wykey House, Wykey, Shrewsbury, SY4 1JA
Tel: 01939 261616 Fax: 01939 261606
E-mail: info@quillerbooks.com
Website: www.swanhillbooks.com

Contents

Dedicated to the memory of Willie Irving and the early LTA members – breeders of real Lakeland terriers.

Acknowledgements

My thanks must go to all who have contributed material and photographs to this publication and especially to Maud and Pearl, Billy Irving's daughters, as well as Alan Johnston of the Oregill prefix, for their generous assistance and invaluable contributions. Also, thanks to all those interviewees and their families for being so generous and hospitable as I went on my travels while researching this book. Every effort has been made to contact any photographers, or their living relatives, in order to gain permission to use some of the photographs included, but that proved an impossible task, so I must apologise in advance to anyone whom I was unable to contact and hope they will appreciate the valuable contribution their work has made to this vital record, before such data and pictorial evidence is lost forever. Many people, most of them from the fell country, have given up their time to speak to me and it is much appreciated. I must also apologise to any breeders I was unable to see, for there is limited space in any book and so I have attempted to represent the Lakeland terrier scene by remaining mainly in those parts of the country where the strains originated. Some of the photographs are old, or were taken using modest cameras, and are not of the best quality, but have been included as they are a vital part of the record regarding the origins and development of Lakeland terriers.

1 Early Working Terriers

"Ay, see the hounds with frantic zeal
The roots and earth uptear;
But the earth is strong, and the roots are long,
They cannot enter there.
Outspeaks the squire, 'Give room, I pray,
And hie the terriers in;
The warriors of the fight are they,
And every fight they win.'"

Ring-Ouzel.

Terriers have existed in the British Isles since at least the time of the invasion of the Celts and have been used in many different ways, but particularly as warriors of the fight underground, where larger dog breeds cannot hope to get. Undoubtedly these early tykes were rather nondescript, and probably rather ugly in the main, but by the mid-seventeenth century two distinct types had appeared on the scene and these were extensively used in the fight against marauding predators such as foxes, badgers and wildcats. Livestock was found at most homes at one time and foodstuffs were regularly swapped between villagers. If one household was short of meat and another of vegetables, then a swap would take place in order to balance such shortfalls. Some of it may have been sold on, but the majority would have been grown and reared for the family table and so a raiding fox, badger, wildcat, or some other predator species, could cause much damage and hardship for folk already living on the so-called 'breadline'.

Some claim that foxes and suchlike do not cause damage and hardship to those who make a living from rearing livestock, whether it be for the table, the market, or for shooting rights, but they are simply fooling themselves, as well as any who are idiotic enough to listen to them. Roger Westmoreland, a Lake District farmer and Joint-Master of the Coniston Foxhounds, is well aware of the damage marauding foxes cause, for he is a shepherd and has lambs

1

First known picture of a terrier-like dog.

taken during the springtime, though he was quick to state that badgers also cause a lot of damage to stock and many lambs taken are actually preyed upon by 'Brock', though the fox often gets the blame. Roger has had his stock taken by badger on numerous occasions. The same is true of Gary Middleton, who lives only a few miles from Windermere, in a remote valley where rock fissure and gorse provide great shelter for foxes. Gary has lost chickens on numerous occasions and the culprit has often been a badger, the tracks unmistakable in the snow. I was visiting Roger's farm during the height of lambing time and he had just had two lambs attacked by a fox. One had perished and the other was severely injured, but with tender care had recovered and was once again growing and putting on flesh, despite bad bites to the back of its head and neck. Make no mistake, foxes, and other predators such as badgers, have for centuries caused much hardship for farmers and others reliant on livestock.

For this reason terriers have been extensively used and by the mid-seventeenth century two distinct types could be found up and down the country. One had a shaggy coat and straight limbs, the other was smooth coated and had short, bent legs. Matters of history often cause much confusion, however, for Daniel, in his *Fieldsports*

A print of working terriers at end of the eighteenth century.

(late eighteenth century), makes mention of two distinct types, one of which was rough coated and short legged, long-backed and strong, with black, or yellowish colour (one can only assume this to be light tan) mixed with white (hound-marked), the other being smooth coated and having a much shorter body, being typey and reddish brown, or black with tan legs. These early descriptions of working terriers are fascinating, though rather contradictory, unless terriers had changed so much during the period of a hundred years, which I think is unlikely.

I believe there were variations of each type and while some of the same stock was smooth coated, others would be rough. Likewise, some from even the same litter would be leggy and short-coupled, while others would be short-legged and rather long in the body. There would be much variety in colour too, perhaps there being hound-marked terriers cropping up in litters of usually coloured origin. Terriers were bred simply for work and the gamest dogs would mate the gamest bitches, whatever the type involved, so terriers would come in all shapes and sizes and it wasn't until shows took off in the latter half of the nineteenth century that more selective breeding began to take place. That doesn't mean, however, that some breeders didn't favour a particular type; breeding stock in an attempt to maintain that type, for this certainly happened, long before shows became all the rage, but few would have the knowledge and skill for such practices and so a hotch-potch of type was the rule, rather than the exception. If a terrier would go to ground and work quarry found below, it was considered game and would be used to produce future game stock, regardless of type. And that is the way things stood for centuries.

Typey terriers were found early on, that is for certain, and writings and pictures tell us that this was indeed the case. The picture of old English working terriers, dated 1803, shows three types of terrier that were around and in use at the time. The one entering the earth is sandy in colour and has a rough coat and looks to be rather up on the leg. The white-bodied terrier is also rather leggy and has a powerful head with small ears, indicating bull terrier blood in its ancestry, the smooth coat also lending weight to this assumption. The third terrier, a rather poor coloured wishy-washy black and tan with some white in patches, is shorter legged and seems to have a dense, slightly broken coat, with a head more akin to a corgi. What a fascinating insight this picture provides of the type of terrier around during those early times. It is obvious that the ancestor of both the fox terrier and the fell terrier, later to produce the border and the Lakeland, are represented in this portrait of early working terriers. The short coupled earth dogs were really quite typey, though they do not have the sharp lines of the modern Lakeland terrier.

Long before foxhunting in the traditional style became the fashion, terriers were used to ground on foxes and they often accompanied a few hounds, which were used to flush and hunt the quarry, or mark it to ground. Two terriers were usually taken along, one on the large side, the other on the smaller side, for working quarry that had got itself into a tight spot. The larger terrier would be straight-legged and short coupled, the smaller bent-legged and long in the back. The terriers would flush the fox from the earth, or they would remain below ground until dug out, or, in some cases, a hard-bitten terrier would be entered and this would then finish its foe below ground (although foxes were hunted as vermin, badgers, polecats, martens, wildcats, rabbits and stoats were also on the quarry list and were hunted with hounds until more organised foxhunting began to take shape during the eighteenth century). Writings from earlier centuries tell us that, if a terrier be required to bay at and bolt a fox, or remain with it until dug out, leaving the fox unharmed in order that hounds could continue hunting it above ground, then beagle blood should be used. However, if a terrier be required to finish its fox below ground, then bull terrier blood, or early bulldog blood, should be added to the mix. The beagle blood produced hound-marked offspring and smooth, or slightly broken coats, while the bull terrier influence, or bulldog in much earlier times, would produce much harder types with good bone structure and smooth coats. Many first cross bull and terriers would be too large in the chest and so whippet blood was added to the mix in order to produce much more refined offspring. Whippet blood was undoubtedly responsible for the narrow chests of many different types of working terrier.

Many ingredients went into the mix early on and different regions began to produce different types of terrier. They were simply referred to as 'terriers', or 'working terriers' at one time, though some regions did give their name to the terrier being bred in that area. For instance, before 1881 the Airedale was known as the water-side, or the Bingley terrier. Many strains originated at a farm, a country mansion, or a hunt kennel. The type of terrier that later became known as the Jack Russell and the fox terrier, for instance, were developed at west country hunt kennels, or at residences associated with the local hunt. These terriers were game indeed and a Mr Lowes tells us of one of his terriers of a type beloved by Parson Russell, which he hunted in the south west of England:

> I possessed many years ago some very good working rough terriers and had pretty well the run of a forest and marshes to kill what I liked, bar the game. On one occasion I was hunting a stream for water-rats or what-not, when my companion, a very old friend, exclaimed: 'Look out! Boxer's got a rat!' But I saw in a moment that it was something more important. The little dog was frantic, threw his tongue, which was not his general custom, and raced under the hollow banks as if something was afoot. I said that it was a polecat, as we had killed those animals in the vicinity before, but then Boxer took to crossing and re-crossing and swimming both up and downstream. I was puzzled and never dreamt of an otter being in the country. But early days in south Devon made me observe that if otters were about, I should swear that one was here. Well, a trail seemed to lie upstream, the terrier flashing too much, over-running it and coming back again, and so on for the best part of two miles. At that point Boxer struck across a meadow and got to some gutters, then another meadow. We let him do as he liked until coming to a clump or small plantation surrounded by water. Into this we threw him and in a moment his small tongue was going, with all the sticks cracking like fire, and in less than a minute out came one of the finest otters I had ever seen in my life. He crossed to another planting before the terrier could get at him, and there, of course, we lost him. As it was four in the afternoon before we first found the trail and five o'clock when we found the otter, we calculated that the trail was at least fourteen hours old, and yet Boxer could hunt him single-handed.

Boxer was a creamy-white, rough-coated terrier bred down from Parson Russell's strain of working terrier and clearly they were wonderful workers. The abilities of terriers hasn't changed much over the years, though, for this hunt, which took place during the latter half of the nineteenth century, reminds me of a hunt with my own team of working Lakeland terriers. I was out hunting on the moors at the start of a new season and, although the broken cloud allowed a few good sunny spells during that late summer day, the wind was rather cool and carried a chill breath of colder times to come.

As we drew along the rockpiles on the side of the moor, just approaching Falcon Crag, my small pack of terriers picked up the drag of a fox and they soon began hunting keenly, right to the foot of the crag and in among the reeds for some distance, until, finally, they entered the large bracken bed close by, now following the line much more eagerly and often keeping together as a pack. Eventually, and after scent had led them all over the place, they emerged at the top of the bracken and now began climbing the steep fellside, heading out onto the open moor until, after quite a long hunt, scent began to fade, no doubt because it was more exposed here to the rays of the sun. However, there were reedbeds ahead and I drew these with my pack, hoping to rouse the fox from its daytime slumber. Scent was patchy as we progressed, until, right out on the moor, at one of the wildest and bleakest spots I hunt, they finally lost it completely and there were no signs of any fox lying up above ground. The long line of Redghyll Crags lay on the edge of the opposite moor and I guessed our fox must have headed there. And there he would remain, for this place is notorious for claiming the lives of terriers and mine would not be entered into such a death-trap.

As I was pondering what to do next, Turk picked up a scent and began hunting very keenly indeed, with the rest of the terriers quickly joining in the fun. Scent was strong and they stuck to the line well, as it took them to a narrow moorland stream. And from then on it was like watching the hunt just described by Mr Lowes, for the terriers crossed and re-crossed the stream and went up and down-stream continually, the scent stronger in some places, weaker in others. Sometimes the pace was slow, at others I was running to keep up and that is how things progressed for the next forty minutes or so until, at a large rock by the side of the stream, the terriers marked a small hole. This, of course, was no otter, but a mink and the small pack went wild to get at their quarry lurking underneath that immovable slab of granite. Digging to the mink was utterly im-possible and so, in the end, after many attempts to bolt our quarry, I was forced to give it best and leave it for another day. It had been an incredibly exciting hunt and was equally as good as a hunt with any pack of hounds. So the ability of terriers to hunt scent has not changed in the least and these examples illustrate the part-hound ancestry of our game breeds of earth dog.

Rough-coated beagles were used in the creation of terriers.

Many claim that foxhound and Celtic hound blood has played a major part in the development of our terrier breeds, and there may be some truth regarding the Celtic hound, though its influence must have been made use of thousands, rather than hundreds, of years ago, but I think it more likely that beagle blood, and, to some extent, basset blood, has played the most part in the creation of small working dogs. This would account for the smooth coat found on many terriers, though a rough coat would also be produced, for the beagle of earlier times was also rough-coated. Many may scoff at the idea of basset blood being added to the mix, but this cannot be discounted. Many terriers, even fell type terriers, of the past displayed a basset-like shape, with long backs and short, bent legs, and this may have been due to a basset influence. Do not forget, basset hounds were used for hundreds of years for the hunting and digging of badgers and so early terrier strains would not have been damaged in any way if such blood had been used. And I believe that it most certainly was used, in order to give nose and improve the tendency to work badger.

The Jack Russell and fox terriers owe quite a bit of their make-up to the basset and beagle and the markings and excellent nose, as well as the inclination to bay at, rather than attack, quarry, gives much credence to this theory. During the nineteenth century a Mr Bates kept Russell type terriers descended from Fuss, a terrier belonging to Parson Russell which saw much service with hounds. Some of this

8

family were also kept in Yorkshire during that time and they had quite a reputation for working fox and badger in that county. The Jack Russell of the latter half of the nineteenth century and the early part of the twentieth, was very popular indeed and easily beat one of its rivals, the Sealyham terrier, in the popularity stakes, though most Russell owners conceded that the Sealyham of those times was an excellent working dog. In fact, one of these early Sealyhams, a bitch of only nine pounds in weight, had proved incredibly game and had killed a fully-grown dog fox with no assistance from any other terriers. By the time of the show craze during the late nineteenth century, the Sealyham was already a well established breed, having been created by the Edwardes family of Pembrokeshire, undoubtedly using a mix of Russell type terriers, together with bull terrier and, I believe, a very old strain of mainly white terrier which came to be known as the Shropshire terrier – a hard-bitten earth dog that had a reputation for killing foxes. The Shropshire terrier was favoured by keepers and was extensively used in an attempt to keep the fox population of that county to a minimum. This breed, or strain of terrier, did not find favour with local hunts, however, for it was simply too hard and damaged, or killed, foxes, rather than bolting them unharmed and thus unhindered from giving hounds a good run. Related to these was a strain of Shropshire terrier, black and tan in colour and with a strong punishing jaw and short legs – undoubtedly a close cousin of the bull terrier.

A terrier of sixteen pounds for dogs and fourteen pounds for bitches was commonly aimed for and a height of no more than fourteen inches at the shoulder was favoured, though many terriers came bigger than this and fifteen, even sixteen inch terriers have been used both with hounds and for private digging. A leggy terrier of such heights, provided it is narrow in the shoulder and not too big in the chest, will usually get and some good 'big 'uns' have seen service at some time or another with all of the fellpacks of the Lake District. In fact, Anthony Chapman, the long-standing ex-Huntsman of the famed Coniston pack, bred some good 'big 'uns' that proved game and useful indeed, even in some of the deep borrans to be found in the Coniston hunt country. Crab, one of Anthony's best terriers, was a big black and tan which did much good work for that pack and he would kill any fox that stubbornly refused to bolt from an earth. Anthony would use Crab for lambing calls, whenever he needed the fox to be killed, rather than bolted, from an earth.

9

Russell type terriers were found mainly in the south-west of England, but their popularity increased greatly because of the growing reputation of Parson Russell and very soon this type was found in several different regions, even into Scotland where Parson Russell's strain was used with the Fife Foxhounds. Other breeds and strains, however, enjoyed strongholds in different localities and one of these was a sandy, rough-coated earth dog, similar in every way to the Irish terrier, bred and worked in Lancashire and Cheshire. In all probability these were descended from Irish terriers which had been brought to English shores during and after the great famine when a great many folk fled to more prosperous shores in search of a more secure and less troublesome life. Also, travelling Irish families would bring their terriers into these areas when they arrived in search of seasonal work on English farms. This sandy coloured strain of working terrier may well have played a part in the development of what would later become known as the Lakeland terrier.

The Elterwater terrier, said to be very much like a border, was another terrier bred in a locality and they were very popular in the west of Cumberland and probably served, not only with the West Cumberland Otterhounds, but also with the old Eskdale and Enner-dale packs before Tommy Dobson amalgamated them into just one fellpack and began hunting them with great enthusiasm such as had not been seen since the days of John Peel. The Elterwater terrier was bred in the Langdales and was simply a type of fell terrier similar to many old fashioned sorts still found in the Lakes today. Far from becoming extinct, the Elterwater terrier will have been absorbed by the Coniston district, and the Eskdale and Ennerdale district, terrier breeders.

Border type terriers were kept throughout the north-east of England and the Scottish borders and they were used in much the same way as the Lakeland bred stock – for bolting foxes and otters and for digging badgers. These had good wiry jackets that could shed water very quickly, with just one shake, but those found around the Lothians were said to have longer and less crisp coats, which may indicate more than a little influence of early working Cairn blood in their not-too-distant past. Squire Thornton of North Yorkshire also kept a strain of coloured working terrier, which had good wiry jackets and they were tan in colour with a black stripe down their backs, indicating they were carefully and selectively bred. One occasionally sees these markings even today, among fell, or Lakeland terriers, and maybe, just maybe, they are throwbacks to this strain.

Another early type of working terrier was the English white. This was truly an ancient breed and was, I am certain, the ancestor of what later became known as the fox and Jack Russell terriers, and this type existed long before a picture of 1670 depicted this particular breed of earth dog. The desired colour was all-white, but many were born with brown, or brindle, markings and this colour, as well as the strong head found on many English whites, suggests a past influence of bull terrier blood, though whippet blood was also added to the mix. Those who attempted to breed out any colour but white, succeeded in destroying this breed in the end, for constitution suffered greatly as the gene pool shrank at an alarming rate.

Idstone believed that the coloured variety was supreme, for the gene pool was much larger, and the English white lives on today in the form of the Manchester terrier, for this is simply a coloured variety, a cross between the English white and old fashioned black and tan terriers of a type that existed in this country for centuries. Pearson, the breeder of the Roocroft strain, bred Tim, one of the best of all English whites and a big winner at shows. Tim was fourteen pounds in weight and was an all-white. He was of good type, but

Very early Old English black and tan terriers. Note the bulldog influence.

11

because of his popularity many breeders had their bitches served by him and this shrank the gene pool even more.

The old English black and tan was closely related to the English white and the Manchester terrier is obviously a cross between these two breeds. This type had much more tan than black earlier on and Squire Thornton's strain of fell type terriers were obviously closely related to the black and tan, for they were similar in every way. The famous rat-killing terrier, Billy, was an Old English black and tan and he was game indeed. Even as an old dog he could kill rats swiftly. He was put against a young bitch and she was exhausted after killing just thirty rats, leaving the rest, as she was unable to carry on (a problem with condition, rather than courage). Billy was then tried and he killed fifty rats in five minutes and six seconds. Billy displayed much bull terrier blood about him and this undoubtedly aided his success as a top rat-killing terrier used in the inhumane rat pits of the time. I wonder how he would have fared in a farmyard, or out among a field of corn, with rats bolting and running all over the place and using every obstacle available to shake off their pursuers. It was in Lancashire that the Old English black and tan was enthusiastically bred and refined until the Manchester terrier at last began to emerge.

The Manchester area is renowned for its many rivers and at one time this was a stronghold for otter hunting. The largest of the rivers, the Roche and Irwell, were regularly hunted with otterhounds (many of these small packs were hounds brought together from local harrier, or foxhound packs, rather than being purebred otter-hounds), until pollution from industry drove the otter out of these areas and this form of hunting died a death long before the otter became a protected species during the 1970s. Rats then moved in in huge numbers and the riverbanks became infested with them until the 1990s when, at last, the local rivers were cleaned up and, according to some, and a friend of mine is certain of his sighting, the otter returned. Fish stocks have risen dramatically too and once again the trout is found in these waters.

It was because of these large numbers of rats found on local water-ways that the Manchester terrier came into existence, after crossing the Old English black and tan with the English white and rag whip-pets which were popular around the south Pennines at that time (the nineteenth century). It all started when John Hulme of Crumpsall crossed a dark brown terrier of the Old English black and tan type (this breed also produced a variety of colours, such as hound-

Ch. Milverton Lady – a Dandie Dinmont around the turn of the twentieth century. Teckel influence is obvious – Dandies were originally shorter-coupled and leggier.

marked, brindle and white, tan, etc.) with a local rag whippet and this was for two reasons. The sport of ratting along rivers, brooks and reservoirs, as well as the infamous rat pits at public houses, was increasingly popular, as was rabbit coursing, not only for competion, but also for putting fresh meat on the table. Hulme thought that if he crossed a whippet with a terrier, he would create a game rat killer that was also fast enough to be a type of lurcher, much the same as northern gypsies and tinkers crossed Dandie Dinmont type terriers with rag whippets in order to produce the Bedlington terrier – a dog game enough to go to ground on large quarry, yet nimble enough to catch rabbits and other game such as pheasant.

The English white showed obvious whippet influence, true, but something hardier was needed. The type that became known as the English white had been around for a long time and a fourteenth century manuscript shows one of the ancestors of this breed, depicting a terrier that Rawdon Lee describes in his book, *Fox Terriers*, saying that this terrier possesses a long, narrow head, is smooth coated and has erect ears. The colour is not discernible, but it may have been all-white, like many English terriers. True, some had heads like bull terriers, but several breeders outcrossed to bull blood before shows became all the rage (but even then whippet, or, in earlier times, Italian greyhound, influence was easily recognisable). Inbreeding among English white enthusiasts caused severe problems in the breed with deafness and, in some cases, blindness, as well as other faults such as overshot and undershot mouths, so it was no surprise that Hulme and other noted breeders sought a much sturdier type of terrier to continue their sport.

Pearson, Joss Kay, Henry Lacey, Openshaw, Barrow, the Fielding brothers, the Fletcher brothers, Joe Walker, Handley, Swinburn, Joe Holt and Rob Lee all contributed greatly to the breeding of the Manchester terrier and some of the early strain were used in the infamous rat pit at the Three Tuns Inn at Bolton, run at that time by the equally infamous Joe Orrell. These breeders became known as 'The Manchester School', though many lived well out of Manchester, particularly to the north of that city. And the Manchester terrier is pretty much as it was back then, but, alas, nowadays few are worked, though there has been some recent interest in using this terrier for work again, if letters in the pages of *The Countryman's Weekly* are anything to go by.

And so the early working terrier was game indeed and came in a variety of shapes and sizes, with coats and colours varying greatly. In fact, not much has changed today, Type has improved greatly, true, in many breeds, but, sadly, although there isn't much difference in the actual physical terrier scene of today, there is a great difference in working ability, for far fewer quarry species are now hunted and, alas, far fewer terrier breeds actually used for the task for which they were originally created – to go to ground and bay at, bolt, or kill quarry found lurking among the dark and often damp recesses of an earth.

2 The Old Strains of Fell Terrier

The Elterwater terrier, already mentioned in chapter one, was much like the early border terrier in appearance, but the early border was quite different from the modern day pedigree stock. They generally had good strong heads and punishing jaws, with some coming quite snipey headed, looking more like cairn terriers than borders. They had good crisp coats and were a little up on the leg, with fairly short-coupled bodies, though they were not as square as a modern day pedigree Lakeland. The broadcast *Lost World of Friese-Greene*, by Dan Cruikshank (BBC), showed an old coloured film from the 1920s which gave very interesting views of different parts of the country. On visiting the lowlands of Scotland, a few old style border terriers were shown with a pack of otter-hounds and they were very much of the type described – good specimens of working terriers similar in type to the dogs kept by Joss Akerigg and Phil Brogden, both of whom have worked terriers with the Lunesdale Foxhounds.

The Elterwater was simply a type of early fell terrier that had originated and had been bred in a particular area for several generations. This way of naming terriers was common in the Lake District and surrounding countryside and so several different names became popular, such as the Patterdale terrier, so-named because these were bred for use with the Patterdale hounds before they amalgamated with the Matterdale to form the Ullswater Foxhounds, which remain in existence. True, many areas did not give their names to terriers, but that is simply because, if a strain built up quite a reputation for itself, such as the Elterwater variety, then other localities would import and use this strain. For instance, the Elterwater district is in the Langdales, yet the popularity of this particular strain was to be found among the western districts and it was the Elterwater that was used in the early days by Tommy Dobson, who amalgamated the old Eskdale and Ennerdale hounds.

This type of fell terrier was undoubtedly the foundation stock of the Dobson strain that is still talked about to this day.

Although the Elterwater strain bred mostly borderish type terriers, it is also true to say that, as is the case with fell strains even today, there was quite a bit of variety among litters and some would throw slape-coated, as well as rough-coated specimens, while some would be leggy and others perhaps rather short in the leg. Some would have powerful heads, while others would have the 'foxy' face of the cairn. Variety was the watchword of early fell terrier breeding, despite the efforts of some to establish strains that bred true to type. In fact, before exhibiting became all the rage, there was quite a bit of variety in all breeds of terrier, though most had features that made them recognisable as belonging to a particular breed or strain. There are no photographic records, obviously, before showing began to take off during the 1860s onwards, reaching a country-wide craze by the 1880s, but I think the word 'variety' well describes the different types of earth dog to be found among the fells. Most farmers kept terriers around the yard in those days and some were very serious breeders indeed. In fact, it is Lake District farmers who have led the field in fell terrier breeding and it is only in more recent decades that fewer farmers continue this tradition. Nowadays most breeders are fellpack Huntsmen, terriermen, or, indeed, 'townies' who enjoy working and exhibiting their charges.

Back in those days, however, before exhibiting took off and work was the only concern, most farmers of the old districts of Cumberland, Westmoreland and Lancashire bred terriers for vermin control, or they walked them for local hunts which took them back to the kennels for the hunting season, and these terriers, apart from a few variations, were pretty much of the same general type. If a particular stud dog had proved a supreme worker to fox, badger, otter, marten and polecat, then he would be used to serve many bitches throughout that local area, and beyond in a few cases, and so the majority of the offspring, at least for a generation or two, would have many of his characteristics, especially if he had proved a potent sire. And that is how things continued until the automobile allowed much easier access to distant places. Nowadays a supreme worker may sire litters up and down the country, and very often does.

This is why certain areas produced certain types. The Langdales produced borderish type fell terriers and the Borrowdale valley may well have produced shorter legged, snipey jawed earth dogs, some of which have appeared in very old fell-hunting photographs.

Whatever the differences in type, however, one thing was certain – the fells produced incredibly game stock that was famous, or, indeed, infamous, depending on your viewpoint, for working in rock, as well as for being capable of finishing foxes that refused to bolt from such strongholds. From where did this ability to work such places so effectively come?

In short, Scotland is the answer. All over Scotland, not just in the Highlands, was to be found a race of earth dog that was both small and hardy enough to work the massive cairns to be found in that country, especially around the mountainous districts, though there are rocky fortresses even in the lower regions. The Highland terrier

The famous John Peel. Peel used old fell strains with his hounds and came into contact with various types at cattle markets, horse fairs and when hunting different areas.

was found throughout Scotland, but in different varieties, much in the same manner as early fell types, due to differing breeding programmes implemented mainly by crofters, todhunters and, later, gamekeepers employed to keep down vermin. It was such folk who shaped the Highland terrier into a very hardy worker that feared nothing and would enter any earth, no matter how vast, or deep. The foundation for this type, I believe most ardently, was the Celtic terrier brought to these shores thousands of years ago. Since the Scottish nation was formed via Ireland, it may be true to say that the little 'Celt' arrived in Scotland by this route, though it is impossible to know for sure. This theory, however, may well account for the fact that, when Irish terriers first began being exhibited, many closely resembled some of the Scottish strains, despite the fact that they had been bred in Ireland for generations, from stock found in Ireland for at least the past two thousand years! It is said that this dog was similar to the corgi, indeed, that it was the ancestor of the corgi. It is probable that this breed produced a variety of differing types and while some would be long-backed, short-coated and short-legged, others would be leggy, rough-coated and shorter in the back. Some of the leggy type were no doubt smooth in the jacket too, just as some of the shorter legged variety would sport rough jackets. Whatever the type, the Scots produced a race of mainly rough-coated tykes with shorter legs (though not so short that they couldn't negotiate rough ground), slightly long backs and rather powerful heads for their size, which would range from ten to twelve inches, or thereabouts.

Some of the fellpacks hunted to the borders of Scotland and beyond. Certainly, John Peel hunted into Scotland and no doubt received invitations to hunt land from his dealings with horse flesh, for, like his father, his business was dealing in fell ponies (and no doubt any breed he could make a few quid from) and this would have brought him into contact with farmers far and wide, and thus gaining ground to hunt would not be difficult. Not that he was short of hunting grounds, for his meets took him down towards Ullswater, across to Penrith and probably to the foot of the Northern Pennines. On the western side he would have hunted right over to Bassenthwaite Lake and probably around the top end of Derwentwater near Keswick. And to the north he would have reached the border country. Peel travelled long distances from home using fell ponies, but he would still have had to stay at farms or inns walking or riding there the day before the meet and possibly

18

remaining in that area for two or three days hunting, before returning home again. He had a farm to run so would not have been able to stay away for any considerable length of time, unlike some of the fell-pack Huntsmen of earlier times who could be away, staying at and hunting different locations, sometimes for weeks at a time.

The Melbreak, before busy roads made it impossible to continue hunting some areas, once had a massive country and Huntsmen of earlier times such as Richard Head, Willie Irving and Harry Hardasty, would have need to stay away from the kennels in order to hunt those areas effectively, for, like Peel, the Melbreak once hunted up to the Scottish border, well out of reach of a day's walk. Peel, as already stated, was a farmer and could afford little help in running the place, hence his use of ponies so that he could reach far outlying places more quickly and thus return sooner, too. He did often hunt on horseback, but only when hunting the low country, for much of his hunting was carried out on the higher fells where following on a mount was, and still is, impossible.

The Scottish strains of terrier were easily available to Peel and other Huntsmen and I believe that, during the late eighteenth and nineteenth centuries, this type of terrier was used as outcross blood

The powerful head of early Scottish terriers influenced early fell strains and, later, the Buck/Breay strain through Black Davy, who was one quarter Scottish bred.

'Harviestoun Madge' on the heath.

The original and unspoilt Skye terrier.

for the old fell strains and that this improved their ability to work in rock; feats for which they have now become famous. Nothing now works in rock like a fell terrier, but I believe there can be no doubts that it was the Scottish strains of Highland terrier that brought about this expertise. A look at an old print depicting a type of terrier that would later be given the name of Dandie Dinmont after a character from one of Walter Scott's novels, shows what are simply a variety of Highland terrier not in any way dissimilar from the strains which gave rise to the Scottish, cairn and West Highland white terriers, indeed, they are also not far removed from many of the early fell strains. This type also gave rise to the Bedlington terrier and a mixture of Bedlington, fell, Irish and small pit fighting bull terriers bred in the northern districts of England, as well as locally bred old working terriers such as the Coquetdale or Reedwater terrier, is what produced the border, but it was this type seen in the old print of so-called Dandie Dinmonts that was the original type to be found throughout Scotland and the border country, with a few variations according to locality. The Highland terrier was probably a little rougher in the jacket than its lowland cousin, but I am certain that they are of the same rootstock. How such terriers got around such a wide area may be a subject for controversy, but I believe dealers in livestock, gypsies and tinkers, and todhunters, those who roamed Scotland and the north of England destroying vermin for farmers, shepherds and keepers, were responsible for this and thus the Highland type terrier became available to the foxhunters of the English Lake District, who made full use of them. And these terriers were game indeed.

A livestock journal of 1879 describes the old Highland terrier in this way; 'wi' body lang and low and strong, at home in cairns or knowes, he'll face a foumart (polecat), draw a brock, kill rats and whitteritts by the score. He'll bang Tod-Lowrie frae his hole, or slay him at his door.' This could easily describe many of the early fell terriers. True, the majority were leggy, but several were 'lang and low' and a good proportion would 'slay' a fox, if it refused to bolt. The harsh, dense coat of the old 'Highlander' also had an influence on fell strains, for a better coat could not be had in those days and even breeders of fox terriers, particularly in the north of England and around Dartmoor and Exmoor, used Highland terrier blood to improve coat in their charges. No date is given for this occurrence, but my guess is this happened somewhere around the mid-nineteenth century. Rawdon Lee wrote about this outcross being used, but, of course, names and dates are omitted. Certainly, Scottish, or Highland terriers, were to be found among English kennels during the early nineteenth century, so this blood was easily accessible to fox terrier breeders, as well as breeders of fell terriers. Granite, Cavack, Povey and Crofter were just a few of the early Highland strains that influenced the breeding of Scotch terriers in English kennels and undoubtedly these were still game and utterly workmanlike at that time, despite the fact that already some breeders had refrained from working their charges. It seems that as soon as showing began to take off during the early 1860s, terriers became simply exhibits to be carted off around the country in order to endure a hard day's 'benching' at each show venue, though a curious system began to be employed by those who wished to have exhibits 'unspoilt' by scars picked up while at work, but at the same time wanting to breed from an unbroken line of workers. We will discuss this later in the book, as well as the effects this curious system has had on even today's working breeds of terrier.

The type we now know today as the cairn terrier is said to be the original and there is quite a bit of truth in this, though the 'Highlander' was generally longer in the back and possessed a better, harsher jacket. Some had stronger heads, especially those bred among the Eastern Highlands, which gave rise to the pedigree Scottish terrier. It is thought that the Old English black and tan was used as outcross blood and that this then gave rise to the little Scotch terrier after much selective breeding. I agree with this theory very much, for, when rare wheaten coloured Scottish terriers appeared in litters in the early days, they had the bar above the eyes that is so typical of Welsh and Lakeland terriers, a characteristic undoubtedly first inherited from the black and tan terrier. The Scottish terrier has a much more powerful head than the rest of the Scottish breeds and undoubtedly the black and tan influence, a breed which had been created using bull terrier blood, was responsible for this. During the very early days of exhibiting, there was much controversy over head size and strength and many claimed that the snipey face of the cairn was the original and that this enabled them to kill foxes quickly and efficiently, while others claimed a more powerful head, displaying an obvious influence of bull blood, was the most useful for fox killing. The fans of the cairn said that foxes only have small, snipey heads, yet they have incredibly powerful jaws, condemning the larger, powerful heads of the Scottish terrier. Whichever breed and type was favoured, all breeds of Scottish terrier at that time were incredibly game and most were still worked, mainly by keepers and todhunters, though most crofts would usually have one or two around the place, the farmer hoping to keep predators at bay by having a brace of hard-bitten earth dogs roaming freely over their land.

There had been differences in type among the strains of Highland terrier according to the regions where they were bred and worked, but all came from the original stock kept and possibly created by the Celts and, by the latter half of the nineteenth century, all of the breeds that had emerged were breeding true to type. A white strain of Highland terrier had been kept on the west coast, as well as on some of the Scottish islands off the west coast, for the past few hundred years, though some cairn breeders, no doubt out of jealousy, for there is much backbiting among exhibitors, claimed that the white strains were simply bred out of cairn litters in recent years. This theory, and that is all it is, can easily be proved wrong by the fact that King James the First, desirous of these white dogs, wrote from London to Edinburgh in order to have secured and sent to him half a dozen 'earth dogges, or terrieres'. He directed that they be got from Argyll, where the best strains were to be found. This occurred shortly after the Union of the Crowns in 1603 and tells us two things. One, that a white strain of Highland terrier was already in existence and, two, that the best of these were to be found in Argyllshire, which suggests that whites were found in other localities and probably all over Scotland, including the lowlands. The now extinct Redesdale terrier, an all-white, rough-haired breed found in the border country, may well have been another strain of white Highland terrier, though it could have been bred from the same early stock that gave rise to the fox terrier, for fox terriers, especially during those early days of shows, threw all-white puppies on occasion.

The Malcolms of Poltalloch have been credited with creating the West Highland white, but this simply isn't true, for whites were around a long time before the Malcolms began keeping this type, though they did much to popularise the breed and, best of all, worked their stock regularly to all kinds of large quarry. Otter, wildcat and fox were certainly on the quarry list and the Malcolms' keepers used this strain for ridding the estate of what was classed as vermin. When Colonel Malcolm began showing his white terriers, an old gentleman approached him and said that he had worked West Highland whites decades before and that they were very similar to the Malcolms' strain. He had hunted otters very successfully with his team of terriers, during the early part of the nineteenth century, especially around Loch Fyne and the surrounding area. And so this breed was in existence and breeding true to type long before shows began, when cairn breeders claimed to have created the West Highland white from their dogs. These white terriers were also used on badgers and in rock, which doesn't seem to be a very good idea, for these earth dogs were usually hard fox killers that would come unstuck at 'Brock'. Maybe they were very sensible workers that would not get themselves too badly knocked about. This must have been the case, for only an idiot would purposely put a hard terrier to ground on a badger lurking among rocks. This type of earth is difficult to dig and even shallow earths can take an age to dig out, so a hard terrier to ground for any length of time would be badly mauled at best, killed at worst, whilst working badger, so these terriers must have possessed much sense, while at the same time being capable of finishing reluctant foxes. Many fell terriers have had this ability too and early fell-hunters would have treasured a dog that could kill a fox, yet would stand

Hunting in the West Highlands in 1835 with gutsy Highland terriers. This ability to work rock was one reason why fell-hunters used this breed on their native strains.

back from badger and guide the diggers until dug out, without taking too much punishment.

Colonel Malcolm's father once had a terrier to ground on badger that became trapped after a few hours below. Highland terriers were usually run in packs throughout Scotland, hunting anything from rats, to polecats, to otters, to foxes, or even rabbits. The trouble with this system is that it is likely that the Huntsmen would be unable to prevent their charges from getting to ground. This may be why many terriers worked badger in rock and probably why Colonel Malcolm's father's terrier, a white 'Poltalloch' that later became known as the West Highland white, now found itself in quite serious trouble. The terrier fell silent and nothing was heard or seen for days afterwards, until, when one of the keepers visited the spot to check on progress, a pair of eyes, eyes which he was certain did not belong to either fox, or badger, could be seen at the bottom of quite a deep hole running through the rocks.

The terrier could not be reached and digging was utterly out of the question, so the keeper thought long and hard about how to go about effecting a rescue. This was now days later and he knew the terrier must be very weak, so it was imperative that he acted with great urgency if the little tyke was to be saved. He attached a rabbit skin to a rope and lowered it down to the terrier, who then grabbed hold of the fur and held on while its master lifted it out of what would soon have become its grave. The terrier was just got out before it passed out, no doubt because of exhaustion and lack of food. Thankfully, rock earths tend to have water among the dark passages, for rain will easily run into a rockpile and pools can lie in among the rocks for days, even during dry spells. Some earth dogs have lived for a fortnight and more, while stuck in rock, eating the carcass of a fox and drinking water running into the earth, or from pools leftover from previous rainfall. After a few days' rest, the terrier had made a full recovery and was back at work.

Colonel Malcolm, and his father before him, ran packs of these white terriers at just about any huntable quarry they could find and they made a name for themselves that surpassed any reputations built elsewhere in Scotland. So much so, in fact, that the Malcolms were credited with creating the West Highland white and one can still read in books of today this legend that is so often repeated. As we have seen, this strain of Highland terrier existed long before the Malcolms of Poltalloch, and not just along the west coast. What this family of enthusiasts did achieve though, was to put this breed, for

Brocaine Righorn Ruadh and Brocaine Turk; of the old type of working Cairn.

that is what it had become by the latter half of the nineteenth century, on the map, popularising this type and producing a strain that now bred all-whites, thus eliminating any coloureds that would have cropped up in litters at one time.

They were certainly plucky dogs, all of the Highland varieties, and worked with noses that almost equalled that of hounds. It is thought that the Celtic hound, a huge beast that could pull down deer and wolf, was used centuries ago as the foundation for the Irish breeds of terrier and there is probably some truth in this, for smaller hounds would also be produced and these could easily have been used to influence terrier strains in order to improve nose and drive, breeding out the large size after only a few generations. Could this also be true of the Highland variety of Celtic terrier? The Irish and Scottish breeds certainly share the same origins, of that I am sure, so maybe the little 'Highlander' did get its wonderful nose from the hounds used by the Celtic race millenniums ago.

They could hunt otter along a river, or around a loch, for hours at a time, following a cold drag half a day old until, at last, the beast was unkennelled, or marked to ground in, and bolted from, a holt.

The keepers and crofters very often shot the quarry as it bolted, treating otters and suchlike as vermin, rather than sporting quarry. Foxes were hunted in the same manner and badgers were also dug out and shot, using this type of terrier, though some must have taken fearful maulings when they could not be dug out quickly enough, they were so game and intent on killing their prey.

A friend of mine, John, has kept terriers for several years and once had one of his terriers, Flint, one with quite a bit of Middleton strain Lakeland in its pedigree, to ground on what he thought was a fox. The terrier had chased a rabbit into quite a large, though not deep, rockpile on the edge of an old, disused quarry, but then began baying keenly. John knew then a fox was home and the stench coming from the rockpile confirmed this. Flint settled down in one spot and after a little time John began digging. The terrier wasn't very deep, but rock is hardly ever easy to get through and so it took at least four hours to break through. Soil had to be dug from around often quite large rocks and these then had to be manoeuvred out of the way, using pick, shovel, crowbar and plenty of sweat and toil. This was towards the end of the season, on quite a mild March day with the sun shining through the broken cloud at times, so these weren't the best of conditions for digging such a difficult earth, but still, the labour had to be carried out and eventually John broke through, the terrier working close to its quarry. It seemed to be in quite a tight space and the terrier suddenly disappeared. The earth was larger inside than it looked and the quarry had taken hold of Flint and had dragged him in. He had seized the quarry in return, though not jaw to jaw, for they seemed to have hold of each other by the cheek, and, every time Flint drew it back towards the entrance, it put in greater effort and drew the terrier back in. This went on for an age until, finally, both antagonists let go. Flint was exhausted by this time and so a youngster just learning his trade was tried.

Rock entered keenly, seized his quarry and drew it out. The quarry had turned round by this time, and so Rock drew it out rear-end first. And John was rather surprised to see a large badger coming out of that earth. It had taken seven hours of toil to break through and finally secure the quarry, after a struggle to get Flint out, and the eventual catch was not the fox John had imagined he was digging, though a strong stench of fox was wafting out of that earth throughout the entire duration of the dig. One can only conclude that Reynard had got himself behind the badger somehow and was skulking out of the way in that tight stop-end. John didn't hang around to find out. He allowed the badger to go free and vacated the place, returning the next day to backfill, once the badger, and any other tenant, had moved on. Foxes do indeed use badgers to escape the attentions of terriers and Gary Middleton once had a fox hide behind two badgers when it was run to ground by the Lunesdale Foxhounds, Gary's terrier's attention being taken up by the two 'Brocks' standing 'twixt fox and earth dog.

One of Colonel Malcolm's young terriers was loaned to a keeper and was entered into a large cairn, similar to a Lakeland borran, though often much larger, and engaged his fox. It is difficult to know exactly what happened from then on, but there may have been a badger lurking in this rockpile too, for the terrier, sometime later, emerged with his stomach badly ripped open and the innards were partly hanging out of the wound. The keeper managed to put them back inside the tear, but the terrier then slipped out of his hands, returned to ground, engaged the fox once more and finally bolted it, the keeper accounting for it above ground with his gun. Truly, these early 'Westies', or, as they were then known, Poltalloch terriers, were game indeed and their courage and ability to work incredibly vast and deep rock earths made them a legend.

Rare light-coloured Scottish terriers with the bar above the eyes that links them to the Old English Black and Tan and probably the Welsh terrier of old from which the English variety probably originated.

Another youngster, at just ten months of age, entered to its first fox, though in a rather curious fashion. An experienced dog had been entered first, into yet another rock hole, and finally succeeded in bolting its fox, which the youngster then grabbed by the throat as it tried to escape, the rocks impeding its progress somewhat. The young entry then held onto its prize until the other terriers caught up and killed the quarry. As I said earlier, these Highland varieties of earth dog were usually hunted in packs and they played a dual role in a day's hunting; that of hound, seeking out, flushing and hunting a fox, otter, polecat, or whatever else was being hunted, and then going to ground on the quarry once it had sought refuge below. And so quite a number of foxes were actually caught on top, rather than below ground. This was not about sport though, though a pack of terriers provides plenty of sport, believe me, but about control, in order to protect game and livestock. And so any foxes that would not bolt from below had to be killed out of necessity. The little 'Highlander' became a superb scenting dog on top, but it also became a wonderful worker below ground and was famed for being capable of killing any fox that refused to bolt. The ten-month young entry then went on to kill a fully grown dog fox just a month after this and quickly went on to fulfil his early potential.

Do you see the similarities between the old Scottish varieties of earth dog, and those of the English Lake District? Like the Scottish strains, the old fell terrier was often hunted on top and in packs, so he mustn't be quarrelsome. The Highland terrier was noted for working in packs and on many occasions several terriers got into the same earth together, without fear of fights breaking out. Maybe the old fell strains acquired this same ability to work peaceably in packs from those same dogs. Also, the old fell terrier became famous for working rock expertly. Another similar feature is the fact that fell terriers were bred to kill foxes that would not bolt, for, again, just like Scotland, the landscape and farming practices dictate the necessity for fox control, rather than a sporting day out. Maybe, just maybe, the fell strains inherited these abilities from the Scottish breeds. There were also similarities in type, such as rough coats and very often prick ears. In fact, the Buck/Breay strain of fell terrier, which is nowadays known as the Patterdale, was partly Scottish terrier bred and this type of terrier continues to throw one, or two, prick ears in many litters. And some of the names have Scottish links. Turk is a traditional Lakeland name for a terrier, but it is a Scottish word, a farming term that is linked with growing potatoes.

Jock, too, is another much-used name in the Lakes, as is Piper, though some may argue that this name originated in North-umberland where the border pipes and the Northumbrian pipes were once common. Certainly, there have been many Scottish families who have settled in the Lake District, such as the Nicholsons, the Jacksons and the Richardsons. It is very likely that these farming families brought their terriers with them and these would surely have entered the local strains of earth dog. Brian Nuttall can remember working Scottish terriers coming to the Lakes and entering the local fell strains, so maybe this has been a long-standing tradition that has resulted in the best type of working terrier for use in a rocky and mountainous landscape! But why work terriers in packs in the fell country when there are fellpacks to take care of the fox population?

It is because the fellpacks can only visit the different localities in their hunt countries two or three times each season, so much of the land is left untouched for much of the time. Hence terrier packs, which, as was the case with many Scottish packs, usually contained a hound or two that were invaluable at checks and for working out cold drags more effectively, were used and, again, otters, polecats, martens, foxes and badgers were hunted and dug and these packs were run with great enthusiasm and effect. John Pool, Eddie Pool's father, bred quite large numbers of terriers and he often ran these at otter during the summer. He would ferry people across Ullswater and take a few of his fell terriers with him, so that he could hunt otter while he waited for the party to return for the trip back across the water. Joe Armstrong, Mowdie Robinson, and quite a few other noted followers of the Melbreak under the Huntsmanship of Willie Irving and, later, Harry Hardisty, also ran terrier packs and they took quite a number of foxes and otters in this way.

The foundation stock for the old fell strains was undoubtedly the same type of terrier that became known as the Old English black and tan, though the smooth variety, which later became the Manchester terrier, was not favoured and rough coats were always aimed for in the northern regions, though smooth coats did crop up in litters at times, and still do. I believe with certainty that the Highland terrier was used as outcross blood, in order to improve the ability to work in rock, as well as to produce much denser coats. Most early fell terriers were a little long in the back and this too, would suggest the influence of such blood. Hardiness and courage would be the inevitable result of using such blood and to illustrate just how useful these Scottish bred terriers were, we must once again look to the valuable records provided by Colonel Malcolm of Poltalloch.

During the last five years of the nineteenth century he took, along with his keepers of course, 603 foxes using his Poltalloch strain of white terrier, and on top of this umpteen badgers, otters, martens, wildcats and stoats were taken too. During the years 1902 to 1905 he took seventy-four foxes and four otters. So one can easily imagine just how useful these terriers were. Many of these Scottish strains were bred to have feet slightly turned out, which, it was thought, helped them scramble up and over rocks. Others stated that foxes have straight legs and negotiate rocks with far more agility than do dogs, concluding that earth dogs are better off with straight legs. I will keep an open mind on this, for I have owned terriers with slightly turned out feet and those with straight legs and all seem to work in rock just as well. For show purposes legs are required to be straight and this in no way detracts from working ability, not in any way that I have noticed anyhow, and the majority of the earths my terriers have worked have been in rock, rather than dug-out rabbit holes, though they also work a large number of drains too, particularly of the stone variety.

All of the Scottish strains, then, have originated from the same rootstock – the little Celtic terrier that was so similar in type to the Highland terrier, and this includes the Skye terrier. These remained tireless workers, even into the early part of the twentieth century, though they were much favoured by the gentry, and, once shows took off, many were prevented from working and became exhibits instead. Up to the beginning of the show craze, Skye terriers were similar in every way to the cairn and the terrier Caius wrote about, calling them 'Iseland dogs', was very different indeed from the Skye we see today. Dr Johnson wrote, in 1773 when visiting Skye, that foxes were 'hunted by small dogs'. The long, soft coat of the Skye would render this an impossibility, so the working Skye was obviously very different from the show type. As early as the beginning of the twentieth century, the show Skye terrier was already too large and too soft and long in the coat for work, though many, even today, do display quite a bit of working instinct and they will readily take to chasing and hunting rabbits. Before the show bench took precedence over the rockpile, the Skye, like its cousins on the mainland, came in a variety of colours such as white, fawn, blue-grey and black.

In 1879 Thomson of Glenisla exhibited a Skye terrier which was prick-eared, dark in colour and with a courage that was said to equal that of a bull terrier, and, best of all, this was a real working terrier, not the long-haired variety which later became so popular. What exactly brought about this change I do not know, but a cross with a Maltese dog is very likely. The Clydesdale, or Paisley terrier, was very similar to the Skye, though it had been fixed in type long before the change in the Skye terrier came about, and this was probably used too. And, I am certain, it was the Clydesdale that changed the Yorkshire terrier into a pampered pet and show dog, rather than the hardy worker it once was, though, again, working instinct can still emerge in some of these breeds even today. I have seen a miniature 'Yorkie' that would readily go to ground in rabbit holes. Whatever went into the mix, an unworkmanlike dog was created and the Skye soon travelled a million miles away from its hardier and more useful cousins.

The Scottish breeds differed according to localities, but the terrier that soon became known as the Dandie Dinmont was just another variety of Highland dog in its original form. And these were courageous indeed. They were described as a rough-haired, short-legged variety of earth dog, long before Scott's novel *Guy Mannering*, gave the terrier its name, and this just about describes the Scottish strains. This type, although found all over southern Scotland, was also a resident of the north of England and was mainly kept by farmers, keepers and travelling folk. That the Dandie and Bedlington share the same roots is seen in the fact that Lord Antrim, in the early days of shows, exhibited two terriers from the same litter and won both his classes. These were the Dandie Dinmont and the Bedlington classes!

It was Billy Allan of Holystone who used such rough-haired terriers for hunting fox and otter and it was he who greatly influenced north-eastern breeders. The Dandie Dinmont, although from the same rootstock as the Scottish breeds, began to undergo a change, probably as early as the eighteenth century, and it seems obvious to me that bull terrier blood was used as outcross, in order to improve bone, jaw strength (some of the Highland variety were rather snipey headed and lacking in bone) and guts. The Dandie has a large head which could only have come about after using bull terrier blood. Later on, teckel, or rough-haired dachshund, blood was added, when the show-craze hit, and the body length was greatly enhanced, though not to the good. True, they were already a little long in the body, but this was a natural body length

Tommy Dobson with a litter of
terrier pups.

which, some say, aided them
whilst working below ground.
The bull terriers used would
be small pit dogs of maybe
eighteen pounds in weight, of
the sort Nuttall's grandfather
used when establishing his
own strain of fell terrier.

Allan, or Piper Allan as he
was known, used much the
same type as that which later
became known as the Dandie
Dinmont, though at some time
Otterhound blood was added
to produce a leggier strain.
Also, whippet blood was put
into the mix and this has
resulted in the roached back
now so familiar on what
became known as the Bed-
lington terrier. But make no
mistake, the earlier stuff
shared a common ancestry and,
while some stuck with the
hard-bitten, long bodied and
short-legged variety, others
bred a leggier dog which was
used for many different tasks, including rabbit coursing and
retrieving shot game. The bull terrier blood from the Dandie
Dinmnont meant that the Bedlington was also used for the
deplorable 'entertainment' of dog fighting.

This leggier type, now with large 'houndy' ears from the
Otterhound influence and a dense shaggy coat, became known as
the Rothbury terrier by the farmers, shepherds and travellers, while
the gentry referred to it as the Northumberland fox terrier, and they
were most impressed with its working ability. Lord Ravensworth
offered Billy Allan a substantial sum of money for his dog Charley,

after he had rid Ravensworth's estate of several otters. Peachem was another favourite and a great finder. Finding ability was most important to Allan and he would not keep a dog that could not find in the often very deep Northumberland earths. Hitch was another superb worker belonging to Allan, as was Pincher, and it is said that this blood was the foundation for the Bedlington terrier. James Allan, born in 1734 when 'Piper' was thirty years of age, carried on his father's breeding programme and he too bred incredibly game stock, though, again, at this time there was little difference betwixt the Dandie and the Bedlington. Pepper was one of James Allan's best and he was the grandsire to Somner's Shem, said to be the ancestor of modern Bedlingtons.

Even during the latter part of the nineteenth century there was a gulf between the show and working type of Dandie and Bedlington terriers, though all would undoubtedly still work. Teckel had been added to the strains of Dandie Dinmont, though this would do little to harm working instinct, for working teckels were used that had a

Jameson's Sport, a good working Irish terrier and ancestor of modern strains. His type was used to improve the old fell strains. Sport made his show debut in 1875.

long history of tackling fox and badger below ground. The Bedlington showed a decided whippet influence, but these whippets were as game as terriers in those days and were often used to take foxes, indeed, it is said that they were created largely from terrier bloodlines, so working instinct suffered little. And Bedlingtons continue to work even in our modern day, though some, after generations of treading the showring, or lying on their owners' laps, have very unpromising prospects as workers.

It is David Hindlee, who farmed a wild part of the Cheviotdale mountains, who is most associated with the Dandie Dinmont, but it is true to say that most farmers kept this type around the place in those days, for keeping down rats and for shifting foxes, badgers and otters from their land, whenever hounds, or todhunters, were not in the area. Again, these were incredibly game and useful terriers and they were very bad cat killers (which suited most farmers) and were also noted for catching fish. One tale told, and supposedly from a reliable source, is of a type of Dandie Dinmont that developed a rather curious habit. It would catch a fish from the local river and then slink away and hide, waiting for a cat to approach. Once a cat was sniffing, or beginning to eat the fish, the terrier would then pounce from the undergrowth, grab the cat across the back and kill it swiftly. The standard for the old strains of this type, including the Bedlington, was to be active enough to follow their master all day across rough country and then to be capable of following fox, otter, or badger into their lairs where they were to fight them. I doubt many Dandies would be capable of such feats these days, not to mention a good number of show-bred Bedlingtons, but back in the eighteenth and nineteenth centuries such terriers were unbeatable in the field and this blood undoubtedly entered early fell terrier strains, adding to the rather alien mix, but the strains being none the worse for that.

It was during the Great War that the fashion for bigger dogs took off and from then on the vast majority of Bedlingtons were unsuited for earthwork, though bigger dogs had been produced long before this time. It was such larger terriers, brought about by the inclusion of Otterhound and whippet blood, that produced the more fashionable large specimens of later years. Some of the most famous of the early type were produced around Rothbury Forest, Morpeth and, of course, Bedlington, this town giving the terrier its name from around 1825 onwards. At this time though, the gentry preferred the Dandie Dinmont type with the long back and short legs, while travellers such as the Andersons, Faas and Makepieces all preferred the leggy variety, which was more suited to poaching rabbits and pheasant, as well as for retrieving shot game. Nicholas Makepiece became a noted professional rat-catcher and he no doubt shifted many rats for farmers using his Bedlington terriers. Flint, born 1782, is one of the early ancestors of the Bedlington, though he was undoubtedly not in any way dissimilar to the ancestor of the Dandie, and Wash was descended from him, a bitch which gave birth to Phoebe, the first recorded blue/black Bedlington. Anderson's Piper was out of this bitch and this dog sired Ainsley's young Piper around 1820. Old Flint was owned by Squire Trevelyan and this dog must have been incredibly game and very hard, for the squire would put down anything that wasn't up to his standard of 'hardness'. Tyne, Tear 'Em and Tyneside became famous terriers during the late nineteenth century and all modern Bedlingtons are descended from these dogs – terriers that were still game, tractable and very useful as workers, though, because of the bull terrier influence inherited from their short-legged ancestors, most were bad fighters and early shows were rather hectic events when large numbers of Bedlingtons

Nelson, a Bedlington terrier of around 1900. Fell terrier bloodlines were once saturated with Bedlington blood, until the improved Lakeland was extensively bred, particularly after 1921.

were thrown together in the ring. It was the Bedlington terrier, because it was so game and a famous fox-killing breed, that was used as outcross blood during the latter half of the nineteenth century and early part of the twentieth in particular. By the 1920s fell terrier strains were saturated with the blood of Bedlington terriers and one can still see this influence even in modern times. Old photographs of fell-hunting often have a Bedlington or two somewhere in the background, along with the more traditional fell types.

So the early strains of fell terrier, the ones so familiar to hunters such as Peel, Bowman and Dobson, were a mixture of Old English black and tan, the same type that gave rise to the fox terrier, for many of the early fox terriers were black and tan, red, or grizzle in colour and it took years to breed out the coloured variety, Highland terrier types that were easily accessible to packs such as Peel's, the Melbreak and the Blencathra, the Bedlington and, especially from the 1840s when the great famine drove millions out of Ireland, old Irish terrier types which were just as varied as the Scottish and English strains. Also, as Plummer states in his *Fell Terrier* book, a superb piece of work that is essential reading, white bodied terriers that gave rise to both fox terriers and Jack Russells, also entered fell terrier strains after Cornish miners came north to work mainly around the Coniston district from 1830 onwards.

Going back to the Scottish strains of Highland terrier, we see a tradition that soon became popular in the Lake District and one wonders if the Scottish settlers were responsible for bringing such traditions to Cumberland. As I have said, hunts were conducted using terrier packs in the main, though often there were one or two hounds also included. The cold drag of a fox, otter, or marten, or maybe a wildcat, was taken up and hunted, sometimes for a good hour or two, until the quarry was unkennelled, either from undergrowth, or usually from a rocky labyrinth, and was then shot, or sometimes coursed using deerhound type running dogs, or greyhound blooded lurchers. These hunts were always carried out on foot, though, in lowland areas, the gentry would sometimes follow on horseback, and afterwards great celebrations were held. Along with the large amounts of food and drink consumed, songs would be sung of the exploits of their terriers, hounds and running dogs. Could it be that the Scottish settlers were responsible for bringing these traditions south into the Lakes country, where such traditions have continued down to our day? I think it most likely.

Johnny Fraser of Glenlivet was a keen hunter and he kept a pack of Highland terriers for working otter, fox, badger, wildcat and marten, which were extremely game and he was called upon many times by crofters from far and near to hunt down and kill foxes that were taking their lambs. He would hunt them with his terriers and then his deerhounds would catch and kill the bolting foxes. Those that refused to bolt were certain to die, if the terriers could reach them, for Fraser's terriers were noted for their hardness at quarry and I should imagine he lost quite a few of them after they became trapped, or badly weakened, from an encounter with a big Highland fox.

No wonder the fell type of working terrier has become so famed as an earth dog, a terrier that has been used, like its ancestors, for a

'Laal' Tommy Dobson at a borran with his terriers, from L–R Dobbie, Brick and Gillert.

variety of different tasks, while excelling especially at working in rock. Some terriers just do not work well in rock and Paul White-head, Huntsman of the Lunesdale foxhounds, was telling me of a terrier he acquired from Wales that had seen quite a bit of work in that country. However, it may have been used mainly in dug-out rabbit holes, for he found the dog useless in the deep and dangerous Yorkshire and Cumbria earths and so the dog was eventually returned to its previous owner. I have owned terriers that do not fare well in rock myself, though I find few fell terriers have this trait. Some do, I know, but not many, for they have been shaped by the hard rock of the north and are more at home in this type of earth than any other.

The old type of fell terrier was bred for courage and any terrier that came to the area, if it proved game, a good finder and was of the correct size, would be used to bring into the local strains, no matter what its type, or breed. And this is how things continued for hundreds of years, though the beginning of the show craze was to alter things quite considerably and even the working strains of fell terrier, not just the show dogs, would be affected.

3 The Birth of the Lakeland Terrier

Terriers found throughout the whole of the Lake District had been known by several different names such as coloured working terriers, working terriers, Patterdale, Elterwater, Coniston, fell terriers and so on, and it wasn't until 1912 that the name of Lakeland terrier began to be used for a race of fell terrier that were superior in looks, and often working ability too, to the old traditional rough and ready strains which were bred for working ability alone. So what changed?

It was in 1859 that the first dog show was held and from then on the craze for exhibiting swept throughout the country rather rapidly. This craze came to the fells too and even the remotest of Lakeland valleys staged agricultural shows that catered for sheep and hounds in particular, with terriers thrown in as a sort of afterthought, though the bug for showing these little tykes also struck home and very soon, by the early 1880s, classes for these were taken very seriously indeed. Just attend any working terrier show today and listen to the crowd once the judge has made his selection. Some will be smiling and looking smug, for the judge has picked the same dogs as they. Some will be pulling their faces and grumbling, criticising the decisions made and telling it 'how it should have been'. Some may be shouting the odds and letting it be known very publicly how they feel about what they see as wrong decisions, while the odd one or two will put their terriers back in the car, sometimes without having yet entered a ring, and exit the show ground rather swiftly in a display of temper that leaves a trail of blue smoke rapidly in its wake. Human nature hasn't changed these past centuries and so one can easily imagine that the early shows were much the same. Exhibiting began to be taken so seriously that changes in the fell terrier scene began to take place, and very swiftly at that.

The old bloodlines of shaggy, raggy terriers underwent a

The Master of Original Wensleydale pack, with a couple of hounds and a fox terrier.

massive change and a much smarter type of earth dog had begun to emerge by the 1880s, type having been fixed by the turn of the century, and possibly before this time, though there was still much room for improvement and improvements did indeed take place over the next thirty years or so. But how did this change come about? Undoubtedly by using both fox terrier and Irish terrier blood, both of these breeds being easily accessible to the terrier-men of the fell country. The fox terrier, even by the early 1860s, was pretty much breeding true to type and not only were these incredibly good-looking dogs, but they were also extremely game and had acquitted themselves well up and down the country against all British large quarry. Many of the strains around Dartmoor and Exmoor were used extensively in rock, and so such blood would do nothing to harm the working qualities of fell terriers. Indeed, bloodlines were already saturated with white bodied terriers from the south west, brought to the Lakes by Cornish miners, who in turn, I am certain, took fell types back to their native land when they returned south. These then entered southern strains and the

Champion Irish terrier 'Sporter' toward the end of the nineteenth century. The Irish had a massive impact on the fell terrier strains.

colour was quickly bred out, after only a couple of generations or so.

This cross was used to improve coat and courage in many of the white terriers of the south, though this occurred long before shows became the fashion in the fells. These white dogs brought by miners, especially to the Coniston district, like the fell strains, were rather rough and ready and it wasn't until fox terrier blood, the smartened variety of white bodied earth dog, was used that type began to improve dramatically. This blood undoubtedly helped shape the improved type of fell, and white terriers were common during the late nineteenth century shows. In fact, even those of predominant colour, such as red, grizzle, blue and tan and black and tan, sported white patches and some were even marked like collies, with huge patches of white on the chest, or across the back. One of the more common markings was white blazes on chest and paws, a sight that can still be seen today. Fred Barker's 'Chowt-faced' Rock had a large patch of white running from his neck all the way down to the deepest part of his chest, with small patches on his paws, indicating an ancestry that included fox terrier. Bowman kept and bred terriers which had much fox terrier in their pedigree, right into his retirement, and Fred Barker is said to have bred his strain originally from Bowman's. There is an interesting picture of Joe Bowman seated on an old horse-drawn coach with a terrier at his feet. Use a magnifying glass on this old photo of a Mardale meet in 1922, two years before Bowman retired as Huntsman of the Ullswater Foxhounds, in order to see this dog, which is red in colour, but it has large patches of white, particularly on its chest and paws. (A magnifying glass is recommended for use on many of the old photos, many of which are poor in quality, but these are a vital part of the record and are included because of their importance.)

This fox terrier influence began in the Ullswater country when Jonathan Wilkinson, father of Sid and Joe Wilkinson, bought a white bitch of the fox terrier type from Yorkshire. This bitch was Lil and Eddie Pool says this occurred before the First World War. The original Wensleydale Foxhounds were disbanded in 1907 after hunting the Yorkshire dales and parts of east Cumberland since the 1700s and they used mainly fox terriers with this pack. Exactly from where they obtained their stock is difficult to say, for the north of England produced some of the very best fox terriers, especially the rough-coated variety, during the nineteenth century and so they

A kill by the original Wensleydale foxhounds.

Champion Lady of Kinniside. Welsh terrier markings are obvious on this Lakeland terrier.

Tommy Dobson and Willie Porter with a fell and white-fell terrier at one of the local borrans. The terrier at Porter's feet shows obvious fox terrier influence.

were readily available to hunt kennels. Indeed, several Masters and Huntsmen bred this type of terrier at that time. My educated guess is that Jonathan Wilkinson bought Lil when the Wensleydale disbanded and then brought her into the Ullswater district where she was put into service at the Ullswater Foxhounds under Joe Bowman and there she was also used extensively as a brood bitch. (Fox terriers that saw service with packs such as the Wensleydale, were familiar with rock holes and had proven more than a match for this type of earth, so they were suitable for bringing into the fell strains. Remember, Parson Russell's fox terriers were often used in rock earths, particularly around the Exmoor district, and so this type of earth dog was well suited to the northern earths.)

The fell terrier of that time was mainly blue, or blue grizzle, and displayed quite a bit of Bedlington influence, with quite poor coats. Fox terriers were used to improve coat, for they were famed by this time for their incredibly hard and dense jackets, which were the result of Irish terrier influence probably during the 1860s when only the best of jackets were good enough to win at shows. Do not

A typey champion Welsh terrier of late nineteenth century. Walter Glynn's 'Brynhir Burglar'.

45

forget, these early shows were usually judged by those who worked terriers and only the best points for work were good enough. The fox terrier, by the turn of the century, was a typey animal indeed, but still an out and out worker and fell Huntsmen had no hesitation when bringing them into the old strains. This outcross blood improved coat and general type immensely, breeding away from the poor coated Bedlington types, though it often produced fox terrier marked offspring in mainly coloured litters, or even collie marked terriers such as the one in the Mardale photograph of 1922. Not all favoured this colouring, though, according to Plummer's *Fell Terrier*, ferreting folk preferred these markings and used such types extensively. Many were used at the fellpacks, however, and Dalton and Bowman, of the Blencathra and Ullswater respectively, often had a white fell terrier or two working at the hunt.

Bowman's Lil, given to Sid Wilkinson when Bowman retired in 1924, was bred down from Wensleydale Lil and Fred Barker may well have brought this blood into his own strain, though Carrick at the Carlisle and District Otterhounds also bred a strain of fox terrier that I believe was the foundation for the improved fell terriers of Jim Dalton's – incredibly typey terriers ahead of their time and stock that played a very important part in the creation of what was to become known as the Lakeland terrier. Carrick owned Lil Foiler, said to be descended from Russell's terriers, and he bred Trick, Tyro and the incredibly good looking and working terrier, Tack, a fox terrier which I believe was extensively used to improve fell terrier type, coat and general working ability. I am certain Lil Foiler's descendants, including Tack, were used by Dalton in order to improve his fell terrier strain, though it seems that some then went on to use the improved fell stock to bring back into their fox terrier breeding programme, for some produced offspring with a silky top-knot and a certain amount of blue colouring (inherited from the Bedlington influence of early fell types), though these faults were bred out by the first decade of the twentieth century.

Bowman used Lil as outcross blood, as did John Pool, Eddie's father, along with other breeders, and this changed the shape of the old fell strains dramatically, improving coat and type and, very often, working ability too. Fox terriers had been put to Irish terriers during the early show days, in order to improve coat in particular, and so some of the early improved fell terriers threw Irish in type. Irish terrier was also used to improve type during the early show days and by the turn of the nineteenth century many displayed such an ancestry. These became unbeatable at shows and so many fell breeders began using such outcross blood in order to make their stock more competitive, for the rivalry at agricultural shows in those days would equal, if not excel, the rivalry we see today at any working terrier show.

I believe Irish terrier blood had entered the fell strains long before the show-bug hit, after the famine in Ireland, though possibly before this time, though these were not the typey red terriers that became so well known and respected during the later decades of the nineteenth century. Terriers in Ireland, like Britain, were varied indeed and many were rough and ready tykes similar in every way to British terriers, though these had probably been bred by Irish crofters for centuries, even millenniums, with possible outcross blood coming from invading nations throughout Ireland's long and volatile history. Terriers of great variety can still be found in Ireland and they undoubtedly represent the old bloodlines that gave rise to the pedigree Irish breeds of today. I have seen such terriers myself. Most are found in out of the way villages, or are bred on farms, and some are short legged, long backed, rather ugly terriers, while others are quite leggy and short-coupled, more typey dogs. Some are red, wheaten, or, one I saw in a coastal village in Cork, was the strangest colour I have ever seen and I can only

Bangor
Dau-Lliw,
exhibited in
1880s.

47

Lady Gwen. How the Welsh terrier had altered by the 1920s (using obvious Irish terrier blood).

describe it as a sort of shade of brown. This dog was a little up on the leg and was definitely not a show dog, but still, it looked a useful sort. Such stock undoubtedly helped shape the early, though certainly not typey, fell strains when settlers came to the Lakes country.

When the Irish first began appearing at shows, type was rather varied to say the least. Quite a few resembled Scottish strains, some looked rather Welsh in appearance, while some were even white. Slasher, first shown in 1875 in Belfast by O'Connell, was a white Irish and he was descended from a white strain bred in that country for generations. Morton's Fly and Jamison's Sport were two other noted early Irish terriers, though Sport wasn't really favoured by the judges. He was red, but black and tan terriers were favoured then. Many were blue and tan or all blue and these resembled Bedlingtons. This type, I am certain, was used to create the modern Kerry blue. Banshee, Sporter and Tanner were three other famous early Irish earth dogs and, like most, if not all, of the others, were workers – used for ridding farms of vermin, as hunt terriers, and as gundogs. Most were also used in bobbery packs hunted by farmers and villagers.

One big winner of 1875 was Stinger, though he was a poor type with a long back and short legs and was blue grizzle and tan, with white turned out feet – the type that undoubtedly gave rise to the Glen of Imaal. The wheaten terrier was developed from less favoured Irish strains, though, like the Kerry Blue, its ancestors resembled early Bedlingtons. Kelly, one of the Coniston Foxhounds' hunt terriers featured in Clapham's *Foxhunting On The Lakeland Fells*, was very much like an early soft coated wheaten terrier and such Irish blood may well have been found in Cumberland during those times. Some early Irish terriers were also brindle in colour, which suggests bull blood had also played a part somewhere along the line. Bull blood was resorted to in order to improve bone and courage, though such blood may have entered native strains via terriers brought in by outsiders. Some were rather short on the leg and weighed as little as nine pounds, but, make no mistake, they were still game and, like their Scottish cousins, were famous fox killers, rather than baying types.

By 1890 brindle and black and tan, along with the whites, had been bred out of Irish terrier stock and reds were now favoured above all others. These reds were similar to Jamison's Sport which, now dead, at last came into favour, though selective breeding had improved type dramatically. Without doubt, before the turn of the century, Irish terrier blood, particularly good red specimens now that the show craze had taken off, were used to improve type in fell strains and many early Lake District bred terriers showed signs of outcross to good quality Irish dogs. Tommy Dobson is famous for his Bedlington influenced fell strain, but he had many of differing type, including white fell terriers descended from fox terrier outcrosses; small, short legged earth dogs displaying a certain amount of cairn blood about them, as well as terriers which were obviously bred down from good quality red Irish terriers. There is an old photograph of Tommy Dobson on the back cover of Jill Mason's fascinating book, *The Eskdale and Ennerdale Foxhounds – The History of A Lakeland Pack*, which tells of some of the terriers being used in those days. The one at his feet is obviously a white fell bred down from fox terrier outcross blood. The one by his left shoulder is undoubtedly a descendant of Scottish outcross blood, the general shape, short legs and coat making this an unmistakable conclusion, while the one on his right is certainly one of the improved type of fell and there is much Irish terrier about this dog. Even when a young man, hunting the Eskdale hounds, before he amalgamated them with the Ennerdale, photographs show him with fox terrier

A fox terrier of the early twentieth century. Some Lakelands came smooth coated through the influence of such blood.

bred fell types rather up on the leg and at least fifteen inches tall. Dobson used a wide variety of terriers and their only required qualities were that they could get to ground and be game enough to tackle a fox.

Early type showed obvious fox and Irish terrier outcross blood and, along with selective breeding, this outcross blood changed the shape of many of the old strains and some were now incredibly typey, though all were still game and all were still worked. The Irish terrier has a peculiarity, or it did in those days, that made it rather uncomfortable when being groomed. In fact, many hated grooming and could hardly tolerate it. I have owned several fell terriers, and my bitch Mist is very much like an early typey Irish terrier who detests being brushed, that are not at all keen on being groomed and I believe this trait betrays the Irish ancestry of many fell terriers. As does the deep, rich red colouring found on many specimens. Before shows became all the rage, most fell terriers were of rather poor colouring, mainly blue and tan, blue grizzle, or wheaten, with a few rather poor black and tan specimens, and a few being red, though this was not the rich red colouring of the Irish that was well fixed by 1890. With the advent of agricultural shows throughout the fell country, colour improved and reds were very much favoured, though good quality black and tans also began to appear. True, black and tans did exist in the Lakes during the nineteenth century, but the black usually contained some grizzle, giving a rather wishy-washy appearance, and the tan was very often quite pale. So how did the rich black and tan come about in the new improved fell strains?

The use of fox terrier blood had created very typey fell terriers, even before the turn of the century, but poor colouring was often the result. Many were white, of course, but those born coloured were rarely of good shade, being either wheaten, or grizzle, and often a poor grey grizzle at that, for this cross diluted what black and tan there was in the strains and good type coupled with good coloration was the exception, rather than the rule. Working ability wasn't badly affected by such outcross blood, though harder terriers lacking the sense of the old fell strains were often the result. Although fox terriers were required to stand back and bay at their quarry, many strains became dangerously hard. They had superb noses and became noted markers, especially of rat (when the unnaturally long muzzles began to appear on fox terriers, they had problems with rats wrapping themselves around their jaws, making a fatal bite nigh on impossible and resulting in severe wounds from the slashing bites of these rodents) and rabbit holes,

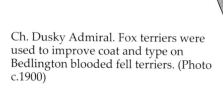

Ch. Dusky Admiral. Fox terriers were used to improve coat and type on Bedlington blooded fell terriers. (Photo c.1900)

51

Arthur Heal, Huntsman to Devon and Somerset Staghounds, with a terrier of a type that was brought north by the Cornish Miners during the nineteenth century.

developing a sixth sense that enabled them to know when and where their quarry was about to bolt, or when the ferret was about to emerge, but at larger quarry they became hysterically keen to latch on, even when at 'Brock'.

One bitch was bought from a farmer and taken out on its very first badger dig. She was entered and eagerly seized her quarry, holding onto it and taking punishment without flinching until she was dug out some time later. Others were hard fox killers, though they were keen to rush in and attack their quarry, rather than cleverly tease until a fatal hold was accomplished and the quarry finished without receiving severe bites. The sense of some of the fell strains made them invaluable to a fell pack Huntsman and Stan

Mattinson, the one-time Whipper-in at the Blencathra and Hunts-man of the Coniston, told me of a terrier bred by Johnny Richardson out of his old strain that was descended from that of Jim Dalton's. Johnny bred Tinker and he grew into a big strong terrier that knew how to handle its fox. He could find in the deepest borran and, if his quarry refused to bolt, as is often the case when a fox finds itself in a good spot, he would bay, nip and tease until, shortly after-wards, he could get a throat hold and quickly throttle his foe. On many occasions Stan has dug down to Tinker only to find the fox dead and the terrier relatively uninjured. Johnny treasured such terriers and his strain consistently produced earth dogs of such high quality. The influence of fox terrier blood during those early times often resulted in less sensible offspring, though after a generation or two, sense usually returned. Richardson's strain was really a continuation of Jim Dalton's, and Dalton used quite a bit of

George Bell looking down into Newlands at Dalton and Blencathra foxhounds. Note White Lakelands coupled in foreground. Jim Dalton was one of the first to breed the typey Lakeland.

fox terrier blood during the latter part of the nineteenth, and early part of the twentieth, century, and no doubt he had problems with lack of sense for a while, but, when Richardson was a lad, Dalton's strain was famous, not only for producing consistently good fox killers, but terriers with sense too, so he obviously succeeded in correcting those faults that pedigree fox terrier blood had introduced.

The poor colouring of the fox terrier influence was partly corrected using Irish terrier blood, producing some attractive red fell types, but black and tan, or, at least, good quality black and tan, was still lacking and the Welsh terrier was used in order to resolve this problem. Welsh terriers had been producing predominantly good quality black and tan colouring and this cross was undoubtedly used in order to correct the problems fell terrier breeders were having with poor colour. Even during the mid-nineteenth century Welsh breeders were producing a jet black and rich tan colouring and this was the favoured colour for the new improved strains of fell types. Also, and this must have been very attractive to fell breeders, the coat of the Welsh terrier was resistant to water and this is why this breed became famous for its otter-hunting prowess. The Welsh also had an ancient lineage, though, as with other breeds, there was quite a bit of variety when they first began appearing at shows. Some were white, others had a touch of white on their chests, while others were grizzled. There *may* have been a touch of fox terrier in the bloodlines, but the coat was quite different from any other breed and so this suggests not.

I have no doubt that the Welsh strains were ancient and native, their terriers probably being descended from the Celtic terrier that was the ancestor of the corgi. (Contrary to popular opinion, corgis will go to ground and there have been at least two that were famous fox killers in the Lake District and one of these regularly worked the bad earths around Appleby and Brough and could finish its fox quicker than the native fell terriers.) However, I also believe that the Old English black and tan was used as outcross blood and that this was responsible for the black bar above the eyes that made this breed so recognisable. While others used white bodied terriers to bring into their strains, the Welsh probably avoided fox terrier blood in the main and eventually succeeded in producing the good black and tan colouring so consistently. Fell terrier breeders had thrown all sorts into the mix, yet Welsh breeders stuck mainly to their native strains and so the colouring of the Old English black

The Blencathra foxhounds in Borrowdale. Johnny Richardson, Huntsman, bred his strain from Dalton's old bloodlines and Thomas Rawling's Rock.

and tan, unlike in other breeds, wasn't diluted and the Welsh, in the main, became fixed in type very early on.

There is certainly an amount of shared ancestry with the old black and tan terrier, though Welsh strains have been bred for hundreds of years in their native land, especially around Carnarvonshire. Indeed, John Jones kept old black and tan terriers that worked with the Ynysfor as early as 1760 and probably long before that time. Could the Old English black and tan have originated from these ancient strains? Possibly, though it is impossible to decipher matters of history that have been lost in the mists of time. Griffith Hughes kept a Welsh strain during the late eighteenth century and these were famed for their prowess at both otter and fox. At the turn of the twentieth century there still existed a painting of him with one of his best, which was said to have killed a great number of foxes.

By the early 1800s strains bred in the south Carnarvonshire area were reputed to be the best and they produced consistently good workers. Lewis Jones, of the Four Crosses district, bred superb workers, known as the Saddler breed, and he kept the line pure for generations. Around Lleyn they were known as the Nauhoron strain. The town of Carnarvon and surrounding areas produced the Rumsey breed and Dolgelly districts kept the Williams strain. Another was the 'Shon go' strain at Harlech. All of these carefully bred strains were not only hunted regularly, producing an unbroken line of workers, but they also laid the foundation for what later became the show Welsh terrier, still an unspoilt native and superb worker during those early days of shows. These dogs became so famous and known for their exploits at work that poets began to write about them. The earliest record is from 1450 and it mentions:

> A black, red-bellied terrier bitch
> To throttle the brown polecat,
> And to tear up the red fox.

This is most certainly a description of an early Welsh terrier that the poet had likely seen at work for himself, for the original poem was written in the Welsh language. The early Welsh terrier was of superb black and rich tan colouring and was noted for its short muzzle and powerful head. By the 1920s and 30s, however, many Welsh terriers resembled fox, or Irish terriers, such blood having been used by the show fraternity in order to 'improve'

A lovely strong champion Morlen Bullseye. The fox terrier pre-Second World War was a worker and such dogs did much to improve type in Lakelands. (Photo c.1900)

type for the showring. What a disgrace that the old undiluted working strains were thought so little of by exhibitors who, after all, were in it for glory, or money. Few worked their charges and racial purity went out the window when breeding to win shows became the rage. Up until at least 1910, most Welsh strains remained pure and I am certain that this blood was used, probably even during the late nineteenth century, in order to improve colouring in fell strains, for the fox terrier blood and white bodied terrier blood brought into the mix from settling miners of the south, had produced mainly grizzle, while the majority were blue, or blue and tan.

True, black and tans were not common before the later 1920s, though some strains did produce this colouring consistently and some of the markings found on early fells were exactly those of the Welsh terrier. Topsy was an early champion and was probably responsible for the longer muzzles that began to appear on Welsh terriers at the turn of the century. Another was Bob of Bethesda, a terrier that worked with the Buckley Otterhounds and was owned and bred by the Master of that pack. Bob was a superb worker, but was killed by the pack while working an otter from a holt. Before this occurred, however, Bob sired several litters and became a cornerstone of the Welsh and no doubt, through his offspring, quite a few fell terrier strains were infused with his blood. Do not forget, as is the case in recent times, packs in different parts of the country were often in contact and friendships were forged by Masters, Hunt servants and followers. Invitations for packs to come to the area to spend a week or so hunting were not uncommon, so it is very likely that Welsh terriers came to the Lakes with visiting hunters, some even being given as gifts to their hosts, and that these then entered local fell strains. Just one strain which consistently produced black and tans during the early part of the twentieth century was that bred by Thomas Rawlings of the Eskdale and Ennerdale Foxhounds, and these had the bar above the eyes which betrayed Welsh terrier influence in his bloodlines (more of this strain in the next chapter). Wales has long enjoyed close associations with the Lake District, indeed, some of the place-names are Welsh in origin, as Plummer so eloquently explains in his book, *The Fell Terrier*, and so it is not unreasonable to assume that Welsh terriers occasionally influenced the breeding of earth dogs in this part of the world.

The original fell terriers, known as coloured working terriers, or

Champion Irish Terrier (Breda Mixer' (nineteenth century) Irish terriers were used to improve coat and type in fell terriers.

named after localities where they were mainly bred, such as at Patterdale, or Elterwater, were rather an unsightly bunch in the main, many with long backs, small heads and poor coats, together with poor colouring, and the advent of the show craze slowly began to change things, particularly from the 1880s onwards. Irish terrier blood produced some very good red offspring, as well as wheaten in some cases (some Irish strains were wheaten in colour), improving type dramatically, while fox terrier blood produced sharp lines, making the terriers much more box-shaped and bringing in the ears tighter to the head. Also, this influence meant that white fell terriers were produced with far more regularity and several can be seen working with the fell packs in early photographs. Many of these may well have found a ready market among ferreting folk, but a large number served with local hunts and all of the fell packs, at some time or other, have had white fells working for them. Fox terrier blood also diluted what black and tan colouring there was in those early days, so much so that, by the 1920s, most, although of superb type, were either red, blue, blue and tan, wheaten, or grey-grizzle. Welsh terrier had already been added to the mix before this time, but was again put into the mix during the 1920s, in order to sort out that bad colouring. The western regions of Cumberland seem to have been producing the best black and tans in those days and it may well have been staff and followers of the Egremont Otterhounds, or the West Cumberland Otterhounds, who first introduced this blood, for Egremont and the surrounding areas seem to have led the field in improving type, the exception being Jim Dalton at the Blencathra kennels at Thelkeld, Paisley of Keswick and Mitchell of the Melbreak (though Mitchell may well have got his improved stock from the Egremont area).

As time went on and great improvements were made in type, exhibiting was taken more and more seriously and quite a number of hunting folk realised they could have terriers that were both typey, and good workers. And so breeding began to be carried out far more seriously and good looking specimens were far more common by the beginning of the twentieth century. These terriers continued to be labelled with several different names and the most common term of 'coloured working terrier' was hardly an apt title for such a superb working, and now better looking, breed of earth dog. And so, in 1912, some of these breeders called a meeting at the Keswick show in the summer of that year and, after lengthy discussions and great debate, the name of 'Lakeland terrier' was proposed and accepted and this was to be all-encompassing, covering all of the fell terriers from all of the different regions. No longer was it necessary to call one strain a Westmoreland terrier, another a Cumberland, or fell, or fellside, terrier, for the name of

A chocolate Lakeland belonging to Diane Barker, daughter of Anthony.

An unregistered Lakeland that clearly owes some of its type to pedigree blood.

'Lakeland terrier' was suitable for every region where the best strains were bred.

It is not known exactly who attended this meeting, but one thing is certain, the numbers were made up of fell Huntsmen, Whips, committee members, and other serious terrier breeders who regularly followed hounds. Robinson, Rawlinson, Long, Pepper, Douglas Paisley, Jim Dalton, Rawlings, Mitchell, Pool, and a host of other noteworthy breeders were likely to have been at that meeting and the name of Lakeland terrier was from now on to be used for Cumberland and Westmoreland based earth dogs. Many did adopt the name, though some die-hards – those who believed that shows would ruin the working fell type – chose not to use this new name and continued with regional titles, or the drab 'coloured working terrier'. It was this new name that gave breeders added impetus to produce better stock that would eventually breed true to type. True, the improved strains, much like the rough and ready fell types, were rather an odd mixture, but they were none the worse for that. The new Lakeland terrier was every bit as useful as the old strains and some Huntsmen, such as Irving and Dalton, and hunt followers, or committee members, forsook the poor type and kept only the better stamp of terrier for work with hounds. The Lakeland terrier had been born and, whether folk loved or hated the new improved type that had inspired the name, it was to have a massive influence on the future breeding of both working and show bred Lakeland terriers for generations to come.

4 The Lakeland Terrier and Early Breeders

Glaister, Mills, Paisley, Rawlings, Fletcher, Spedding, Irving, Johnston, Bruce, Long (grandfather, father and son), Dalton, Pool (both Anthony and John), Allen, Crellin, and several others, were responsible for breeding the new improved Lakeland terrier and some made a massive impact on strains, while others had a much smaller, though still valuable, part to play. Even as early as 1912, and before this date in fact, fell type had improved in leaps and bounds and there was some very typey stock around at this time, which was winning well at agricultural shows, but after this date, now that the new name had been adopted, breeders began attempting to iron out the many faults still cropping up in litters such as poor coats and weak heads. These breeders were all hunting folk and worked their stock regularly to fox, badger and otter, as well as polecats and pine-martens, and several continued to work them in packs, together with a few hounds and often farm collies too. It is true to say that Irish blood in particular had produced more quarrelsome offspring and that breeders did experience problems with kennel fights, even in those early days, but the majority were quiet and non-aggressive and several could be kennelled together without any problems whatsoever. Even two dogs were couple companions in many cases and there were no problems with fighting. Some became aggressive if not regularly employed at work but the vast majority were peace-able and it seems that only those fanciers who didn't work their stock had severe trouble with their charges, with many being killed in kennel fights, for they were bored and frustrated because of not being able to exercise their incredibly strong and persistent working instincts. The breeders mentioned above do not fall into this category, for they were first and foremost working dog folk who would not tolerate non-workers.

Foxes, badgers (in lowland areas, for they were not found on the fells in those early days), otters, rats, polecats, pinemartens and stoats – all were worked regularly by the top breeders of the early twentieth century and the new type of Lakeland terrier was fully tested as to gameness during the years after the 1912 Keswick meeting. The Eskdale and Ennerdale, Melbreak and Blencathra packs led the field in working the improved Lakeland and it was the fell packs that led the field in terms of breeding programmes too, for the new strains were bred first of all for work, and then in order to compete much more successfully at shows, which remained the old agricultural shows where classes for terriers took third place, after sheep and hounds of course. And so they were not particularly well organised affairs, though the judges were usually fell pack Huntsmen, Whips, or committee members.

As time went by, some who were only interested in glory and money began keeping the new type and work was only a mere after-thought, if it was a thought at all. The decade after 1912, therefore, proved rather unsatisfactory and the leading lights of the Lakeland terrier breeding scene decided they must do something about the situation, for, not only were non-workers winning at shows, beating good typey stock that worked regularly with hounds and also privately (most of the fell country was keepered in those days and

Early Lakelands exported to Europe.

terriers were often used to bolt foxes to guns, or for fox and badger digging) for the hunting of foxes, badgers and otters, but the shows themselves were poor affairs with inadequate prizes on offer to the winners.

Something had to be done and so, in 1921, many of those same enthusiasts who had secured the name of 'Lakeland terrier' in 1912, now called another meeting at The George Hotel, Keswick, where, again, after much discussion and debate, The Lakeland Terrier Association was formed. This was to be a governing body that would guide the future breeding and work of the improved type and ensure that good, well-organised shows be staged where proper prizes would be awarded to worthy exhibits. But, again, work came first and prizes awarded must only be given to working stock, unless it be in puppy classes of course, and usually working stock that served at one, or more, of the Lake District packs. Prizes were awarded specifically to such working dogs. Bruce, Paisley and others, in fact all of the founder members of the association, worked terriers regularly with both fox and otterhounds and, no matter how smart a terrier was, if it did not work it would not be tolerated by such folk. This meeting in Keswick proved to be a great success and from then on the LTA would stage shows that would be far better than the agricultural affairs. Also, shows were sometimes staged during the season itself, after a hunt and usually combined with a stick show – a tradition that survives to this day. But how could so many breeders all keep terriers that served at one of the fell packs? The way in which hounds were hunted in those days meant that almost an unlimited number of terriers could be employed on a fairly regular basis.

The structure of the fell packs was unique, though, to some degree, it was based upon that of the travelling todhunters who roamed northern regions in pursuit of troublesome predators. Before the fell packs as we know them came into existence, the landowners paid a Huntsman to keep a few hounds, terriers, sometimes running dogs too, which were used to protect the tenant farmers' livestock. This was not about sport and very often foxes were driven to waiting guns, or running dogs, rather than hunted until caught, lost, or run to ground. And not just foxes were hunted, for 'sweetmarts' (pinemartens), 'foumarts' (polecats) wildcats and badgers were also on the quarry list, as well as otters during the summer months. Hard-bitten terriers were used, for bolted foxes could escape and the tenants would not tolerate such neglect, so, if a fox was found skulking, it was usually killed underground, unless, of course, it got out of there before the terrier reached it. This service was provided all over the Lakes country and was usually paid for by the tenants giving the landowner some of their produce each year. Several packs were kept, far more than we see today, though they were much smaller and very often trencher-fed, the hounds coming together on a hunting day after the Huntsman climbed to the top of a prominent hill and gathered his pack using the horn.

It is said that some hounds, after a lamb, or poultry killing call, jumped through windows of farmhouses and outbuildings because the farmer hadn't been informed of a hunt that day. Normally, on an appointed hunting day, the hounds were loosed probably at dawn, just as the Huntsman would begin blowing 'the gather', but, on unexpected call-outs, informing all of the farmers was impossible and so some hounds were locked in. This old system continued into the nineteenth century and from early on things began to become much better organised and the system we see today was gradually adopted. All of the smaller packs dotted around here and there, and there were packs at Keswick (the Keswick hounds were moved to Threlkeld in 1826 and they later became known as the Blencathra Foxhounds we know and love today), Coniston, Ambleside, at the bottom end of Windermere, at Patterdale, Matterdale, Workington and a host of other places, eventually amalgamated and became the Coniston, Lunesdale, Eskdale and Ennerdale, Melbreak (probably the most ancient of all Lake District packs), Ullswater and the Blencathra Foxhounds – all of which, despite the ban in 2005, are still in existence and continue to carry out fox control, though in a more limited form, throughout the fells.

Hunting in the Lakes country is ancient and it seems that, before the landed gentry began keeping packs that were supported by tenants giving some of their produce in order to help pay for the upkeep of the kennels, many smaller packs were in existence that were maintained by farmers, though yet another curious system existed that enabled these packs to operate, mainly on a call-out basis when poultry and lambs were taken. My researches have led me to the writings of Ritson Graham who recorded the following in 1932. He gives a fascinating insight into the ancient form of hunting that had existed in the Lakes before the fell pack era.

He wrote:

When in the 17th and 18th centuries the rest of England was being rapidly depopulated of most of the noble of its wild creatures, Lakeland churchwardens were paying heavy toll for the capture of eagles, hawks, ospreys, wildcats, foxes and foumarts. The disbursement of the 'parish pence' continued in the more remote dales up to 1750. The reward varied not only for the species of vermin procured, but for the same creation in the various parishes. In the chapelry of Martindale where the record of payment for wildcats runs almost consecutively from 1706–1755 we find that the sum of one shilling was placed upon the head of the offending feline. Almost every Lakeland parish was at this time paying head money for foxes, though packs of hounds were being kept at the expense of the dalesmen in some districts. Thus from 1824–37 the churchwardens of Martindale had contributed £1.16s.1d for the feeding of hounds. Records covering a period from 1659–1849 show payment for a fox head at 12d, a badger 6d, an otter 6d, a pinemarten 4d, a polecat [foumart] 4d and a wildcat 4d. During the year 1725–6 24 foumarts were paid for, and in 1794, in which year a great slaughter of vermin was effected, as many as 173 foumarts are included. Even the much misunderstood and comparatively harmless badger [many Lake District farmers would not agree with this sentiment] was not exempt from this insidious persecution. In the parish of Dacre 36 badgers were slaughtered between the years 1685–1750. The fox, being more numerous and destructive than the wildcat, was paid for at a higher rate. In the parish of Asby in Westmoreland 2s.6d appears to have been the usual fee. The now almost-defunct pinemarten was also the object of a paid persecution and, though never as numerous as the fox or wildcat, it has survived the latter in Lakeland by half a century and still holds a precarious footing in the rugged heart of the district. Martindale, Patterdale, Greystoke and Kendal are the only Lakeland parishes which show a return of pinemarten payments. The earliest record is from Martindale dated 1598. The price for a dead pinemarten at Martindale had reached 2s.6d by the middle of the 19th century, though at Kendal the price for such a trophy in 1684–88 was but 4d.

What a fascinating insight into how pest control was carried out in the Lakes country in ancient times, though undoubtedly the bounty payments brought about unnecessary persecution and probably attracted professional Todhunters, or, to give them their proper Highland name, Brocaires, into Cumberland. Indeed, Todhunter is not an unknown name in the Lake District (Isaac Todhunter was Huntsman of the Blencathra 1843 to 1869, and Barry Todhunter is the current Huntsman of that pack) and undoubtedly has its origins in Scottish professional pest controllers settling in the area. This also gives us another clue as to how Scottish, or Highland terrier blood, entered the old fell strains very early on, giving the Lakeland bred terriers a knack for working in rock. No doubt many kept terriers and running dogs for controlling such pests, though, as the writings tell us, packs of hounds were kept by the dalesmen themselves, with churchwardens helping maintain these packs. They hunted everything with these hounds, from fox, to badger, to foumart, to wildcat, and so on, until, in later times, and that would be well into the twentieth century, the Lakeland packs began hunting fox exclusively, while otterhounds and beagles also came into existence in the area, the hunting becoming much more organised.

Once certain leaders in the world of hunting with hounds (such as Crozier, who formed the foundation pack of the Blencathra) realised how much enjoyment and satisfaction resulted from watching a pack at work, running dogs and guns were dropped from the proceedings, though guns did continue to play a minor role in fell pack hunting in certain areas at times, especially in more recent years because of roads becoming busier and more dangerous for the hunting of hounds. The Lunesdale, for instance, when working areas close to the M6, have traditionally allowed the use of guns in order to prevent a situation that could result in hounds getting onto the motorway.

Professional Huntsmen and Whips were employed, though during the very early days most packs could only afford a Huntsman (a scenario that has returned in these modern times), and then very often on a part-time basis, and, now that all of the smaller packs had forged into just a few, large areas had to be covered, which meant hounds had to travel great distances in order to hunt the more outlying places. Some hunts operated on Saturdays, though hunting often took place on weekdays only, usually three or four, starting on a Tuesday and continuing on Wednesday. Thursday would be for resting, while Friday, or Saturday, would be the next day of hunting. Some hunted Tuesday, Thursday and Saturday, while others hunted four days a week. And, during the spring when lambing calls came in, hounds would sometimes be out for as many as seven days in a week.

It was a very hard life, which, to some degree, has been made easier these days by motorised transport. The fact that much hunting took place on weekdays alone, meant that many folk could not attend hunts, especially when hounds were hunting another area, though some of the keener followers, many of them farmers and shepherds, managed to organise their workload in such a way that they could get out with hounds. And it was mainly farmers, or the more wealthy folk of the community, very often the landed gentry (or, rather, their kennelmen, or keepers), who bred the terriers. This remains true to some extent today, but terriers are mainly bred by hunt staff, villagers and even 'townies' in modern times. So, when hounds were visiting that particular dale for the week, the terrier breeders in that area had a good chance of using their terriers to ground. True, the Huntsman and Whip always took out with them a few brace of earth dogs and the Huntsman (the Whip in his absence) always had the say on which terriers were used, but the nature of the terrain meant that others often got a look in too, when a fox was either marked, or run, to ground.

If a meet was at Troutbeck, for instance, then foot followers would be scattered around the surrounding fells, with each hoping to keep

George Bell, Huntsman at Blencathra, and Johnny Richardson (Whip) just after the Second World War, with terriers bred down from Dalton's Lakelands. Note their size and good type – at least fourteen to fifteen inches.

in touch with the hunt for as long as possible. Some might climb out to Wansfell, or onto The Tongue, or maybe even onto the High Street range, while others might climb out to the head of the valley. If a hunt then occurred, and a find was often sure in such places, then, if the fox was either marked, or run, to ground, then the nearest person with good enough terriers would be the one to use their earth dog. The Huntsman and Whip might be a long way off and it could take an hour or two for them to reach the spot, and then only if they knew where hounds were, and so, in order to save much time, a terrier would be entered as soon as possible. This is how several folk could work their terriers with the same pack. Well over a hundred foxes would be hunted, probably nearer two hundred in an average season, and many of those would be marked, or run, to ground by hounds, and so there would be ample opportunity for any regular foot follower to make use of their terriers. Some loaned their earth dogs to Huntsmen and even keen breeders such as Willie Irving and Jim Dalton took terriers on loan, many of them unrefined in type, unlike the stock they bred, while others walked terriers for such breeders, in much the same manner as hounds are walked.

Hound puppies are reared by the keener followers, very often farmers, or villagers living within the hunt country, but these return to kennels when they are old enough to join the pack. However, because the hunt servants have to find work for three months during the summer, until the new season begins, hounds return to their walkers for that period, as do some of the terriers too. The keener terriermen of the fell packs, such as Jim Dalton, Johnny Richardson, Willie and Arthur Irving, to name but a few, bred their earth dogs in quite large numbers and put them out at walk during the summer off-season. The very best of the stock then went into kennel for the season, or they were kept by the walker, if that person was a regular and keen follower. And so large batches of terriers found work at each fell pack, as well as privately, working for keepers and farmers who had need to control foxes when the hunt was not in their area. And that is how the Lakeland Terrier Association could put classes on for terriers serving at one or more of the Lake District hunts and thus preserving the working qualities, while still enjoying a 'pleasing to the eye' sort of earth dog. The new improved Lakeland terrier was certainly pleasing to the eye, though they worked just as well as they looked.

In more recent years walkie-talkies and motorcars have meant that Huntsman and Whip can usually keep in close contact with

Champion Irish terrier, Paymaster, descended from Breda Mixer. The Irish was used to produce red terriers and improve coat on Lakelands. (Photo c.1900)

hounds and so waiting for hunt servants to arrive at a borran when a fox has run in, is often not a very long process, so fewer folk have used their terriers lately, with usually three terriermen being on the register and using their dogs when requested to do. So there is far less opportunity, or there was before the recent ban I should add, for using one's terriers than in former times.

The Irish blood had produced some fighters among the new improved Lakeland terriers, but, generally speaking, they were quiet and well behaved, even when several were together. Mrs Spence, Douglas Paisley, Dalton, Willie Irving, Glaister and a host of other folk, bred quiet, reserved Lakeland terriers that could easily be kennelled, or coupled, with other dogs, though they became hysterically keen when at quarry and several did not have the sense of the old fell strains. These often took fearful punishment, mauling their fox to death and being driven on to greater and wilder efforts with each strike of Reynard's powerful jaws. When at badger they very often suffered severely and many of the new stamp were actually killed by badgers. Harold Watson, Willie Irving, Dalton, Rawlings and several others all lost terriers when 'Brock' was un-expectedly found lurking in an earth; usually a rock spot from where they could not be dug out quickly enough. Though they may not have been hyperactive and eager to latch onto anything wearing fur, or even feather come to that, they were certainly hyper-game and came with no reverse gears when they found themselves in a little difficulty with a big hill fox, a badger, or an otter. Some strains of fox terrier, although originally bred to stand off and bay at fox and badger, were of a similar disposition and many are the pedigree fox terriers of yesteryear that were badly mauled by fox and badger, some even killed. Indeed, many of Rawdon Lee's contemporaries complained that their dogs were severely savaged by quarry before they could be dug out. One can only guess that the pedigree fox terrier influence was responsible for this lack of sense, for the Welsh and the Irish, although they could be hard killers of large quarry, usually had sense too. Plenty of bull terrier went into the fox terrier mix during the eighteenth and nineteenth centuries and I guess this is where the 'fool-game' qualities originated.

It has to be said, however, that, although there were many hyper-game Lakeland terriers, there were also several that were sensible and these proved excellent workers. Thomas Rawlings' many terriers, for instance, were used extensively with the Eskdale and Ennerdale pack, some for six or seven seasons plus, so they must have been game and sensible to last so long in the field. Rawlings' terriers played a huge part in the development of the early Lakeland terrier, both working and show specimens, and I believe the good quality black and tan terriers that have served at the Eskdale and Ennerdale hunt throughout the years are descended from his dogs, for he bred mainly black and tans when others were producing mainly reds, grizzles, blue and tans and wheaten coloured puppies. Some of the new good-looking strains were actually superb badger-digging and otter-hunting terriers as they would stand back, bay at and drive out their quarry, or stay until dug out without receiving too much injury to themselves. Joe Armstrong, for instance, a big pal of Billie Irving, worked several of Irving's Lakeland terriers and dug badger with them. Irving's stock were noted as stayers, but many had sense enough to stay out of trouble and some would not tangle with a fox, but cleverly bay and tease until their quarry fled to open ground. The new improved Lakeland terrier had its critics in those days, but one thing is for certain – they were game indeed and extensively used with the local fell packs.

The very nature of the terrain over which hounds run and the earths inhabited by fell foxes would ensure that the improved strains were suitable for the task of assisting hounds in controlling foxes and any that couldn't live up to the challenging circumstances surrounding every hunt, would be put down, no matter how

Anthony Chapman with Coniston terriers. The bitch at the front is very much of a type bred by Willie and Arthur Irving and may well have been bred from such stock.

good-looking, or typey they were. And so, even though much neater, more pleasing to the eye terriers were bred, their work continued to dictate their stamp, for the Lake District earths are testing indeed.

Borrans, or bields, abound in the fells, usually made up of rock that has fallen from tall crags above and piled up, one on top of another, over thousands of years. Many of these borrans, despite being hollow, are so deep that even the most noisy of earth dogs just cannot be heard and many are the tales told of terriers that entered such places, bayed a few times until going out of earshot in pursuit of their fleeing quarry, and were never heard, or seen, again. The late Anthony Chapman, in his memoirs, *Hark For'ard*, tells an awful tale passed down to him by his father, George, who hunted the Coniston Foxhounds from 1908 until 1931 when he was forced to retire due to a severe ankle injury. A fox was run in, a rather common occurrence in the fells, and, this being a large borran, two terriers were entered and later killed their fox below ground. However, they could not get out and the diggers soon encountered large, immovable rocks that meant extracting them was now utterly impossible. Food could be passed down to the terriers through cracks in the rock and it was decided, no doubt after much soul-searching and heated discussion, that it would be kinder to pass down poisoned meat to the pair, rather than leave them to suffer over several days, before they died of either exposure or starvation, whichever claimed them first. Hunting in the fells is not for the faint hearted and many gruesome tales of failed rescue attempts can be told. Borrans are terrible places and some are so bad that they are not worked anymore.

When talking to Barry Todhunter I asked him about bad earths in the Blencathra country and he went on to say that, even in recent years, he has discovered new earths and is amazed at some of the places he didn't know existed, despite his long service of hunting this landscape. They have run foxes into earths numerous times that Barry was unaware of and some of these were unsuitable for entering a terrier. But how did he know these were bad earths if he had never worked them before? Because they were either walled-up, or a rusting iron bar had been left jutting out of the piles of rock boulders as a warning to future generations not to enter a terrier here. Walling-up has not been practised for many years, but in the old days, up until the early years of Johnny Richardson (1940s), this was a common practice where terriers had been lost and a rescue had failed. If the borran could not be walled-up, then some sort of

L–R:
F. Pepper, G. Bone, Alf Johnston, unknown. All these early dogs were worked.

73

reminder was left at the scene and this was usually the iron bar aforementioned. The Lakeland fells are littered with walled-up borrans and rusting iron bars pointing to the sky as some sort of sad and lonely reminder of the fate of some poor terrier, or a number of terriers, of past generations. In time, many of the walled-up borrans have worked loose due to the horrendous weather conditions that plague the felltops, and foxes once again get to ground there, though only a fool would enter a terrier into such a place. Barry moves his hounds on every time a fox gets into one of these bad places. The new improved Lakeland terrier was certainly tested to the full when working out foxes from borran earths.

Dug-out rabbit holes can be bad places too, for a terrier usually has a tight squeeze to get up to a fox and has much less room to manoeuvre than in a drain, or rock earth (some rock earths are like caves in places), and so an earth dog can be severely punished under such circumstances before either bolting its fox, killing it, or being dug out. Anthony Chapman always said that a terrier had a much harder time with a fox in this type of earth and there is much substance in what he says. I have had my own terriers in dug-out rabbit holes on numerous occasions and they have usually had to dig on a bit to their fox, which meant that there was hardly room to move. A terrier thus situated cannot dodge the lunges of a fox and will sometimes be quite badly bitten.

Peat hags are another hazardous earth in the Lakes and the Blencathra country has some bad ones, particularly among the northern fells behind Skiddaw and Blencathra. Stan Mattinson has much experience of working such places and he says that a terrier will often suffer from the icy waters underneath these hags and it is sometimes this, rather than bites from a fox, that sees off a brave and game earth dog. Gary Middleton knows of some bad hags around the Lythe valley area, for he once had a bitch to ground in such an earth for hours before he finally located and dug her out. Not only is the icy water a danger, but, especially before the days of locators, hearing a terrier in a peat hag was often nigh-on impossible, no matter how loud and yappy it may have been. Peat kills sound and quite a shallow terrier may not be heard. One that is deep would be very difficult to locate in the old days. And digging in such material is incredibly difficult too, for peat sticks to the spade and is not easy to remove.

Stan has had terriers to ground in some nightmare peat hags, the worst being on the fells around Uldale and Caldbeck. One of the worst spots was out on the tops of the Skiddaw range after a meet at West Head farm with Jim Benson, who had called out the Blencathra pack after losing lambs. This was Stan's first hunt as Whipper-in to Johnny. Hounds, once the drag had been taken up, ran across the wide-open spaces of these fells on rather a good scent, leaving followers far behind, including hunt staff. Stan had climbed out higher than Johnny, the Huntsman, as is the usual custom for the Whip, and so was first to come upon the hounds at the spot where they had found their quarry to ground. They were marking a gryke in a crag and there was a borran above. Stan had never worked this spot before and he soon loosed a brace of terriers, Paddy and Wander. Paddy was out of Richardson's Paddy, which had been bred by Harry Corr of the Dungannon Foxhounds of Ireland. Corr always remarked that he 'never keeps rubbish' with regard to terriers and so this tried and tested Irish line of Jack Russell terrier had proved superb at work in the Blencathra hunt country.

The brace of terriers disappeared into the earth and no sound could be heard from them. Stan became a little worried after some time, but even more so when Johnny arrived and informed him that

Fred Barker's 'chowt-faced' Rock – (right) ancestor of Barker, Wilkinson, Irving, Hardisty and Middleton strains, to name but a few. Anthony Barker as a nipper with two Ilfracombe Badger digging club terriers.

this was a particularly bad place where terriers should not have been entered. Stan wasn't to know, however, so Johnny shrugged his shoulders and moved on with hounds, leaving his Whipper-in by the crag in order to wait for the terriers to emerge, if, indeed, they did. After a long wait, Wander, a blue bitch from the ancient Blencathra lines, did indeed scramble out, from the borran above, and she was, to quote Stan, 'completely clagged up with peat'. Paddy, alas, never emerged and Stan surmises that he killed his fox, along with the bitch, but couldn't find the strength to crawl out, due to the peat and the icy cold of the peaty water. Exposure to cold certainly sees off many game fell terriers.

All of the fell packs have their fair share of bad earths, some very bad earths in fact, yet terriers bred for service with these packs, including the new improved strains which, don't forget, were bred by fell-hunters in the main, continue to work such places successfully. Of course, some of the very bad spots are completely avoided nowadays, though there have been times when a terrier has been entered into a bad spot because of a lamb, or poultry, killer having to be accounted for. Eddie Pool was once out with the Coniston Foxhounds, during the 1950s when Chapman had his best terrier, Crab, serving with the pack.

The fox was either a lamb killer, or a poultry killing fox, for it was run to ground at Broad Howe borran, a notoriously difficult place where normally a sentry stands in order to keep out a hunted fox. The fox either ignored those standing guard at the borran and dived into the place despite their every effort to send it on its way, or there wasn't anyone keeping guard that day. Hounds were taken away from the spot and the field stood well back, hoping for a bolt, and then Crab was loosed from the couples. He entered the borran, found his fox after some time and eventually, after a little 'persuasion', bolted the quarry to hounds. Eddie says he was most impressed with Crab that day, for foxes will often not bolt from such strongholds. The Ullswater country too, has some very bad earths and Eddie, as well as other regular followers, can soon tell a novice which earths should be avoided in that area. These borrans can be several feet deep and locators are useless for such places, for the bleeper goes out of range in a very short time. I once had my bitch, Bella, in a crag earth with a locator collar fitted, while she searched for a trapped terrier, and the bleeper went out of range within about six seconds, it was that deep. I had a very vociferous bitch down to a vixen and cubs and, though she was in for two days and eventually got herself out, I never heard a thing throughout the duration of the dig.

Lead and copper mines are honeycombed beneath the Cumbrian fells and the worst places for these are the Coniston mountains, such as the Old Man range and the Borrowdale valley where graphite was clawed from the earth for use in pencils. Some of these mines date back to prehistoric times, though the majority were dug from the Elizabethan era onwards, with the nineteenth century being a particularly busy time for miners. Lord Burghley had the task of defeating the Spanish Armada and he knew that putting copper onto the bottom of ships would make them faster in the water. A ship that can outpace those of the enemy will often be victorious and many battles were carried out using copper mined in the Coniston district in particular. Anthony Chapman, hunting the Coniston area, was following in the wake of his pack when one of his terriers, Patsy, fell into one of the old disused Burghley copper mines. She fell for quite some way, but was safely pulled out by a rock climber after several hours in this predicament. Foxes will sometimes use these old mineshafts and many terriers have been lost in them, very often because of rock or soil collapsing into the tunnel after a fox and terrier tussle disturbs the long-rotted supports.

The North Yorkshire areas hunted by the Lunesdale and

Champion Zip with champion Lady of Kinniside.

Wensleydale Foxhounds also have bad earths, ranging from borrans, to peat hags, to grykes that can plunge hundreds of feet into the pitch-black, icy world that makes up those rocky labyrinths. Around Pen-y-ghent, above Horton in Ribblesdale where the Lunesdale hold their annual Friday night terrier and stick show, there are some very bad places, some of which look like innocent soil holes, but in reality are nightmare deathtraps where terriers should not be put in. However, those earths that are deemed workable, must be worked out by a competent terrier and only the very best will do in such a landscape. With now at least two decades behind them of working such places, the new improved strains were proving more than useful and, by 1921, several terriermen were seriously breeding much better looking stock that could both work, and compete at summer shows. Now that the Lakeland Terrier Association had been formed, things could only get better for the Lakeland terrier itself.

5 The Work of the Lakeland Terrier Association

By 1921 a much better looking terrier was in existence in the fells, yet many breeders continued to work the old unrefined type which was mainly made up of Bedlington blood. These had poor coats and Willie Irving, writing to George Newcombe in the 1960s, explained why he abandoned this type of terrier for the new improved strains. Shows played a large part in breeders' efforts to produce good looking stock that worked well, as well as being pleasing to the eye,

Joe Bowman (1922) (seated on carriage) with a terrier at his feet bred down from J. Wilkinson's Lil. This bitch is probably Lil, the terrier given to Sid Wilkinson two years after this photograph was taken, in 1924. This setting is a Mardale Meet.

but Willie, and many other fell-hunters, experienced problems with the old type of earth dog during spells of bad weather. Willie mentions that he had to carry semi-conscious terriers home on several occasions after they had suffered from the elements. They were game enough, even too game in some instances, but they were not well suited to conditions that are classed as 'Arctic', especially on the high tops where many borrans are found. Now that the Keswick meeting had resulted in The Lakeland Terrier Association being formed, one of the main aims of the members was to improve coat, for many breeders experienced the same problems when their charges had been out in bad weather. Irving goes on to say that the old type fell terrier was mated by fox terriers and the coloured offspring were kept back and used for work and show and then carefully bred from.

The fox terrier had one of the best coats at this time and they were also incredibly typey, so breeders had no hesitation when it came to using them. Irving did not use fox terrier on his bitches, but he certainly used Lakeland Terrier Association stud dogs that had been produced via this route. The immediate result was better coat and

'Chappie' with coupled black and tans which show a large influence of pedigree Lakeland in their make-up. Note the black terrier, possibly one of Buck's given to Logan during the 1950s.

Ch. Lady of the Lake. Entered to fox like Wildfire at 6 years of age.

type and from then on the terriers improved yet more, with Irish and Welsh terrier also being used. Thomas Rawlings and Frank Pepper produced some very typey black and tans in those days and Willie Irving certainly used their terriers in order to help shape his own strain of Lakeland, as did Bob Gibbons who bred some very typey black and tans from such stock. It is my belief that Welsh terrier blood, possibly from the Ynysfor Hunt, was responsible for this quality black and tan colouring and Irving himself referred to these as being 'rather Welsh in type'.

Frank Pepper lived in the Borrowdale valley, though it seems he hunted with the Melbreak, as well as the Blencathra (both packs hunt parts of the Borrowdale valley), though his stock may well have originated with Jim Dalton. Rawlings and Pepper were breeding good quality black and tan terriers and these may well have been related stock, but who first started breeding these terriers is a matter lost in history. Whoever led the field in those days, I am convinced that Welsh terrier blood played a major role in the development of the Lakeland terrier. These Welsh earth dogs were as yet unspoilt by professional show people who cared nothing for work, and the improved Lake District strains were no worse off for such outcross blood. In fact, these dogs had been used for working all large British quarry and in a similar landscape to the fell country, so they were well-suited for use on Lakeland bred stock. Even into the 1960s and 70s, some strains of unspoilt typey Welsh terrier were still in existence and Gary Middleton used such blood in order to produce much better colouring in his strain of Lakeland terrier.

Douglas Paisley was one of the driving forces of the Association formed in 1921 and it was he and his wife who donated a challenge cup that was to be awarded to any terrier that had earned a working certificate with any of the fell packs, though the owners had also to be members of the Association. This shows that work was of paramount importance and Willie Irving stated that all of the Lakeland terrier breeders, or the vast majority anyway, continued to breed with work foremost in mind even into the 1950s and 60s. In those early days especially, Lakeland terriers belonging to the Association were worked both privately and with fell packs and it was Paisley and Irving who led the field in this regard. Work was so much an important factor during the 1920s and 30s in particular that The Lakeland Terrier Association was referred to, unofficially of course, as The Lakeland Working Terrier Association and even those members who didn't hunt always had access to work for their dogs through friends or family members who hunted. The fell country communities were very tightly knit in those days and many families were related in one way or another, through blood ties and marriage, so there were no problems getting dogs entered to fox, badger and otter. Irving himself, would take terriers on loan for Association breeders and several of the Oregill strain (Alf Johnston, who was also Meagean's kennelman) worked with the Melbreak.

Billy Irving had an endless supply of work for his terriers, of course, for he did all of the hound and terrier work himself, and so would have need of a large supply of earth dogs (if Willie couldn't get to an earth because of distance, or he lost touch with hounds, then others on the scene would use their stock for bolting, or digging out, foxes). Douglas Paisley was Honorary (unpaid) Whipper-in to the Blencathra and had plenty of work for his dogs too, so he could easily help other association members out who didn't hunt, or who only hunted on occasion. These breeders, Tom Meagean and Bob Gibbons among them, were bitten by the show-bug, but they made sure their charges were entered to large quarry, for the aim of the Association was not only to improve and fix type, but to make certain that working qualities were preserved for future generations. The early Association members were passionate about preserving both show and work qualities and non-workers were

82

simply not tolerated. At the Eskdale and Ennerdale pack, it fell to Thomas Rawlings to make certain that working qualities were of uppermost importance for the new improved type being bred in that hunt country.

The 1920s were spent fixing type and making certain that the improved strains were just as useful, if not more so, than the old strains and, in some ways, they were of better type for work. The old strains had come in many different shapes and sizes and large chests and shoulders were often a problem, making it impossible for some to reach their quarry, especially in borrans. Others were so short in the leg that covering rough ground was a nightmare for them. Middleton can remember being out with two very short-legged terriers belonging to a hunting companion and, after crossing a fell covered in deep heather, their bellies were scratched to ribbons and bleeding. Most of the early types had poor coats and many suffered badly from the elements. Also, many were fifteen inches plus in height, so size was an issue at the time.

The meeting in 1921 resulted in a breed standard that was full of

Unspoilt Welsh terriers of late nineteenth century. The characteristic bar above the eyes is found on many pedigree and working Lakelands.

common sense. The acceptable colours were black and tan, red, blue and tan, wheaten, grizzle, mustard, black, and all of the above could include a small amount of white on feet and chest, though several breeders were not at all keen on these markings and Billy Irving did his utmost to breed out flecks of white on his terriers (the result of fox terrier blood). Predominantly white terriers, though worked with hounds, were not accepted in Lakeland classes. This is something working terrier judges should consider before allowing white Lakelands in Lakeland classes. Some judges even suggest to owners that such exhibits should not be in Lakeland classes. The original standard, set by the creators of this breed, prohibits putting white Lakelands in such classes and, if show organizers do not wish them to be in Jack Russell classes either, then they should provide separate classes exclusively for white Lakelands. The trouble is, at many shows the Jack Russell classes would be nigh-on empty!

Weight in dogs was not to exceed seventeen pounds, while bitches were not to weigh over sixteen pounds. Colour, of course, has little to do with working ability, but one can see the workmanlike standard beginning to emerge, for such weights are just about the maximum for a terrier to be required to work in the fells. Also, because this was not an average weight, allowing a little more or a little less, terriers weighing quite a bit less, but no more, were accepted and there are places in the Lakes where a smaller terrier is very handy, such as in deep borrans. Johnny Richardson, Stan Mattinson and Willie Porter all favoured smaller, lighter terriers for working particularly deep rock places.

Height had not to exceed fifteen inches at the shoulder and, again, because this was not an average size, smaller terriers were accepted, for they were used in the fells at work. Many of the new improved strains produced smaller terriers, ranging from twelve to fifteen inches. During those early days many of the fell terrier strains were larger, rather than smaller, and this was probably due to the inclusion of Irish terrier blood, for this breed, even in the early days, was usually on the larger side. The LTA had certainly got size and weight correct and, again, the emphasis on work, rather than show qualities, is obvious.

The head had to be square and the jaws powerful and not too long, the nose black and the teeth meeting in a scissor-bite, for maximum biting power. Missing teeth, though not mentioned in the breed standard, were acceptable, for such resulted from regular work to

Bob Gibbons with one of his Kinniside Lakelands. His strain served at the Blencartha and possibly the Melbreak too.

fox, especially on harder dogs. A baying terrier will usually keep all of its teeth, but one that grapples with its fox and kills it, will inevitably lose a tooth or two. The ears were to be small, V-shaped and carried on top of the head preferably, though a little to the side wouldn't be considered too much of a fault. Even the small ears had a purpose regarding work. For one thing, this was implemented in order to breed away from Bedlington blood, for this produced poor coats and often dangerously hard terriers which were often killed, or badly maimed, when encountering 'Brock'. Secondly, large ears do get bitten, and sometimes quite badly, while at work to fox, so the smaller ears were partly to avoid this. The eyes were to be dark, or hazel in colour, with a keen, alert expression.

The neck was to be of good reach, but not too long like a whippet, enabling a terrier to grapple with a fox round a rock, or suchlike obstacle, while the chest was to be reasonably narrow, the forelegs and front straight, narrow and well-boned. A light-boned terrier would fare badly against fox, especially a big hill fox, so again one can see the emphasis on work in such statements. True, some preferred feet turning out slightly in order to scramble over rocks better, but, as someone said, foxes have straight legs and feet and nothing is more agile than they. The feet were to be small, compact and well padded, and for good reason. Working rock and covering rough ground for miles on end would badly damage unsound paws, so there is much common sense in this standard.

The back was to be strong and short-coupled, but only moderately, not so short that agility suffers, for a terrier must twist and turn through narrow crevices inside borrans. The hindquarters were also to be strong and muscular and well balanced.

The jacket, and this is most important, was to be dense and weather resistant, harsh and with a good undercoat. Many of these fell-hunters had been forced to carry their poor-coated terriers home, or to the nearest farm, after bad weather, and some had died, so one can see the common sense coming through yet more in this workmanlike breed standard. And finally, the tail was to be well set on, meaning of decent length, enough to get a good handful should a terrier have to be lifted out of a tight spot, and carried gaily, but not curling right over the back. The general appearance was to be smart and workmanlike, alert and fearless.

This is such a good, practical breed standard that judges of today, whether of Kennel Club appointment, or at working terrier shows, should keep this close in mind when judging Lakelands and adhering to such a standard would produce worthy winners (if terriers matching this standard can still be found at Kennel Club shows today). What this standard did was to produce a more uniform type that was just as useful, if not more so, at work than the old and unrefined fell strains. We hear a lot of folk go on about 'working type', casting out of the ring smart Lakeland types, for often more mongrelly terriers. What short-sighted people these are. This standard for Lakeland terriers was set by working terrier enthusiasts who hunted over some of the worst terrain in Britain and it was practical, not meant just for producing show dogs. Also, it was designed to do away with excessively large terriers and those too wide in the shoulders, or too deep in the chest, to 'get'. When the Kennel Club made changes to the standard and introduced such things as average weight and height, they began to ruin the working standard, for terriers nearest to those averages, with some exceeding the original limits, were put up and many champions have been unworthy, being too heavy and too big for work. That original 1921

Alf Johnston (centre) with Mrs Parks at the Mealbank kennels at Kendal. This strain may well have influenced breeding at the Coniston Hunt.

standard should have remained as it was, though liver colour, for some reason, was not included and this was put right in 1937, when the average system was introduced – wrongly in my opinion. From then on, the Lakeland terrier, as far as work is concerned, went into decline in some ways, especially with regard to weight and height, though it would take quite a number of years for the bad effects to show.

Even in the early days of the 1920s some breeders were producing large specimens that were a little on the heavy side too, though the LTA standard would mean that few, if any, would do well at shows. Irving, Gibbons and Paisley in particular, bred smaller, neater dogs, which worked regularly to fox. Some were bad fighters, true, but the majority were kennelled together and with hounds and so were not in the least bit quarrelsome. Irving and other breeders only usually experienced problems when two dogs, or two bitches, took a dislike to one another, the seed having been sown after a slight disagreement at feeding time, when a bitch was in season, or maybe a bit of jealousy at an earth, but that can happen with even the quietest and least quarrelsome of breeds, including the old strains of fell terrier. Maud Vickers, Billy Irving's eldest daughter, showed me the famous and much used photo of her father at Crummock Water in the spring of 1934 (the Good Friday meet), going on to name some of the terriers. Two of them, Rock and Jerry, took such a dislike to one another that, though easily kennelled with others, if they met in the yard they fought vigorously and had to be drowned off each other in the water trough. Both were extremely good workers and served regularly with the Melbreak, being tolerant of each other when out with hounds (though not being coupled together), but they hated one another and attacked at the first opportunity back at the kennels. Generally speaking though, the new strains of Lakeland were quiet and docile and only gave problems when not worked.

Who exactly began the breeding of these more typey terriers is difficult to say, but Peter Long was instrumental in producing many of the early terriers. He obtained his stock from Robinson, a road worker who may well be the same Robinson of Maryport from whom Breay obtained Tink, one of the founder terriers of the

Hamilton Docherty (L) and Glaister with white Lakelands. Docherty kept fell terriers infused with Irving strain Lakelands.

Buck/Breay strain. The other alternative is a chap known as 'Doggy' Robinson who was described as 'an old fell-hunter' in the early 1950s, though, of course, they could be one and the same person. Peter Long took bitches from Robinson to Jim Dalton's stud dogs, such as Turk and sons and grandsons of Turk, and he produced many of the foundation stock for what later became known as the pedigree Lakeland terrier. It is my belief that many of the early breeders, including Alf Johnston, Meagean and possibly Thomas Rawlings, obtained their stock via Peter Long.

Douglas Paisley undoubtedly used the fox terriers and improved fell terriers belonging to Glaister and Carrick who hunted around Carlisle and much of the fell country too, especially around the northern regions where the Blencathra and Melbreak also hunted. Carrick was master of the Brampton Harriers which hunted both hare and fox, and Glaister was with the Carlisle and District Otterhounds, both packs covering much of the same country, though the otterhounds hunted into the fells and up into Dumfriesshire too. Both of these breeders produced top quality fox terriers and they also used crossbreds; typey stock that resulted from fell and fox terrier crosses. Dalton used these fox terriers and typey crossbreds on his fell stock, and it seems likely that the Paisley brothers, both Douglas and Joe, followed the same route, including the use of Dalton's stud dogs (Turk was the gamest and smartest terrier in the fells during the first decade of the twentieth century and he is undoubtedly the founding father of the Lakeland terrier), while Rawlings, Irving and Pepper used terriers with Irish and Welsh ancestry in the main, though, of course, fox terrier blooded fell types also went into the mix. Pepper lived where the Blencathra hunted, so it may well be that he also used Dalton stock in his breeding programme. Irving used Pepper, Gibbons, Johnston, and Meagean bred terriers on his own strain of Lakeland and this resulted in one of the best looking and best working strains to ever come out of the fells. Indeed, Irving's terriers had a massive impact on the working, and exhibiting, terrier scene throughout the 1920s, 30s and 40s in particular. But from where did Irving's strain originate? The next chapter will discuss further the breeding programme of Billy Irving and others associated with him, but first it is appropriate to discuss the progress made by the LTA in those early days.

Selective breeding carried on in earnest throughout the 1920s and several breeders from the small town of Egremont were instrumental in producing top quality Lakelands. Some of these breeders were able to use their stock with the fell packs, often when Huntsman and Whip were too far away to use their terriers, though the majority did not use their stock in this way. This meant that certain classes were inaccessible to them at LTA shows; classes open to stock working with fell packs only, but still, these terriers were workers through and through, used for fox and badger digging and otter-hunting in particular and worked in bobbery packs throughout the countryside surrounding this area. Make no mistake, they may not have worked with any of the fell packs, but they were still extremely game and often worked with small packs of hounds kept by a few enthusiasts. The otterhounds were made up, especially in the early days, of hounds walked from the Melbreak and Eskdale and Ennerdale packs and many Egremont breeders used their terriers with such packs.

At Egremont, Irish, Welsh, but mainly fox terrier blood went into the mix and the old Bedlington type of fell became far less common. In his early days, Willie Irving had crossed small bitches from the Eskdale and Ennerdale pack with blue fell terriers of obvious Bedlington ancestry and had produced some incredibly game stock from these unions. However, on wet and icy cold days, he had been forced to carry near-dead terriers to the nearest farms, and then home, after they had suffered from the elements due to very poor coats. This was one reason why Irving abandoned the old type of fell for the improved Lakeland. The use of fox and Irish terrier in partic-ular, had improved coat dramatically. Steve Robertson of Tebay, a good terrierman of the modern era, has also been forced to carry poor-coated terriers home for treatment after they have stood out in icy wind and rain for any length of time, and he says that the prob-lems often come not when a terrier is to ground working (wet drains and damp peat hags excepted) where the toil and body heat will help keep a terrier warm, but when it has to wait outside an earth, often for hours, while the fox is either bolted, or dug out. That is when many terriers with poor coats suffer and for that reason the improved strains of Lakeland had to have good coat that would keep the wind and rain at bay. The Lakeland certainly had a much better coat than many of its predecessors and this was very often attained after the very first cross, with improvements made with selective breeding. If a terrier had a poor coat, then it was not used for breeding, and the same rule applied to working ability. The early Lakeland had to prove game and all of the original stock saw work of some sort, either during private digs and/or with Otterhounds and Foxhounds.

As the twenties progressed the LTA sought Kennel Club recognition and in 1928 this was at last accomplished. It was feared that working ability would suffer and dogs fit only for the show bench would result from this, but the LTA was determined to keep working ability to the fore and breeders such as Pepper, Irving, Paisley, Farrer and Mrs Spence, a later member of the Lakeland Terrier Association, were determined to keep this alive. It was they, together with several of the Egremont breeders, who made working ability a priority and it was they who maintained that ability – none more so than Billy Irving and Paisley in particular. The meeting at Keswick show in 1912 had produced the name of Lakeland terrier that was to be all-encompassing – a name which even the scruffiest of fell terriers would be known by, and proudly, but by the 1920s an ever-widening gap had begun to emerge and the new strains of Lakeland were vastly different in looks from the old strains, though, again, it must be stressed that working ability did not suffer at this time and the vast majority of Lakelands saw service at all large British quarry. Nevertheless, several breeders stuck with the old strains of fell terrier, while others brought into the mix the typey Lakeland, but had not sufficient enough knowledge of genetics to keep the better type going. Some breeders attempted to produce good looking and competitive stock, but failed, abandoning their breeding

Egton Crab of Howtown; looker and worker. Mrs Spence's Lakelands served at the Ullswater once they had become champions – Crab was full brother to Zip.

Egton Surprise, a black Lakeland exported to Sweden. Modern blacks are descended from this dog, which, I believe, could be traced back to Parker's black Turk, through Irving's dogs.

programme and returning to the old type, which still showed characteristics of Lakeland terriers years later.

Lakelands were first seen on the show bench at a Kennel Club show in 1928 and Douglas Paisley won first, second and third prizes with his terriers – dogs that worked regularly, alongside those of Dalton's, with the Blencathra Hunt. By 1931 far more exhibitors were seen in the ring and Mrs Spence and Tweedie were among them. Tweedie won with Evergreen's Double, while Mrs Spence won with Lady of the Lake. Alf Johnston wasn't keen on Evergreen's Double, the first Lakeland champion, however, and he stated, in a letter to Miss Morris of Kelda kennels, that this terrier was used all over the country and that he produced poor offspring that set the Lakeland back years. Lady of the Lake and others such as Egton Rock and Paisley's Huic Holloa, were quality terriers that bred good stuff – workers as well as lookers. In fact, all of these early champions were bred out of workers and all were worked. Paisley served as Whip for the 'Cathra and he also used Bob Gibbons' strain of Kinniside Lakelands with the same pack. Irving used his strain with the Melbreak and often had Alf Johnston's Oregill terriers out too. Meagean's terriers also saw service with this pack, for the early breeders were determined to keep working ability alive and they deemed that honourable scars were not to be considered a fault by association judges. Also, non-workers were not to be tolerated. Maud and Pearl, Irving's daughters, stated that Billy's dogs carried scars picked up at work and that is how they were exhibited, whatever the opinions of the judges regarding this occupational hazard, though such scars prevented his terriers from doing well at Kennel Club shows.

Mrs Spence paid Braithwaite Wilson, and later Joe Wear, generous tips to try her terriers when hounds ran a fox to ground and several of her stock worked with this pack. However, by the 1930s, scars were not looked upon with favour by ignorant Kennel Club judges (LTA judges, on the other hand, were not to penalise a terrier with scars picked up at work) and so serious breeders such as Mrs Spence, Gibbons and Alf Johnston, introduced a curious system that would ensure working ability remained alive in pedigree stock. A terrier would maybe do the show rounds for four or five years, gain a championship or two and then retire as a stud dog, or brood bitch. A terrier might retire at the age of six years and that is when Kennel Club exhibits were entered to quarry. In 1933, just before he left the

Egton Lakeland terriers belonging to Mrs Spence. L–R; Crab, Stormcloud, What a Lad, Egton Rock and Fearless. Rock was used by many breeders including Joe Wilkinson, Joe Wear and Willie Irving. Many of the Egton terriers were fearless workers to all large British quarry.

Ullswater, Mrs Spence paid Braithwaite Wilson £1 to try a six-year-old bitch at fox. A fox was 'run in' by hounds and the bitch entered and she went like wildfire, quickly finding her quarry and seizing hold of it. She gave it no chance of bolting and a dig was soon underway. When they finally dug out the terrier, she had such a hold on the fox that she would not let go, no matter what they did. In the end, overcome with excitement, hounds 'broke' and rushed in on the fox and terrier, grabbing the fox, but leaving the little bitch unharmed. This 'legend' does not name the bitch, but I am certain that it was Lady of the Lake; the first bitch to win a certificate at a Kennel Club show. Her sibling was already serving regularly with the Ullswater pack and, because it was so narrow, was used in particularly deep borrans where its finding ability made it a legend. Egton Rock, the ancestor of Sid Wilkinson's famous Rock, was another of Mrs Spence's Howtown strain to be used with the Ullswater and he

Johnny Richardson's Lakelands. The terrier on the right is possibly Tinker and Pedigree Lakeland blood, the unspoilt early strains, is obvious. Tinker was a sensible worker.

Alf Johnston with My
Masterpiece.

impressed Joe Wilkinson (Whipper-in to Joe Wear) so much that he
brought him into his strain, which, again, served at the Ullswater.
Egton Rock was so game, in fact, that even Frank Pepper used him
on one of his bitches and no doubt he served several brood bitches
throughout the Lakes during his reign in the 1930s. Rock, like the
other show Lakelands of the time, was entered after his show career
was more or less finished, but before he was used at stud by working
terrier enthusiasts. Pepper's Blossom was by Egton Rock, out of
Myrtle, and this bitch was incredibly game, used at otter and fox
with the Melbreak.

This curious system was continued for many years after the estab-
lishment of the Lakeland terrier at Kennel Club shows, but it seems
that few outside of the Lakes practised this system of keeping
working ability alive. Many Fell terriers are slow at entering and I
wonder if this curious system of entering terriers so late began to
have an effect on some of the offspring, making them slow to mature
and thus making them not ready for work until maybe two or three
years of age. Border terriers are notorious for being slow to mature
mentally – the key to settling down to work – and this could be for
the same reasons. The early Border was just as easy to enter as the
early fell strains, but maybe the mix of show stock entered late, as

95

well as non-workers, has produced this trait. It is impossible to say why many fell and Lakeland terriers take time to mature and settle down to work, but maybe, just maybe, it is a result of Kennel Club show stock being entered at around five or six years of age and then being used to breed future stock.

Even into the late 1960s some breeders, especially in the fells, continued to use the system of entering terriers before they went at stud, or as brood bitches, in order to keep the working qualities alive. Kennel Club judges have a lot to answer for, for it was they who brought about this system, for it was impossible to win with scarred exhibits which had maybe lost a tooth or two in a tangle with a fox, and so breeders had no choice but to introduce this way of having both show, and working, stock. Ted Rigg was one such breeder. He lived near Cartmel in the south Lakes country and he was a professional pest control officer. He also hunted with the Lunesdale and North Lonsdale Foxhounds. Ted would enjoy a successful show career with each of his terriers and then, before they went at stud, or as brood bitches, he entered them and many then saw regular work at fox, and, in the early days when it was legal, badger too.

As he got older, Ted struggled a bit with digging and so he asked Gary Middleton to work one of his last champions, before he went at stud. This was a large, powerful red dog taken on by Middleton in the late 1960s and was probably Ranthorn Arkle, registered at stud in 1970. Gary cannot remember its pet name however, but he says that the dog was as game as they come. He was rather on the large side, the reason why Gary did not bring him into his breeding programme, but he could still often get up to his fox and when he did he killed quickly, cleanly and efficiently. Arkle was as good at killing foxes as any of Middleton's stock, though Gary says he had not the sense of his strain. This pedigree champion charged at his foe and killed it with hysterical glee. Middleton also entered the dog at badger (badger digging was then legal and Middleton shifted them for farmers and then released them into unused setts elsewhere), but Arkle was unsuited to such work and Gary could not enter him into deep places. He would put him in shallow setts and he dug quite a few badgers with this Lakeland, but he would not learn to stand back, the hard bites of 'Brock' only driving him on to greater and more savage efforts. Middleton once dug a fox in woodland at the side of the Wild Boar hotel, near Crook, and by the time he dug down to the dog, the fox was stone dead. And this was fairly typical of a dig with Arkle. He was then returned to Ted and began his stud career. Gary is pretty certain that Rigg's terriers were sometimes used with hounds too, though certainly not on a regular basis.

Allan Johnston, grandson of Alf, continues to breed the Oregill

Above left: Johnston's unregistered Lakeland, Bridgett.

Above right: Allan Johnston's black Lakeland from Europe.

Rightt: Alan Johnston with Oregill Pocket Rocket.

strain and one of his, Oregill Hacksaw, was used by several terrier-men in the 1970s for breeding typey stock that were as famous for gameness as they were for looks. One of Hacksaw's sons was put to ground close to the end of a badger dig. Two terriers were to ground, but 'Billy' had dominated the situation and the pair were stuck behind their quarry in a stop end. Hacksaw's son was now loosed and seized the badger, drawing it, and the pair of terriers holding grimly on to their quarry, from the earth. The 'Brock' was humanely dispatched, but still this son of the Oregill pedigree Lakeland would not let go his hold and in the end he had to be drowned off the cadaver in a nearby beck. Spluttering for breath, the terrier released his hold, but was wild with excitement to latch on to his prize once more. Several half-bred Oregill working Lakelands were used at the end of badger digs in order to draw out any that had gotten themselves into an awkward spot.

A Mr H. Fell left the Lake District for Australia in the 1960s and he took his working pedigree Lakelands with him. He was another who had worked hard to keep the working instinct alive, but, it has to be said, this was rather a losing battle. The Lakeland began to develop a much longer neck, a narrow head with weak jaws, and

The right sort; Alfie, bred by the author and owned by Neil Wilson.

A good Stamp.

chests too deep to be effective in rock. The founders of the Lakeland and the strains of the 1920s, 30s and 40s were still game, workman-like and extensively used in the fells in particular, and the same can be said of some strains during the 50s and 60s, but the majority were now unworked and unworkable and the situation only got worse, with unspannable and weak-headed Lakelands becoming the rule, rather than the exception. Some, like Billy Irving and Ted Rigg, continued to breed for work as a priority, even into the 1960s, but far fewer breeders, even in the Lake District, the breed's native home, showed any interest in earth work, or in producing terriers capable of working an earth.

Poor judges are to blame for this, as they would put up unworthy champions unsuited to work and then most would use that stud dog, or buy puppies from a champion bitch, despite its lack of ability and hunting instinct. Up until 1937 the standard size was not to exceed fifteen inches, but in 1937 an average size was introduced and that meant that many now bred as close to the fifteen-inch mark as possible. This created terriers of sixteen inches and above and much heavier than a working sort, which were put up as champions by judges who knew nothing of earth work, either in the fells, or down in the shires. Others bred extensively from these champions and hence a swift ruination of the original Lakeland was brought about. But the early dogs must not be confused with current pedigree Lakeland dogs, for the original strains were workers indeed, of the very highest order.

The Lakeland Terrier Association had been officially formed in 1921, though a group of enthusiasts had been working hard to breed a better type since the 1912 meeting at Keswick show. They did their utmost to promote work and all association studs were indeed workers, though there were already a few who had no interest in work at all. Classes exclusively for terriers serving at the fell packs were introduced in Association shows in order to ensure non-workers didn't take all of the prizes (non-workers were rare at this time) and the more serious exhibitors, especially during the 1930s, entered their stock after the best of their show career was over, in order to keep working bloodlines alive. They were doing good work and would continue to do so for a number of years to come.

As time went by and pedigree terriers that were worked became far less favoured, far fewer breeders, even in the Lake District, continued to work their exhibits and so the pedigree type fell more or less completely out of favour with those who worked unregistered strains. After Billy Irving had retired from the Melbreak in order to take up a post with the Hound Trailing Association, even his stock was looked upon unfavourably by many working terrier

A good quality modern Lakeland.

Steve
Robertson
with a
working
Lakeland.

enthusiasts, though Irving still bred for work, continuing to hunt with the Melbreak whenever possible and using his terriers when an opportunity arose. Others knew the value of Irving's strain and quite a few working terrier lads, both inside and outside the Lakes, used his stud dogs on their bitches, or bought pups from him, and these were first rate workers, used for both fox and badger digging. In fact, Pearl and Maud can still remember terrier lads from Wales travelling up to the Lakes during the 1950s in order to buy both entered stock and pups for fox and badger digging. Major Roche of the Ynysfor Hunt made a yearly pilgrimage to the fells in those days and undoubtedly took back to his native land Irving-bred working Lakelands.

By the 1960s the LTA had lost any influence it once had regarding the direction the breed must take and a few years later, during the early 70s, the Association became defunct. Breeders and judges who had no idea or ambition regarding working dogs had completely taken over the pedigree Lakeland terrier scene and type suffered greatly, until few exhibits were suitable for working underground. True, some, such as Oregill Hacksaw and Henchman, displayed a strong working instinct and produced excellent working terriers when put to unregistered bitches, and even full pedigree dogs such as those belonging to Ted Rigg, were still extremely game, if lacking in sense (though some pedigree Lakelands were sensible at work

Will Pinkney of the Golden Valley Foxhounds judging Lakelands at the Pennine Hunt Puppy Show (2006).

and Arthur Irving stated that his dogs were not as hard as the native Eskdale and Ennerdale unregistered terriers belonging to the Porters), but the majority by this time were unsuited to a day on the fells, let alone a few hours underground. The LTA had come to an end and, with it, the good old fashioned working Lakeland terrier.

I hunted with a pedigree Lakeland during the mid-1980s and, although it would go to ground and bay at its quarry for a time, it would not stay and showed little inclination to find quarry in deep earths. True, this was a young dog and may well have matured into a good worker in time, but I was not impressed. However, I was recently in Ireland and one of the terrier lads I was talking to regularly hunted with a pedigree Lakeland bitch and she was killing foxes for fun. He had taken her out a couple of times and she had shown a bit of interest in a couple of foxes they dug, but things didn't look too promising. On the third outing, however, the bitch suddenly clicked and entered eagerly, quickly killing her fox. She is also a good finder and works regularly to large quarry, so, obviously, some pedigree bloodlines still produce workers when given a chance and when they are small enough 'to get'.

George Newcombe, from his own handwriting in a letter to Willie Irving, was an enthusiast of pedigree Lakeland terriers and his Rillington strain was descended from Irving's dogs. Jock was bought directly from Billy and he was a superb worker at both fox and

An
unregistered
Lakeland bred
by Alan
Johnston.

103

George Norman with his Middleton bred Lakeland.

badger. Newcombe bred working Bedlingtons, some of which could get to a fox, others couldn't, and he would use these larger tykes as drawing dogs, or seizure dogs, at the end of digs; digs that were carried out using his Irving bred pedigree Lakelands.

The pedigree Lakeland in general is a sad creature that would have no chance whatsoever of enduring life as a working terrier up in the fell country. I believe they could be saved by using good typey working unregistered Lakelands, such as those belonging to breeders like Gary Middleton (Middleton breeds a type of Lakeland that is a near-replica of the foundation stock of the pedigree strains, but these are fixed in type and are generally of better conformation), Barry Wild, Brian and Andrew Meeks, Terry McLoughlin of Ireland,

Steve Robertson and others who enjoy a good working terrier that is also pleasing to the eye. The pedigree gene pool continues to shrink and outcross blood to such unregistered strains would easily correct the faults associated with unworkable pedigree stock today. I doubt my advice will be heeded, in fact, I know it will be rejected with scorn, for breeders of the quality of Paisley and Irving, who put working ability ahead of looks, no longer exist in the pedigree world. Allan Johnston, of the Oregill strain, agrees that working qualities should be bred for, just as his grandfather bred for them, but one man cannot change the way things are. The future looks bleak for the pedigree Lakeland as it moves further and further away from the good old working type of yesteryear.

6 Billy Irving and Associated Breeders

Robinson and Peter Long seem to have been the first breeders in the west to have begun breeding better type, as early as the late 1880s, but by 1920 there were several breeders and Egremont in particular would produce almost two-dozen terrier enthusiasts who helped shape the early Lakeland. Spedding of Egremont was one such breeder and his dog, Scamp, a half-bred fox/Lakeland terrier, became the foundation for future breeding programmes. Bill Mawson, father to Joe of the Rendale kennels, bred and worked wire fox terriers, as well as Lakelands, during those early days and many breeders used such bloodlines. I think it more than likely that one of the parents of Scamp would be owned by Mawson. Bill Mawson was certainly one of the co-founders of the pedigree Lakeland terrier and

Kitchen's Central Midge, 1928, founder of many top strains of pedigree Lakeland terriers.

106

The first Lakeland terrier champion, Evergreen's Double, bred from Irving's Crab, Nettle and Pippin.

his strain of fox terrier was widely used to improve type on what were mainly Bedlington blooded fell terriers.

Scamp mated Flower Girl, owned and worked by Fletcher, also of Egremont, and bred Castle Buglar (Castle comes from the district near Egremont castle ruins) and Fletcher's Peggy. Scamp was then put to a bitch called Meg and this bred Kitchen's Grip. Edmund Porter is certain Kitchen hunted a pack of otterhounds at one time and used his terriers with this pack, but he couldn't say whether it was the Egremont Otterhounds, the West Cumberland Otter-hounds, or just a private pack kept by himself and a few enthusiasts. What is certain, is that Kitchen senior (his sons also kept, worked and bred terriers) was a working terrier enthusiast and non-workers would be useless to him. True, he was blinded in an explosion in an iron-ore mine in the mid-1920s and was rather limited by that time, but he had family and friends who would gladly work his stock for him. Kitchen's Grip now mated Fletcher's Peggy and from this union came one of the most famous terriers in Lakeland history and ancestor of all modern pedigrees, as well as much of the working stock. This was Vic of Wastwater which was owned by J.J. Crellin of Thornhill – a village only a mile or so from Egremont. Also in this litter was Midge, owned by Kitchen and more popularly known as Central Midge, after Central Avenue, Egremont, Kitchen's home and centre (no pun intended) of early Lakeland terrier breeding. Central Midge played an important part in the foundation of pedigree stock and this bitch played an equally important part in the breeding of Willie Irving's strain.

Vic of Wastwater was mated by Crab of Wastwater, another famous terrier that founded a dynasty of both working and show Lakeland terriers, and from this union came Egton Rock of Howtown, a black and tan terrier that saw service at the Ullswater kennels (no doubt once he had become a champion) and was used, not just by LTA members, but by several of the fell pack followers interested essentially in work, including Joe Wear, Joe Wilkinson, Sid Wilkinson, Jim Fleming and Frank Pepper, for Pepper's bitch, Blossom, the one he is holding in the photograph opposite, was sired by this pedigree dog, out of Pepper's Myrtle. Egton Rock, make no mistake, sired top quality workers and he was bred from a long unbroken line of working stock, stock that saw service at badger, fox, otter, polecat and pinemarten, as well as rats and very often rabbits too.

Egton Rock was certainly well bred. Tramp, a looker and a worker, mated Kitchen's Peggy and produced Bookwell Bristles, belonging to another breeder, Mr Hartley, of the same estate where Alf Johnston and Kitchen lived, for this is the Bookwell estate, built directly after the Great War. Hartley's Bookwell kennels would have terriers bred by Billy Irving a few years after this time, as would most of the Lakeland terrier enthusiasts. Bookwell Bristles now mated Egton Lady of the Lake and this bred Rock's sire, Crab of Wastwater. Robinson's Gyp was also sired by Bookwell Bristles and Gyp was used to produce a great many offspring in the 1920s. It was Robinson's Gyp who sired Scawfell Guide, when put to Central Midge, and he was another terrier that played an important role in Irving's breeding programme. Robinson was a road worker and he was well known for not only having superb working terriers but good-looking stock too, stock he had been using at work and for shows since the nineteenth century.

Sandy Boy of the West Cumberland Otterhounds mated Nellie and produced Tramp, the sire of Bookwell Bristles. Peggy was bred out of Prospect Pirate and Joyful News. The dam of Scawfell Guide was Fletcher's Peggy, bred out of Spedding's Scamp and Flower Girl.

Frank Pepper with an otter in his right hand and Blossom in his left hand. The terrier on the rock is Peggy, given to Irving in the early 1930s. The original photo has the following written on the back. "The finish of an otter hunt just below our house taken a while back. Terriers are Blossom and the bitch I sold Irving which he still has. You will notice the otter in my right hand shows dark." Pepper lived close to the Bowderstone in the Borrowdale Valley.

Spedding's Scamp was out of Gillert and Peggy, the bitch probably belonging to Spedding and undoubtedly serving at one of the otter-hound packs that hunted the area. Gillert, I am guessing, was a wire fox terrier belonging to Bill Mawson, for, according to Alf Johnston, Scamp was a half-bred.

Egton Rock of Howtown, when put to Egton Sting of 'Cathra, produced Zip, an early Lakeland champion and a real workmanlike dog. Egton Sting was out of Bant and Bet. Bant was out of Tinker and Floss, Tinker probably being Paisley's Tinker, a prolific sire of lookers and workers which Irving brought into his own strain. Tinker was out of Grip and Pim, while Floss was bred from Ben and Judy. Some of these terriers were Paisley's, while others belonged to Dalton, for Jim Dalton, long-serving Huntsman of the 'Cathra, was one of the first to begin breeding for better type. He was using fox terriers, those at the Carlisle and District Otterhounds, as well as outcross blood from Major Williams of Barrow-in-Furness, who probably supplied many of the Egremont breeders, Bill Mawson included, with 'wires', long before Spedding's Scamp and other 'half-breds' were being used to improve type in West Cumberland. Peter Long used Robinson terriers for work and show, and his bitches he took to be mated by Dalton's strain. Many of the founda-tion stock of the Lakeland terrier were bred, or partly bred, from the Dalton strain. And why not, for no better lookers, or workers, could be found than these Blencathra terriers and Turk, working at this hunt during the first decade of the twentieth century, was certainly ahead of his time, as he would easily win at shows today. It was Turk and his offspring that helped shape the typey terriers of the Long family and other Egremont breeders, as well as the dogs bred by Douglas Paisley.

Alf Johnston's foundation stud dog was Terry, a son of Spedding's Scamp. Terry sired Bullet and this dog mated a wire fox terrier belonging to a relative of Alf's, Wilton Benn, who lived only a short distance out of Egremont, and from this union came High Lea Laddie, which was later bought by George Long, son of Peter. High Lea Laddie was both a looker and a worker and he became the ancestor of Irving's superb worker and good-looking dog, Burtness Lady, used, when put to Mick of Millar Place, to breed superb working Lakelands. Pearl Wilson, Billy's daughter, told me of a dig to one of her father's dogs and it was probably Mick, though she cannot be certain, but this dog was certainly his best at that time. The Melbreak Foxhounds had been hunting for quite some time when

110

they ran a fox to ground in an earth at a big sandbank close to the railway at Branthwaite. Irving entered a terrier, and it was probably Mick, which quickly found and began working his fox. However, Reynard refused to bolt and so a dig was on the cards. Irving got stuck in, but the going was very difficult and anyone who has attempted to dig out a sand earth will sympathise, for several falls occur and very often more sand falls in than is taken out. Willie stuck to the task however, for he was by now a seasoned veteran at this game, and eventually made progress, though rather slowly it has to be said. More falls occurred and the site was becoming rather dangerous, for Billy had to tunnel into the bank in order to reach terrier and fox. He put his jacket on the floor of the dig and began tunnelling in, instructing the onlookers to pull him out by his feet if the tunnel roof collapsed. Meanwhile, Mick was hard at his fox, though in a precarious situation, for the roof of a tunnel can collapse when fox and terrier are at each other, so Irving was keen to reach his dog. After a gruelling and dangerous dig, Billy eventually reached his terrier and the quarry was secured. Mick, a direct descendant of Irving's famous Turk, served for at least five seasons with the Melbreak and he was truly a wonderful worker.

High Lea Laddie was registered with the Kennel Club and the sire

Willie Irving judging Lakeland terrier, Scafell Guide.

111

shown is Terry, while the dam is given as Oregill Lady. However, this wasn't so and the correct breeding, from Alf's own hand, is as stated above. So why High Lea Laddie was registered under these names is rather a mystery, though it may have had something to do with the fact that he was out of a fox terrier bitch! Alf Johnston got the breeding of Bookwell Bristles wrong in his letter to Miss Morris of Kelda fame, saying he was bred from Bill Mawson's Jim. While I have no doubts at all that Jim sired many Lakelands, he did not sire Bristles, for, from Kitchen's own hand, the sire was Tramp, from a West Cumberland Otterhounds stud dog. Alf was writing these things in 1951, however, so maybe his memory wasn't quite what it had been in the 20s.

Studholme and Moore were two important breeders during those early days and their terriers figured prominently in several breeding programmes. Sheik of Kinniside, bought by Bob Gibbons and bred by Studholme, was another looker and was a blue and tan dog. He was born in 1929 and was sired by Thomas Rawlings' black and tan dog, Gillert, which saw much service at the Eskdale and Ennerdale pack, as did all of Rawlings' strain. Gillert was from Scamp and Peggy, Peggy again being of the Eskdale and Ennerdale Foxhounds. Scamp was a red dog and the pedigree doesn't say who owned him,

Billy Irving at Crummock Water, Good Friday 1934. The first terrier far right is Jerry, coupled to Nan. Rock is the leggy terrier at Irving's feet.

though he was bred from Sandy, a West Cumberland Otterhounds terrier which was probably the same ancestor to Scawfell Guide and may have belonged to Kitchen of Egremont, and Tyke, a fox terrier bitch possibly owned by Bill Mawson.

Peggy was from Sandy, a blue and tan Eskdale and Ennerdale dog, again possibly one of Rawlings', or maybe Porter's stock, and J. Moore's blue dog, Vic, another terrier that played a major role in the breeding of early pedigree Lakelands, especially Irving's strain. Nell was the dam of Sheik of Kinniside and she was bred from Studholme's Turk, a black and tan, and a blue and tan bitch, Squib, which Studholme had bought from the Coniston Hunt. Turk was sired by Grip, a blue and tan belonging to Studholme, and his dam was a bitch belonging to a Miss Lutton, another blue and tan. The sire of Squib was Fred Mitchell's Turk, possibly Irving, or Pepper bred, which served with the Melbreak pack. The name of the dam isn't given, though it would be one of George Chapman's, for he was still Huntsman of the Coniston at that time.

Fred Mitchell bred Border terriers in the main, so Turk was unlikely to have been of his breeding. Pepper and Irving were two of the top breeders of Lakelands then, so I am guessing Turk would probably be from either of those strains. Of course, Turk could have been an early border terrier, though I think it likely that Mitchell did run on a few Lakeland terriers now and again, which saw service at the Melbreak.

Champion Evergreen's Double was well bred too, despite the fact that Alf Johnston believed he ruined the Lakeland type for a few years. Crab of Wastwater was his sire and he was bred from Bookwell Bristles, his dam being Egton Lady of the Lake. Lady of the Lake was bred from Castle Buglar and Vic of Wastwater. The dam of Evergreen's Double was Albermarle Pippin and she was by Blencathra Boy (Douglas Paisley), by Scamp out of Jess, probably Dalton bred Blencathra terriers, while the dam was Ribston Pippin. This bitch was by Crab out of Nettle, a bitch who served at the West Cumberland Otterhounds and the same dam of Irving's Turk of Melbreak. It is possible, of course, that Irving owned this bitch and put her out on loan at this hunt. It is also possible that Rawlinson, or maybe Kitchen of Egremont, owned this terrier.

Rex of Melbreak was the sire of Turk and he was from Willie Porter's Riff and Irving's Floss, which served at the Eskdale and Ennerdale before Irving took up his post at the Melbreak in 1926. Riff, born circa 1918, was bred by Irving, from Jack, a terrier belonging to J. Hodgson, the Blencathra Whip at the time and a terrier either Dalton or Paisley bred and Rose, another bitch serving at the Eskdale and Ennerdale and bred from Brant and Maud, Irving's first terriers, probably obtained from Willie Porter and of the old Eskdale and Ennerdale bloodlines that included the dogs of Tommy Dobson, Jim Kitchen, Thomas Rawlings, Will Ritson and Billy Tyson in their pedigrees. These were game stock and many of the old Eskdale and Ennerdale terriers were extremely hard and they would kill reluctant foxes quickly and efficiently and often without taking too much punishment, for sense is rated highly among fell-hunting folk. A terrier serving at a Lakeland pack must be capable of killing a fox and emerging without too many injuries, for he must go again a day or two later. A terrier that gets constantly mauled by its foe and that needs weeks to recuperate is nigh-on useless to a Huntsman.

The young Willie Irving hunted with the Eskdale and Ennerdale from being a young lad and eventually went to work for Willie Porter, helping around the farm and assisting Porter on hunting days. Billy lived with the Porters for three years and learnt much from the master of hunting fell hounds. Porter was also a very serious terrier breeder, considered to be one of the best of his day, and no doubt Irving got his enthusiasm for earth dogs from working with the legendary Willie Porter. Porter became fond of the young apprentice and I am certain this is from where Irving got his initial stock, Brant and Maud, in 1916, for this is when Willie first started with his own terriers, when he was eighteen years of age, though he already had a wealth of experience of hunting the fells by this time, with both hounds and terriers.

Rex was walked at the Horseshoe Inn, Lorton, with the Benson family and it was this dog, one which served at the Melbreak hunt, which sired the famous Turk, when put to Nettle of the West Cumberland Otterhounds. Turk was born in January 1930 and he entered quickly to fox during the very next season. From then on he never looked back and quickly established himself as one of the top working terriers in the fells at that time. Turk had a fearsome temper and would finish reluctant foxes quickly and eagerly. Irving used him on lamb- and poultry-worrying foxes, or at the close of the day, when darkness was approaching and a fox needed to be accounted for, not bolted. As early as 1932 Turk had become a legendary worker and many bitches were taken to him to be served. At that time Albert Benson was Whipper-in to the Blencathra Foxhounds and it was while he was serving with this pack that he bred his famous Red Ike. Ike was an incredible worker – a big, bold terrier who feared nothing and who could be worked in the deep borrans of the Blencathra country, despite his size. Gary Middleton, when he came on the terrier scene long after Ike was dead, can remember this dog still being talked about, he was that good a worker, and Gary says he was typey, out of pedigree stuff – a big red dog of the type Irving certainly bred at that time. It is a mystery how Red Ike was bred, but my money would be on a Blencathra bitch, probably Dalton bred (Jim Dalton had retired a couple of years before Ike was born and George Bell, the new Huntsman, carried on breeding this strain) being the dam and Irving's Turk being the sire. The Melbreak was the place to find good quality red terriers at that time and Albert Benson was certainly a friend of Billy Irving. So it is not unreasonable to assume that Ike was bred this way.

By 1932 Turk had established himself as possibly the best working terrier in the fells and he served numerous bitches. Also, he was a looker; a big, powerful black and tan and he won everywhere with Irving. In the summer of 1931 Billy won fifty-one prizes with Turk, earning him £31.00, which was quite a sum in those days. Turk was registered with the Kennel Club and he was used to breed quite a bit of the pedigree stuff at that time, though he sired many typey working terriers when put to fell bitches. With Turk being so prolific at that time, at shows, but, more importantly, at work, it seems likely that a good deal of the terriers after that time were bred from this dog, including Red Ike. Ike served for four seasons with the Blencathra, until Benson moved on from his post at this famous pack, and then the terrier was loaned to Anthony Chapman, who worked him with great success at the Coniston Hunt when he was Whip to Ernie Parker. Ike was such a good worker that Walter Parkin, the Lunesdale Huntsman, based his strain of working terriers on this dog and Walter bred many wonderfully game dogs after he had taken his bitches to be mated by Red Ike.

George Long saw Turk at work for himself and was most impressed. He would use Turk as an example whenever anyone mocked the pedigree Lakeland as being a non-worker. Sadly, similar examples are nigh-on impossible to find nowadays, though I have no doubts at all that some pedigree stock of today would kill foxes if they got the chance. However, could they stand up to twenty miles across rough ground before entering a vast rock earth? Could the pedigree dogs of today stand up to hours below ground and then

Willie Irving (centre) after a successful hunt, with Melbreak hounds and pedigree terriers.

having to walk miles to get home? Could they stand up to hours of waiting outside a borran for a fox to be bolted, or dug out? The early pedigree dogs were tested to the full in all of the above conditions and they often stood up to the elements far better than some of the unregistered strains which sometimes suffered from bad weather, especially while waiting outside an earth in freezing temperatures. Also, the pedigree Lakeland of those days, in many cases, had sense while at work, while having the ability to finish a fox quickly indeed. No fox could live for long with the likes of Irving's Turk, yet this dog, along with many others, could come out of an encounter with fox without serious injury and such qualities are priceless to a fell pack Huntsman.

From 1930 onwards, Irving brought into his strain the earth dogs of Frank Pepper and no gamer strain entered an earth than these terriers belonging to Pepper. He worked a wide range of quarry and also regularly followed the Melbreak, where no doubt Irving had been impressed with their abilities. Irving also dug badger at that time, particularly during the summer months, and no doubt enjoyed plenty of digs with Pepper. Frank gave Billy his bitch, Peggy, which is seen in the photograph with Blossom. Peggy was an outstanding working Lakeland of the new type and Irving used her for several seasons with the Melbreak. She worried any fox that would not bolt and Billy stated that she was a superb finder, even in deep borrans. Peggy was also very useful on badger and Irving rated sense highly when digging such quarry. He stopped using harder Lakeland terriers for digging badgers, as these took terrific punishment and most of his pedigree stock encountered 'Brock' accidentally, when seeking a fox in an earth. Maud can remember treating the wounds of several of Billy's terriers that had encountered a badger skulking in a fox earth and some of the injuries were horrific, so Irving looked with disdain on those who used such hard dogs for working badgers. Peggy, however, was very sensible at 'Brock' and emerged from encounters without too many problems.

Billy used literal border/Lakeland crosses for badger digging in the main, for these had more sense. He put Mitchell's border terriers to his Lakeland bitches and produced a few crossbreds, which he ran on from time to time, using them at times with hounds, but mostly for the digging of badgers. His main stock, however, were pedigree Lakelands and Art' Irving, his younger brother, stated that he had never known Billy breed a quitter from his pedigree stock. 'All were worked', said Arthur, as Billy would not tolerate a non-worker. He tried a few border terriers at work, but had little success. Maybe this was because he was used to the Lakeland terrier temperament that is bold and begs for work, usually from a very early age, literally self-entering when allowed to go in an earth. Borders, however, even back then, were more sensitive and required different entering methods, which didn't suit Billy at all, though he found his crossbreds to be much more suited for work.

Peggy, the bitch given to Irving in the early 1930s, was very well bred. She was sired by Pepper's Nip, who was from Pip (Pepper) and Kitchen's Central Midge. The dam was Pepper's Peggy, which was from Tuce's Bin and Pepper's Fan. Irving's Peggy was from a long unbroken line of workers, but they were lookers too and Pepper, like Kitchen, Irving, Paisley, real working terrier enthusiasts, among others, enjoyed exhibiting his terriers at summer shows, though I don't think he registered any of his stock with the Kennel Club, though quite a bit of the early KC stock came from Pepper's terrier strain. Peggy was used to bring into Irving's strain and Trigger, a famous Melbreak terrier of the late 1930s/early 40s, was descended from this bitch, which was mated to Rock, the leggy terrier in the famous 1934 photograph of Irving at Crummock Water. I cannot find the breeding of Rock, but I think it likely that Turk sired this dog.

Irving's strain was certainly hardy and Maud tells a tale that illustrates just how hardy they were. Billy was out hunting and one of his bitches, Nan, the terrier coupled to Jerry in the old photograph at Crummock Water, must have been loose, for she broke from her master and went off hunting with hounds. At the end of the day, although Billy gathered in his pack successfully, there was still no sign of Nan and so hounds were taken back to kennels where Billy hoped she would turn up by next morning. However, on rising, there was still no sign of her and the family began to be worried for her safety, for she was more or less a family favourite; one of the terriers Billy allowed into the house on a regular basis. And they were right to be worried, for the little bitch had still not returned several days later and so they eventually gave up all hope of ever seeing her again.

The routine at the kennels continued and more hunts took place and the little bitch, though certainly not forgotten, became a memory; one put in the 'lost to ground' category. But then, many days later, a rather thin and bedraggled terrier came walking down the lane and up to the house. To the delight of the Irving family, it was Nan, looking rather worse for wear, but alive and on her feet, despite her ordeal and lack of food. One can only surmise that hounds ran a fox to ground out on the high fells where no followers had yet reached, and that Nan, once she had caught up to the pack marking furiously, had then gone to ground, bolted her fox and had become trapped. Hounds then carried on their way, in pursuit of the fast-fleeing quarry, and the little bitch was lost without any trace whatsoever. And then, after several days had passed, Nan became so thin that she was at last able to pass the obstacle in her way and got out, now making her own way back to kennels. Only the toughest of earth dogs could hope to stand up to the rigours of such a life and Irving's pedigree stock were obviously constitutionally as hard as iron.

Twist was another of the early terriers and he was born in the mid-1920s, just as Irving was settling in as Huntsman at the Melbreak. Twist sired Wasp, which was the ancestor of quite a few of the Mockerkin terriers belonging to Tom Meagean. Twist was another grand worker of the new improved type and he was sired by J.

Arthur Irving with terriers bred down from Willie's classy strain. Arthur's terriers were excellent workers in the deep borrans of the Eskdale and Ennerdale Country.

Moore's Tinker. This dog, in turn, was from Paisley's famous and incredibly game dog, also named Tinker, and Moore's Vic. Vic was bred from Barwise's dog at Yearton when put to Moore's Mist, a bitch from Moore's famous Vic. All of these terriers were workers serving at one, or more, of the fell packs and Irving could not have found a better line for producing good-looking stock that could serve him well at the hunt. The dam of Twist was J. Norman's red bitch, which was of Mossop Nelson's strain. The Nelson family were

119

shepherds who bred a long line of terriers which saw service at the Ullswater and were of the old Patterdale type with good harsh jackets. It seems that these had their roots in the Eskdale and Ennerdale country, however, for Nelson's strain was descended from Bill Tyson's and Will Ritson's line of working terriers. Braithwaite Wilson was rather cagey about where his strain of working terrier originated, but my guess is he used either Mossop Nelson's strain, or that belonging to Kitty Farrer, which were no doubt related anyway. Farrer's strain was typey and was a mix of Dalton and Ullswater terriers, probably the hard-coated strain belonging to Nelson.

Felix was another of the early Melbreak terriers, born in the same year as Twist, and this terrier was sired by Mac, which was by Sir T. Ainsworth's dog, Hughie, which was in turn by Blencathra Rock (Paisley or Dalton?) out of Jack Hodgson's bitch, Vic. Jean was Mac's

Irving's Turk won both these cups. The cup on the left is the one donated by D. Paisley for the best terrier serving with a fell pack.

120

dam and was sired by Kitchen's famous Grip, the sire of Central Midge, and her dam was J. Moore's equally famous Vic, another grand worker. The dam of Felix was an ageing Rose, the bitch bred from Irving's first terriers, Brant and Maud.

What Irving succeeded in doing by using such a breeding programme – one that included some of the best working stock to be found in the Lake District during the 1920s and 30s in particular – was to produce a strain of earth dog that was both typey and incredibly game. They had to be game. Billy Irving was a professional Huntsman and if his terriers couldn't work out a fox from even deep borrans, then, not only were they useless, but he would have been too and would have become surplus to requirements, for a fell pack Huntsman must control foxes for the farmers in his area and control is impossible without game earth dogs.

Turk was probably *the* gamest terrier Irving ever bred, though several others were incredibly good workers too and had such reputations that the lads from the Welsh valleys, serious digging men, journeyed north to buy stock from Willie Irving for fox and badger digging back home, particularly around Monmouth and Carnarvon. Turk won well at shows and he it was that won the Paisley donated cup for best working terrier serving at one of the fell packs in 1932. Irving won it again with Turk's son, Roamer, another superb working Melbreak terrier, in 1933 and was allowed to keep the trophy after winning this class for two years running. I have photographed this cup and it has fascinating inscriptions, telling us that Logan's Crest, a Coniston terrier, won it in 1926, Farrer's Gyp in '27, Ernie Parker's Nigger in '28, Thomas Rawlings' Gyp in '29, and then 1930/31 are omitted for some reason, with Irving's Turk and Roamer winning the cup in '32 and '33 respectively. Ernie Parker served at the Blencathra before becoming Huntsman of the Coniston in the early 30s. His terriers were rather leggy, typey terriers and they may well have been bred from Dalton and Paisley stock, for he was Dalton's Whip from 1919 to 1929.

Willie Porter gave Riff, the terrier Irving had bred from Jack and Rose, back to Billy when he took up service at the Melbreak in 1926 and this terrier was a very good worker indeed. On 11 February 1927, a fox was found and hunted by hounds and was eventually run to ground in a rock earth; a scenario that often ends, or interrupts, hunting with hounds in the fells. Riff was put in and quickly found and engaged his fox, seizing it and drawing it from the earth. In the struggle, the fox broke loose and bolted and the hunt continued on. It takes a game terrier to draw a fox from any type of earth, so this hunt tells us something of the abilities of Billy's terriers.

It was probably Riff who was entered when a fox was run to ground near Cleaves Ghyll, where it was worried by one of Irving's terriers, though at the time (1927) Billy had plenty of earth dogs he could use, including those belonging to followers. On 16 November of the same year, a fox was hunted for quite some distance by hounds and was eventually run to ground in a big rock spot. Riff was put in, but, no matter how hard he tried, he couldn't shift it and so, in typical early Lakeland terrier fashion, he finished his foe below ground. As Willie put it, the fox 'was worried by Old Riff'.

Riff had served both Willie Porter and Willie Irving well, at the Eskdale and Ennerdale and the Melbreak packs, but tragedy was to strike on 1 February 1928. A fox was again run to ground by hounds and Riff was entered, but, as is often the case in fell country hunting, Reynard wouldn't bolt and so the terrier engaged his quarry, tackling it as the diggers made their way to the scene. Unfortunately, the roof of the dig fell in and poor Riff was smothered. The faithful terrier was an old dog by this time, close to retirement, but still, it was a sad end for such a gallant working Lakeland.

On 28 March however, we have an account that tells us that a fox was run to ground after a very long hunt on the northern side of Cockermouth at Andrew Bank. Tess and Riff were put to ground and then went on to worry a stubborn fox that wouldn't bolt. So, obviously, Irving had more than one Riff. The fact that he referred to the other Riff as 'Old Riff' shows that there was a youngster of the same name. I am certain this must be Scalehill Riff, a terrier born in the 1920s and the one put to ground with Tess. Scalehill Riff was another very well bred terrier and, obviously, a worker. His dam was Trim, by Ainsworth's Hughie out of Jean of Kinmont. His sire was Jock, a terrier from the hard working Mossop Nelson strain, bred out of Nip, by G. Mossick's dog (Nelson) and a Turnerhall bitch probably bred by Irving. Jock's dam was Meg, a bitch from Irving's Crab and Nettle. This Crab, Nettle and Meg feature quite prominently in the breeding of early Lakeland terriers and Nettle was the dam of Turk of Melbreak, a bitch Irving acquired from the West Cumberland Otterhounds. I wondered if Billy actually owned this bitch, but it seems that he did, for he bred quite a bit of stuff from her and he may well have bred her in the first place, sometime during the early 1920s. It was the same Crab and Nettle that bred Ribston Pippin, the ancestor of Champion Evergreen's Double.

W. Irving with Trim and Mick – superb workers and typey terriers, winning at Patterdale sheep dog trials terrier show.

Squib, the terrier in the pedigree of Sheik of Kinniside, a blue and tan belonging to C. Studholme, was put in service at the Melbreak and she was a game bitch indeed. On 1 April 1927, Willie was called out on a lambing call, which means that a fox was killing lambs at one of the farms within the Melbreak hunt country, and hounds were taken around the low-lying pastures where the scent of a lurking fox was taken up. They followed the drag to a large borran on the fells at High Crags, near Buttermere, and two terriers were entered. It is best to work one terrier at a time in most types of earth, but in borrans a fox can give one terrier the run around all day, so two, and sometimes more in the vast rock spots, are usually entered so that the fox has far less options, forcing it to bolt, hopefully. In this case, the fox wouldn't bolt and so the two terriers, Floss and Squib, were entered and they worried their quarry among the rocks, though both terriers were badly bitten, especially around the legs, which suggests that Reynard had got himself into a tight spot and the terriers had to shuffle towards it, their front legs extended, or maybe it was on a ledge and, as they jumped to get a hold of their foe, it put in several strikes, catching them around the legs in particular. The early Lakeland terrier was fully tested and only a fool would question the abilities of the stock that works with a fell pack. Floss was the ageing bitch who was the dam of Rex, which became the sire of Turk of Melbreak. Irving bred terriers that could finish reluctant foxes, especially the dog terriers, but many of his bitches had the same ability to worry any fox that refused to bolt.

It was Squib who was to ground for a good twenty-four hours in the December of 1927. Hounds had hunted a fox and it eventually ran to ground in order to escape its pursuers. However, Squib was put in, in the hopes that the fox would bolt, but it remained below and Squib quickly killed it. However, there was also a badger in the earth and she turned her attention to this, refusing to leave her quarry. Willie moved hounds on, but still she never showed and a digging party returned at first light next morning. A hard dig then

Young Maud Irving with a Melbreak hound and the famous Turk; legendary worker and champion show dog.

ensued, which lasted all morning until, finally, they dug Squib and the badger out of that earth. They found the corpse of the fox, and the bitch still at her badger, by the end of the morning after a gruelling dig and this tells us of the quality of some of these early Lakelands. To kill a fox that refuses to bolt is a feat in itself, but then to turn its attention to a badger skulking in the same earth, and to stay until dug out the following day, enduring a freezing winter night in the process, is almost beyond belief, yet such tales can be told over and over again in the fells, for such a harsh country has been producing high calibre earth dogs for centuries.

Squib was in action again in October 1928. Hounds had a good hunt, after a find at High Dyke Woods, and eventually ran their fox to ground at Bardshaw Crag, on the high fells west of Lorton. Squib was put in and, after a bit of a tussle, bolted the fox, but got herself trapped in the process. A bolting fox can easily dislodge a small rock, which can then block the exit for the following terrier. However, after a dig she was got out safely. In the November of 1928 hounds had a rattling hunt in the Buttermere area and, after quite some time and after successfully pressing their quarry hard, Reynard was run to ground at Wandup Crag above Buttermere. The fox had been harried from place to place and had been pressed by the oncoming pack, so it was reluctant to bolt and Squib and Felix then worried it among the piles of fallen rocks. This was the same Felix bred from Irving's Mac and Rose and she had a long line of superb workers in her pedigree, including the dogs of Dalton and Paisley at the Blencathra. Felix, when put to Jock, was the dam of Irving's Boss and Tiny, born in April 1931.

On 19 April 1927, a fox was holed by hounds inside a borran near Crummock Water and, again, Reynard refused to bolt, preferring to take its chances with the terriers, rather than seek open ground once more. It should have bolted, for J. Moore's Vic and Bob Gibson's Jack worried the fox below ground and another predator was accounted for by the Melbreak pack. Gibson was another who bred the improved type of Lakeland terrier and, like many other breeders of that era, kept only working stock. True, several of these early breeders were serious exhibitors of their charges, but work always came first and Billy Irving felt the same long after he had retired as Huntsman. Crab and Nettle seem to have played a very important role in establishing the founding strains of Lakeland terrier and these two were very game indeed, making them ideal earth dogs from which to begin breeding a line of both lookers and workers.

On 22 February 1927, a fox was holed after a short run and Crab was entered. He quickly found and got stuck into his fox, eventually killing it below, but during the dig a stone fell in and landed on his leg. He was 'badly lamed', as Irving put it, but he doesn't say if his leg healed properly, or whether the terrier was lame for the rest of his life. A lame terrier would have to be retired if such an injury was permanent, for a lame earth dog would struggle badly to negotiate both rough ground, and borrans. Saturday 29 October 1927 saw yet another fox run to ground by hounds and Vic was put in. I presume this was J. Moore's terrier, though I cannot be certain, for Irving too, may well have owned a bitch by this name. However, the bitch either killed her fox, or bolted it, the account doesn't say which, though it does tell us that Vic then became trapped and it took until Monday to dig her out. For sure, these Lakeland terriers have much to endure and need plenty of pluck and spirit in order to work with a fell pack.

Many breeders used Willie's pedigree Lakelands to smarten up their own working terriers and Hamilton Docherty and Bancroft of Sullart Street, who originally bred all blacks, which Irving says were common around Windermere and Grasmere in the early days, when George Chapman was still Huntsman and possibly into Ernie Parker's time at the hunt, were among them. Irving was of the opinion that Frank Buck's strain of terrier got its black colouring from the Coniston hunt terriers. He may well have been correct, though more of this in a later chapter. Many turned to this strain because it was both good looking and sensible at work. True, many of Willie's terriers suffered badly when encountering a badger skulking in a fox earth, but at fox they could kill their quarry without taking severe punishment, which is an invaluable quality to a fell pack Huntsman. Tales are told of pedigree dogs lacking any sense whatsoever, but that wasn't true of all strains during those early days, for many, including the Egton Lakelands, were sane and sensible and incredibly game. Willie was given quite an ugly terrier, a crossbred. It was a game and useful worker and Irving kept it, but it was in no way superior to his pedigree stock. Albert Thomas, Billy's first Whipper-in, also kept the Irving strain of Lakeland and these served him well indeed.

Irving knew such noted breeders as Thomas Rawlings, Jim Fleming and the Wilkinson family of the Ullswater country, very well indeed and I am certain that such breeders, especially Fleming and the Wilkinsons, used Willie's dogs in order to improve type in their own strain. They certainly used Egton terriers and many of them carried lines back to Irving's dogs. Billy was very successful over the years at the Patterdale show, so I am certain a few of the Ullswater breeders would have used such stock. Indeed, Willie was related to them. He was Rawlings' cousin and was related to Jim Fleming through the Rawlings family. Willie was big pals with Joe Wear and the Wilkinson family and even the Tysons, a top hunting family in the Lakes, had Willie's strain of terrier, also being related to the Irvings.

Both Maud and Pearl are certain Jim Fleming used Billy's terriers on his famous strain at Grasmere. Fleming bred black terriers at times, which suggests Coniston bred dogs went into the mix, though he hunted with the Ullswater in the main and often loaned his terriers to this hunt, being a big mate of Joe Wear. Tear 'Em was a big blue and tan dog of the type Irving bred and it can be said with some certainty that this dog carried lines back to Irving's strain and ultimately to Turk of Melbreak, though he was no pedigree. He was not ugly either, but a big, bold, housewrecker of a dog who feared nothing and was more or less impossible to control. Tear 'Em was a fearsome dog and no fox could live with him (see interview with Eddie Pool in chapter 7) and several breeders, including Frank Buck and Cyril Breay, used this dog to serve their bitches. Anthony Barker told Gary Middleton that Tear 'Em had been used on his strain, just after the war, for he commented to Gary, after seeing a dog called Mac draw a badger from under a huge boulder close to the shores of Ullswater, that he worked just like Tear 'Em, his ancestor. Middleton's strain of working Lakeland are famous for good heads, heads which Gary refers to as being 'like a brick'. Tear 'Em, as well as other terriers in this strain, had a massive head with huge, powerful jaws, so maybe the big heads found on terriers such as Wilkinson's Rock and Middleton's Rags and Old Rex, were partly due to the inclusion of Tear 'Em blood in the Barker strain.

Some say that Irving had two types of terrier, smart show dogs and an unrefined type of fell terrier that he used for work, but his hunting diaries prove beyond any doubt that this is a fallacy. Some just cannot accept that a smart terrier will work just as well as unrefined stock, but this is a ridiculous theory that breeders such as Kitchen, Irving, Wilson, Farrer, Dalton and many others proved to be totally unfounded. Irving did have some less typey stock, this is true, but often these were terriers given to him, or, more often than not, were his literal border/Lakeland crossbreds. These he would

Oregill Cracker, decended from Irving's Melbreak strain.

use particularly if there was a risk of badger being to ground. Brian Nuttall said that Irving had 'some damn good terriers', but that they were rather too game, especially at badger. They had no reverse gear and attacked 'Brock' as they would a fox, receiving terrific punishment as a result. Pearl and Maud confirm this, remembering treating wounds on Billy's pedigree stock when they had met up with a badger after a fox had been run in by hounds. Buck and Breay had the same problem. Nuttall told me that they would search around an earth diligently for any sign of badger, when hounds had put a fox in, for, he said, they knew many of their stock would get torn to pieces if 'Brock' was found at home. Irving's border/Lakeland crossbreds, and he only had a few during his time at the Melbreak for the vast majority were pedigree stock, could work a badger without receiving too many injuries and that is why he kept them.

I have concentrated on Billy Irving simply because he is probably *the* most important of all the early breeders, for his pedigree stock were not only top winners at shows, especially at LTA shows, but they saw regular work and most could kill a reluctant fox without too many problems, though, as already stated, they were often too hard for use at badger. Some were baying types and these were most useful at 'Brock', but baying dogs, even bitches, seem to have been the exception, rather than the rule. The Lakeland terrier was required to kill a fox, more so in those days than in recent times when bolting foxes has become more the fashion, but back then the focus was much more on accounting for foxes and bounties were still being paid in some areas. In the Yorkshire Dales, for instance, bounties for foxes were still being paid into the 1960s and Frank Buck took hundreds of foxes under the bounty system.

The famous 'Dalesman' and his contemporaries, approached Irving, I think it was at Lorton show, and told him that he had done more for the Lakeland terrier than anyone else, and they were probably correct, though other breeders of the time did much to promote the working Lakeland terrier too. Even Mrs Spence promoted work, though, as stated earlier, she would wait until they were champions before having them entered, sometimes as late as six years of age. Many breeders, more so those within the Lakes country, continued this system of entering once they had gained champion status well into the 1960s, but after that it seems that few, if any, bothered about work and Lakeland terrier temperament now made most unsuited for work at a fell pack. This was true in many cases when Irving was still alive and Willie condemned what he called professional show men who were ruining the Lakeland terrier. Some blamed Willie for ruining temperament in Lakelands, but it was those who had no idea about work who were to blame for this. Even Willie's later stock was both game and easily worked alongside other terriers, so those accusations were completely unfounded and downright wrong. Most pedigree stock would rather kill their fellow terriers, than go to ground, these days. Irving had died in 1966 and his working strain of Lakeland terrier was now mostly lost, though George Newcombe, a lonely soul in a sea of Lakeland terrier breeders who hadn't a clue about working type, continued to work and breed Irving pedigree stock and he found them to be just as good as any of the unregistered strains, as did the Welsh lads from the valleys who went to Irving whenever they needed game terriers.

For those who cannot accept that typey terriers make superb earth dogs when given a chance, I have included more extracts from Billy's diaries from those early days when his terriers were being used to fix type in the Lakeland terrier, as well as to spice up many working strains of fell terrier. Willie Irving was a champion fell runner and he was one of the old type of fell walking Huntsmen who would cover well over twenty miles in an average day's hunting, and then often having to face a ten mile hike back to kennels, or wherever hounds and hunt staff were staying for the week. Like Willie Porter, Walt Parkin, Johnny Richardson, Anthony Chapman, and others of their generation, Irving walked everywhere and hadn't transport to rely on for getting him back in touch with hounds and his stamina was as legendary as his hunting skills.

Hunting the Loweswater area in January 1929 the Melbreak pack found a fox and then hunted it for a long time, up and over fells, down into the valleys and through woodland, until, finally, they ran it to ground at Low Fell End. It had been a good hunt and this had proved a game fox. Two terriers were then entered, Nit and Twist, and they eventually found the fox after searching the borran, but it wouldn't bolt. Twist and Nit then killed their foe and it was dead by the time the terriers were dug out, accounting for a large dog fox. This was the same Twist who was bred out of Moore's Tinker and J. Norman's Mossop Nelson bred bitch.

In March 1930 hounds had a fast hunt and eventually holed their fox at Big Wood, Isel, and Rex, the sire of Turk, was entered. Again, the fox refused to bolt and Rex promptly finished his foe below ground. Rex was a superb worker and a looker too, being bred by Irving out of some of the best looking and working terriers to be found throughout the fells.

It was on 10 October 1932 that Billy recorded that he had a 'disastrous hunt'. Why? Because Major and Crummock, two of the Melbreak hounds, and Gyp and Turk, Irving's best terrier at that time, picked up some poison at Red Lowe Wood, near the kennels at Lorton, and died as a result. Willie was devastated for the loss of all of these gallant working dogs, but especially because of losing Turk who had already won scores of shows and had become a legendary worker, despite the fact that he wasn't yet three years of age when he died. He was a sire of good-looking stock too, but, better still, he passed on his working ability to his offspring. It was a tragedy Billy found hard to get over, for he talked about Turk and his abilities for the rest of his life, as did others such as George Long who saw this dog at work.

Boss and Tiny were bred from Jock and Felix in the April of 1931. Billy Irving must have entered his terriers early, for they started their working career in the December of that same year, making them just eight months of age. Hounds had put a fox off from Tarn Crags and

Trixie '58, a
very typey and
unspoilt
pedigree
Lakeland bred
by Willie
Irving.

they enjoyed a long hunt over Red Pike, finally holing a fox at Scaw, near Buttermere. Boss and Tiny must have been keen to go, for Irving entered this pair for the first time and they searched the borran and quickly found their quarry. When foxes find a good spot to hide from hounds, it is often difficult to shift them, especially from rock earths. This was the case now as Reynard stood his ground. The two young terriers were not to be deterred though and Billy records that they worried their fox inside the earth – not bad for a pair of novices. Many Lakeland terriers will enter early and, while I am sure Billy didn't enter all of his stock at such a young age, there must have been something about this pair that made him enter them at eight months of age. Maybe they were mature for their age, or just begging for work, or maybe they were frustrated and had become trouble-some in kennels and he needed to calm them down. I do not know, but I doubt he would have made it a usual practice to enter his stock so young.

Hounds were out on a lambing call in April 1932 and they followed the drag from the low-lying pastures and finally un-kennelled their fox on the fells, which then gave them a fast hunt. They finally holed the fox in a borran under Black Crag, close to Loweswater, and Turk and Boss were entered. This tells us some-thing of the temperament of Irving's strain of Lakeland terrier. A dog and a bitch can easily be worked together, but here we have Irving putting two dogs to ground and he would not have done so if his dogs showed any sign of aggression towards one another. It is obvious that the early pedigree Lakelands, especially those allowed to exercise their working instinct, were not bad fighters and that two dogs could be both kennelled and worked together. The fox would not leave its refuge and so Turk and Boss quickly finished their foe. Turk needed no assistance of course, but borrans can be difficult places for a lone terrier to corner its foe and that is why two, sometimes more, are entered.

Again, in April of that same year, hounds were called out to deal with a lamb-worrying fox and the drag was soon picked up. They followed the scent and finally unkennelled their quarry, which took them on a fast hunt to Dove Crags and on to Grasmoor fell, where it was at last run to ground. Irving didn't want his quarry bolted, so he entered Rex and Tramp and they quickly killed an old dog fox, which, once it had been dug out, was found to be 'full of lamb' when they cut open its stomach.

In November 1932 hounds followed a drag to Burtness Combe where Reynard was quickly afoot and they ran him to ground at White Cove. The fox refused to bolt and this must have been a particularly big and difficult place, for three terriers were entered, they being Tiny, Tatters and Tick, and they worried their fox below. On 5 November of that same year, a fox was run to ground and Boss and Tiny were put in again. As was the case when this pair first entered, they worried their quarry, which would not bolt. During that same month, hounds pressed a fox hard and ran it to ground after a long hunt, into an old stone drain near Whinlatter where it was worried by Boss and Whisk. Boss had been used at least twice in that same month (Billy didn't record all of the terrier work, just accounts that were outstanding in one way or another) and both times he killed his fox, so obviously he could account for his foe without receiving too much punishment, telling us that the early Lakeland terrier, unlike the pedigree of later years, was indeed sensible at work.

In February 1933 a fox was bolted by one of the Melbreak terriers and was run to ground again by hounds. Willie entered Boss and Whisk and this time the fox would not bolt and so it was worried by the terriers as a consequence. In March of that same year a fox was run to ground at Sandholes, Calva, in the Whinscales area, and Wisp and Merry were put in. As was often the case, their fox refused to bolt and the terriers finally pinned down their quarry, worrying it below ground. During that same month hounds had a very fast hunt on a game fox and it went to ground at Wythop Hall Fell. Irving's terriers, although sometimes worked in pairs at big, difficult places such as borrans, were noted for their determination at work and they could do the job single-handed with few problems. This was the case now, for Willie entered Whisk and the terrier quickly finished its fox below ground. When Irving dug out his terrier and its foe, they found it to be an old dog fox.

At the Good Friday meet in April 1933 hounds enjoyed a fast hunt in the Buttermere area and they eventually holed their fox at Blea Crag. This is a difficult rock earth and well known in the Lakes as quite a bad spot, though it was found to be workable as Willie entered Peggy and Mist. This Peggy is the same bitch given to Irving by Pepper and one that served at the Melbreak for several seasons, working both fox and badger. Irving bred some fine black and tan terriers from Pepper's stock, from 1930 onwards, and Willie comments in his letter to Newcombe that Pepper's terriers were 'rather Welsh in type'. Peggy and Mist not only killed their fox below at Blea Crag, but they drew the carcass out of the earth too, which would save a lot of digging, for the fell-hunting man always tries to recover a carcass, just to make sure the fox is indeed dead. Not that fell and Lakeland terriers will leave a fox alive, not good ones anyway, but foxes can 'play dead', going suddenly limp and lifeless and an inexperienced terrier in particular, can be fooled in this situation, coming off its quarry and leaving it still alive, while believing it to be quite dead.

23 April saw hounds called out to deal with a lamb-killing fox and they soon picked up the drag around the lambing fields in the low country. They then unkennelled their quarry and had a hunt from Crummock Head to High Style, finally holing their fox at Blea Combe. Irving wouldn't require his terriers to bolt such a fox, so Jewel and Tiny were entered and they didn't let their master down. They worried their fox in among the rocks and put a swift end to its crimes.

During the autumn of '33, in the month of October, hounds had a long hunt over Whiteside and eventually holed their quarry at Boat Crag, above Crummock Water. Two terriers were again entered and these were Tramp and Roamer, the son of the unfortunate Turk. Reynard refused to face the Melbreak hounds once more and paid for his obstinacy, as the two terriers quickly worried their quarry among the rocks.

On 12 October 1933 a fox was hunted around the Lorton area and was eventually run to ground at Rogerscale, a couple of miles out of the village. Ruffler and Peggy were put in and they worried the fox, as, again, it wouldn't bolt. Two days later, on 14 October, a fox was found at Dodd, Lorton, and was hunted for quite some time, eventually running back to Dodd and going to ground. Ruffler had killed a fox just a couple of days earlier, but was used again on this occasion, alongside Jewel, showing how sensible some of Irving's terriers were at fox, though many were just too hard for working badger. The two terriers quickly got the better of their fox, worrying it below, as it refused to bolt.

17 October saw hounds having a superb hunt round Whinlatter and to Sunnybrows where Reynard crept into a rock earth, attempting to evade the oncoming and relentless pack. Jewel and Roamer were entered and they soon overcame their quarry and worried it among the piles of rock. On the 31st of that same month, hounds had a good hunt around woodland and eventually ran their fox into a drain. Good old Whisk was entered and the terrier was soon up to a fox that wasn't for bolting. It should have done, for Whisk worried it and the fight was won by the time the

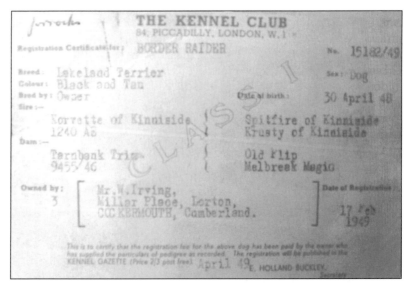

Pedigree of Stowbank Queen. All of Irving's stock, pedigree and crossbreds, were regularly worked.

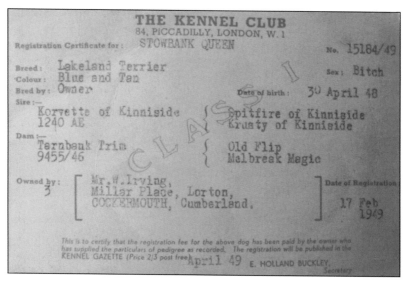

THE KENNEL CLUB
84, PICCADILLY, LONDON, W.1

Registration Certificate for: STOWBANK QUEEN   No. 15184/49

Breed: Lakeland Terrier   Sex: Bitch
Colour: Blue and Tan
Bred by: Owner   Date of birth: 30 April 48
Sire:—
    Korvette of Kinniside   { Spitfire of Kinniside
    1240 AE   { Krusty of Kinniside
Dam:—
    Tarnbank Trim   { Old Flip
    9455/46   { Melbreak Magic

Owned by: [Mr.W.Irving,   ] Date of Registration
    3   [Miller Place, Lorton,   ]
           [COCKERMOUTH, Cumberland.   ]   17 Feb
                                                      1949

This is to certify that the registration fee for the above dog has been paid by the owner who
has supplied the particulars of pedigree as recorded. The registration will be published in the
KENNEL GAZETTE (Price 2/3 post free) April 49   E. HOLLAND BUCKLEY,
                                                              Secretary

Pedigree of Border Raider (Jorrocks) one of Irving's best.

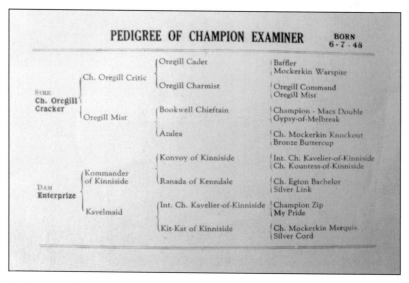

PEDIGREE OF CHAMPION EXAMINER   BORN 6·7·48

SIRE **Ch. Oregill Cracker**	Ch. Oregill Critic	Oregill Cadet	Baffler / Mockerkin Warspite
		Oregill Charmist	Oregill Command / Oregill Mist
	Oregill Mist	Bookwell Chieftain	Champion · Macs Double / Gypsy-of-Melbreak
		Azalea	Ch. Mockerkin Knockout / Bronze Buttercup
DAM **Enterprize**	Kommander of Kinniside	Konvoy of Kinniside	Int. Ch. Kavelier-of-Kinniside / Ch. Kountess-of-Kinniside
		Ranada of Kenndale	Ch. Egton Bachelor / Silver Link
	Kavelmaid	Int. Ch. Kavelier-of-Kinniside	Champion Zip / My Pride
		Kit-Kat of Kinniside	Ch. Mockerkin Marquis / Silver Cord

Pedigree of Ch. Examiner. Shows ancestry includes terriers bred from all
LTA stock, which was worked with various fell packs.

diggers broke through. Willie did much of his own digging in those days, for there were no car followers to keep happy. These days Huntsmen will usually leave a terrierman to do the digging, moving hounds on and keeping the hunt flowing, especially for the sake of car followers who make up a large part of a fell pack, but back then the Huntsmen usually did the terrier work themselves and men such as Dalton, Parker, Wear and Irving would often be found at the head of any dig.

7 November 1933 saw hounds out on the western side of the Melbreak country and they had a good hunt, finally running a fox to ground at a rock spot at Gale Fell, Ennerdale. Tramp and Felix were tried and they soon found and bottled up their foe, worrying it quickly below ground. 2 December of that same year saw a fox run to ground in a drain at Rogerscale and Ruffler and Tick were put in. The fox wouldn't bolt and paid the price in full. Again, by the time Willie dug out his terriers, they had finished the job and were ragging a carcass. 1934 came around and in January hounds had a fast hunt, finally holing their fox at Cat Howe. This fox would not face the pack again and took its chance with Wasp and Tick and was duly worried among the rocks. Wasp was out of Twist and quite a number of pedigree Lakelands, including several Kinniside dogs belonging to Bob Gibbons, can be traced back to this dog.

22 February 1934 saw hounds hunting the low country near Cockermouth and hounds marked a fox to ground at Dunthwaite. Jewel was entered and soon engaged her quarry, but it would not bolt and the bitch then worried the fox below ground and was dug out in good time. Jewel was a superb working Lakeland bitch and she may have been a daughter of Roamer. It is difficult to fathom all of the breeding of Irving's strain, though much of it has been recorded and I was recently sent the details regarding Gypsy of Melbreak, a bitch that features in many Lakeland terrier pedigrees, including those of the Oregill strain. I thought she may have been bred from Turk, but she was born in 1934 when Turk was already dead. Her sire was Majore and her dam was Myrtle. Majore was by High Lea Laddie, a renowned worker bred by Alf Johnston and later owned by George Long, and Irving's Nettle, while Myrtle was bred from Trip and Peggy. Trip was probably Irving's dog and Peggy was probably the dam of the Peggy that Pepper gave to Billy in the early 1930s. Mick of Millar Place, one of Billy's best working and looking terriers and a top-winning dog during the late 40s and early 50s, was

descended from both Turk and Gypsy of Melbreak and, in turn, was descended from High Lea Laddie.

Billy Irving was passionate about the new improved type of Lakeland terrier and always strived, right up until his death in 1966, to produce pleasing to the eye terriers which were game enough to tackle the fell foxes of the Lake District. He succeeded in his endeavours for fifty years and, as we have seen, he certainly produced game stock. As Nuttall so eloquently put it, 'Irving had some damn good terriers' during his lifetime. Every fell and Lakeland terrier one sees with that characteristic bar above the eyes is sure to have at least some blood in their veins from the working pedigree Lakelands belonging to Willie Irving.

7 The Real Lakeland Terrier

(With Thoughts on Breeding, Entering and Exhibiting)

The 1912 meeting at Keswick show resulted in the name of Lakeland terrier being given to the motley collection of what was formerly referred to as coloured working terriers and I use the name in this book in the original form for which it was intended – to cover both pedigree and unregistered working types. True, one associates Lakeland terriers with a box-shaped, square-headed type of earth dog, but in the first instance this name was given to all fell terriers working in the English Lake District. As was the case back then, type differs greatly today, but one thing is certain; the early pedigree Lakeland had a massive impact on working strains of fell terrier during the twenties, thirties and forties in particular, when the pedigree type was still a game and sensible worker. It wasn't until after the Second World War that working qualities began to decline in many strains, because of the huge growth in breeders who had no interest in work, or qualities that aided such work.

The LTA made it a practice not to fault terriers with scars and even the Lakeland Terrier Club, formed in 1932 by mainly southern breeders, had no problems with honourable scars found on exhibits at their shows, though very often Kennel Club appointed judges did not feel the same and scarred exhibits didn't do particularly well under some of them. However, by the early 1940s, breeders began experimenting and put more Irish and Welsh terrier into the mix, as well as more fox terrier blood, and type altered even more, slowly but surely moving away from a type suited to work in the Cumberland fells. After the war, when shows resumed, many Lakeland terriers were indistinguishable from the Welsh and to sort out this problem the Welsh colouring of black and rich red-tan was faulted. True, Welsh terriers had been used even during those form-ative years and Thomas Rawlings and Pepper had charges which

displayed a rather Welsh influence, but bloodlines became saturated during the war years.

Allan Owen, of the Nantcol Valley Foxhounds, was told that
several Welsh miners went working in the Lakes from around 1900
onward and that these took their terriers with them. I can well
believe this to be so, as Welsh terriers had definitely gone into the
mix during the early part of the twentieth century, for some of the
early Lakelands carried the exact markings of the Welsh terrier of
that time, before it became ruined with fox and Irish terrier blood.
Maybe some of these miners worked at Coniston and these may
possibly have been responsible for the pitch-black and rich tan
colouring found on Coniston hunt terriers in particular. Anthony
Chapman had several earth dogs of this colouring, but whether
they were descended from the dogs of those Welsh miners, or
whether they were influenced by Welsh terriers brought north by
Major Roche of the Ynysfor Hunt when he visited the Lakes, is
impossible to say.

Gary Middleton can remember Major Roche leaving one of his
Welsh terriers with either the North Lonsdale or the Coniston pack
many years ago, but this colouring was found on several of
Chapman's fell terriers long before then. It is just possible that
Major Roche loaned or gave some of his terriers to the Kendal and
District Otterhounds and that this is where such rich colouring
came from. Brian Nuttall, however, says that, though Roche's
terriers were of a rich red-tan, the black had flecks of blue and grey
running through, which suggests these were part-bred from fell
terriers with a Bedlington ancestry. My guess is that those Welsh
miners did indeed bring their own chunky, attractive and workmanlike Welsh terriers to the Lakes and that these were then
responsible for the good black and rich tan colouring found on
many of the early Coniston terriers.

All of the fell packs used early pedigree Lakeland terriers, not
only for killing and bolting foxes, but also for improving coat and
bringing down the size of shoulders and chest on unregistered
strains (making them more suited to working the narrow fissures
found among the twisted mass of rocks in borrans and suchlike),
and this continued into the 1950s and, in some cases, beyond, for a
few of the Lake District breeders had stuck close to the old lines and
these were still breeding some excellent workers. Many pedigree
strains, however, including some within the Lakes, had lost sense
and several were now far too big for serious earthwork, so they lost

favour during the 1950s and 60s and from then on the pedigree type, except for one or two breeders around the Egremont area, was not used on unregistered strains, for a good working pedigree dog was increasingly difficult to find. Irving was still breeding working pedigree stock after leaving the Melbreak in 1951, but he had problems with fertility and skin troubles on his terriers at Cockermouth, the town where he settled after leaving his former home at the kennels, and so the once glorious Melbreak strain gradually declined, especially during the 1960s. However, the working fell, or Lakeland, terrier of today displays an ancestry closely linked with the early pedigree working Lakelands and such strains will be discussed in the following pages of this book, together with their breeders. Although many are not the box-shaped traditional Lakeland in type, all have earned the right to be called Lakeland terriers as they are true workers which are of the correct type for working with a fell pack – ideally suited to working the landscape that is known as 'The English Lake District' where foxes are controlled out of necessity and not for 'sport'.

Steve Dawes

Steve has hunted with the Coniston Foxhounds for much of his life, though he originally comes from the Ullswater country where his dad had a farm at Patterdale. He hunted with the Ullswater during his early years and began keeping Jack Russells to start with, which he found well suited to working the fell country. One of his Russells, Sam, was a corgi cross, a small brown and white dog, which, Steve says, was very hard at fox.

He left school and moved over to Grasmere where he worked as a shepherd. He came to know Joss Hardisty well, who farmed around this area, and he says that Joss had the old type Lakeland that he thinks were probably bred out of Harry Hardisty stock, for Harry, the succeeding Huntsman to Willie Irving at the Melbreak and Whip to Irving, was his brother. Sid Hardisty of the Eskdale and Ennerdale though, was the main terrier breeder of the family, so maybe Joss had terriers bred out of Sid's stock; terriers that produced the famous Melbreak terrier, Turk.

Steve can remember Joss's terriers sometimes going missing when they were accompanying their master around the farm and often they had to be dug out of fox holes and badger setts once they

Steve Dawes' first Lakeland, Rock, which was Cowan-bred and a good, reliable worker.

had been located. They were game stock, but Steve stuck with his Russells until he bought Rock, a Cowan-bred Lakeland bred down from Irving and Hardisty stock, having plenty of old pedigree bloodlines in his breeding, from Willie Stevenson who worked his terriers with the Ullswater. Steve was twenty-one years of age by this time and Rock entered to his first fox, which was run to ground by the Coniston pack. Rock wasn't hard, but he was game and was a good bolting and digging dog with plenty of sense.

Steve then bought Tess from Ken Harrison. She was a black bitch who was bred from Middleton's old stuff and, true to these blood-lines descended from some of the hardest dogs to work with the Ullswater Foxhounds, she became a hard fox-killing bitch. Like Rock, she entered to her first fox with the Coniston, after they had enjoyed a short hunt around Skelghyll, running their fox into a rock spot. Steve entered his black bitch and she quickly found, engaging her fox and tackling it hard, though it would not bolt and had to be dug out in the end. After a few hours of gruelling work, Steve uncovered his bitch and accounted for not one but two foxes. Tess received quite a mauling that day, but she never looked back and became a very sound worker. Another fox was run to ground after a hunt around Loughrigg Fell, which stands above Ambleside, and

Tess was put in, accounting for her fox below ground, for, again, it wouldn't bolt.

Rock and Tess were not only superb workers, but they were lookers too and Steve did well with them whenever he exhibited at Lakeland shows. It was inevitable, I suppose, that he should breed from this pair and they produced Tag, a superb working dog with quite a poor open coat, but a nailer to fox. Hounds had hunted a fox for two hours in the Crosthwaite area near Windermere and they eventually ran it to ground at Lords Lot. Stan Mattinson was the then Huntsman and he asked Steve to try the young Tag. He obliged, of course, and Tag entered, found his fox and engaged it, not allowing it to bolt. Steve and Dave Dixon then dug the earth and came upon Tag and his quarry, which he had seized by the throat and turned over on its back. Steve says that Tag had a knack of doing this and several foxes he dug were found in this position when Tag was to ground. I saw Tag work a fox in a difficult place near Grasmere, which had found itself a good vantage point inside a borran earth, and was most impressed, Reynard eventually being dug out by Steve and Dave Dixon. Tag worked for some ten seasons with the Coniston and he accounted for several foxes during that time.

One of the hardest digs Steve took part in with Tag was after a fox had been run to ground at Skelghyll. The Coniston pack had been called out by a local shepherd who was losing lambs to a fox and they took up the drag around the lambing fields, unkennelling their quarry and hunting it for well over an hour, before it at last went to ground. Tag was entered and the digging commenced. This turned into a gruelling dig of a good few hours, but eventually they dug out their fox, which had found itself a good spot behind a rock. Tag took quite a mauling that day but still he stayed with his quarry and worked it hard until finally dug out. Terriers of such quality are essential in such a landscape, with nigh-on impossible earths of this type around every corner.

Steve has unique ideas when it comes to the entering of terriers and what he says makes a lot of sense. He will allow a youngster to rag a carcass or two during the early part of its life, but he will not put a terrier to fox until it is eighteen months, or even two years of age. He wants his terriers to be fully mature both mentally and physically when they start their vocation and he says that this gives the teeth, jaws and bones time to develop fully. Remember, Lakeland terriers are traditionally bred to kill, rather than bay at, foxes and so I suppose it makes sense to be patient and allow such full maturity to be reached.

Now a made and reliable worker, Tag was mated to Freddie Downham's working Middleton-bred bitch and this union produced Rip, another grand worker. After hounds had hunted a fox for about three hours over the Tongue and around Troutbeck Park, finally running it to ground, Rip entered a running drain at Troutbeck and, despite their only being a two-inch clearance above the water, quickly found and bolted her fox, but it went back in, unwilling to face the waiting pack once more. Steve then had to dig his bitch and fox out of there and this took quite some time. Despite the icy water almost filling that drain, Rip stuck to her task and was eventually dug out, but she had suffered due to the cold and afterwards needed to be wrapped in a blanket and kept warm in the car. Hardy indeed, are these Lakeland terriers!

A fox was run to ground in a big earth at Skelghyll and Rip was entered. Reynard wouldn't, or maybe couldn't, bolt and so a dig commenced, with the bitch and fox being dug out a few hours later.

Steve Dawes (standing) with Tiny and Tan. Freddie Downham (right) is holding Tag and Rip.

Rip had developed into a superb working bitch that could bolt reluctant foxes, or stay with them until dug out and Steve took many foxes using this bitch.

His next terrier was Tan, a bitch from Willie Stevenson of Penrith who worked his team with the Ullswater Foxhounds. The parents to Tan were both sired by Rock, the first Lakeland terrier Steve owned, with the dam being possibly Buck/Breay bred. Like her grandsire, Tan is not at all hard, but she will stay all day and has made a good fox-bolting terrier. It may seem quite an easy thing for a terrier to bolt a fox and it possibly is in many places, but in the Lakes, after a fox has been put in by hounds and is reluctant to face them again, with a rocky stronghold around them, it can be very difficult indeed and can take quite some time. Many hunting reports state that a fox was bolted after being run to ground, but one does not get the sense of the effort put in by a terrier in order to get that fox on the move. A good bolting terrier in the fells means one that will work close to its fox, continually harassing and striking at its foe until it leaves the chosen den. Tan is such a terrier and continues to work at the age of twelve years!

At Kentmere, hounds hunted a fox for three hours until it even-

Steve Dawes with Tag and fox taken using this terrier.

tually went to ground in a rock earth on the fellside. Steve was asked to try the young Tan and she entered keenly, found and bayed at her quarry and eventually bolted it. Hounds took off in pursuit, but Tan remained below, having found another fox skulking among the rocks. Steve and Dave Dixon then dug to her and accounted for a second fox. This was a promising start for a young terrier and from then on she never looked back.

Tag was mated to Rip and this union resulted in Tiny, a hard dog who became another good worker with the Coniston pack. At the Brown Horse, Winster, a fox was run to ground by hounds and it had gained quite a stronghold in among yet another rocky lair. Tiny was keen to go and Steve entered his dog, which soon found its quarry and settled down in one spot. The fox had jammed itself in 'twixt a couple of boulders and it was very difficult for the dog to get on terms with his quarry, but he stuck to his task and was dug out a couple of hours later, along with the fox. Tiny had taken a bit of a mauling that day, yet he hadn't flinched, nor given an inch, sticking with his foe until finally reached by the diggers. When he was eight years of age, and after a distinguished career with the Coniston, Tiny suddenly lost the use of his legs and had to be put down, but before this happened he mated Tan and this resulted in Tess, who entered to her first fox at Grasmere, after it had been run to ground at Broadrayne. The fox had sought shelter in quite a large earth, but the bitch quickly found and began baying at her foe. However, the fox wouldn't bolt and so digging commenced and, after an hour, Tess and her fox were successfully dug out. This was another promising start for a youngster and from then on she improved rapidly.

In the Cartmel Fell area Steve and Dave found a fox lurking in an earth as hounds were hunting another. This was a soil hole that led under a wall and Tan was put in and dug to. However, it was a very awkward spot, right under the wall and Steve replaced Tan with Tess, taking another full hour to make enough room to get at the fox, being careful not to dig too much ground away, just in case the wall collapsed. It was a dangerous dig to say the least, but eventually the quarry was reached and successfully accounted for.

One of Steve's current dogs is Rock, a black Lakeland bred by Steve Robertson of Tebay, his bloodlines going back to Middleton stuff. He is a good looking terrier that was begging for work when I visited Steve's kennels in the spring of 2006 and I am certain this terrier will make a very good fox dog. He is powerful and has a

Steve Dawes' current dog, Rock (left) bred by Steve Robertson of Tebay.

massive head and is just the type for a fox that has a stronghold from which it will not bolt.

Sam, Steve's corgi cross Jack Russell, was a very good little worker and he once stayed three hours when put to a fox at the New Year's Day hunt from the Drunken Duck, Hawkshead. This was yet another rock earth and Sam stuck with his quarry until Steve and Dave finally reached him after a long, gruelling dig. The photo (p.144) showing Tag with a fox was taken at another meet at the Drunken Duck at Hawkshead. A fox was run to ground by hounds, into a soil hole, and Steve dug it out using his best dog, Tag.

Hunting in the fells is a hard life for all concerned and many dangers present themselves through the course of an average season. Hounds can get trapped on ledges, which lead them onto steep and dangerous crags, followers can slip and fall, and terriers can become trapped to ground. Also, during heavy rainfall the mountain streams can suddenly swell and Steve can remember one day when he was hunting with Chris Ogilvie of the Coniston Foxhounds, when one of the Huntsman's terriers was swept away by a swollen beck and never seen again. Steve has owned and bred some very useful terriers over the years, many of which could kill a fox that refused to bolt, while others were baying dogs, staying until dug out if they couldn't persuade their quarry to bolt. Terriers of this type have been bred in the Coniston country for centuries and it is good to see people such as Steve Dawes keeping up the tradition.

Roger Westmoreland

After speaking to Steve Dawes I headed up the Kirkstone road and killed time at the Kirkstone Pass Inn, and then the Queen's Head at Troutbeck, in order to check and organise into good order, my written notes, before going to see Roger Westmoreland who farms on the edge of this famous hunting village. No, I am not an alcoholic, but wanted to check if any of these public houses, with strong connections to fell-hunting, had any old photographs which I may have been able to use for this book. I met Roger at his farm a little later and enjoyed a very enlightening interview with this once close friend of both Cyril Breay and Frank Buck, two of the most important breeders of working Lakeland terriers of recent times.

Roger took up this strain of working terrier many years ago, so it is fitting to discuss the history of this type of fell terrier, before expanding on Roger's breeding programme. Cyril Breay came north from South Wales during the 1920s and he brought his working Sealyhams with him; terriers he and his father used for fox and badger digging among the rolling Welsh hills. Cyril, however, found them a little unsuited to the North Pennines, where he settled at Mallerstang, and so crossed them with early Lakeland terriers. This produced a leggier type that was more suited to rough ground and rock earths. The first all-black terrier in this strain now famous for such colouring appeared in 1936 and this colouring was probably due to a Bedlington influence, which came mainly through the Coniston line. Turk, the only terrier to emerge from a borran in the Kentmere valley in the 1930s, after four terriers had been lost to ground, was a black terrier and this was possibly Ernie Parker's famous Turk, a hard fox-killing dog with a vile temper.

Billy Irving stated that all-black terriers were found around Windermere and Grasmere in those days and it was through a Coniston hunt terrier, I am certain, that the black colouring was introduced into Breay's famous strain. Breay put a red Coniston hunt terrier onto his white Sealyham, Wendy, and bred Tubby. For some reason Brian Plummer, writing in the *Shooting Times* during the early 1980s, stated that Tubby was a misprint and that this terrier was, in fact, Jummy, the famous short-legged Coniston bitch photographed for Clapham's book, *Foxhunting On The Lakeland Fells*, but Brian was mistaken, for Tubby was born during the 1920s, after Jummy had been retired from hunt service. Jummy was born long before then and so these two terriers were different animals. It was Tubby who continued Breay's breeding programme.

It was during the 1930s that Buck and Breay first met, and in rather dramatic circumstances. Tommy Robinson was hunting his pack of Lunesdale Foxhounds in the Bishopdale area and they ran a fox to ground at a bad spot, a large rock earth that was rather a stronghold for foxes. Breay entered two of his bitches into the earth

Roger Westmoreland's chocolate fell terrier, Cocoa.

and, after killing their fox, they became trapped to ground. Digging commenced and, after a long, gruelling session on the exposed fells, one of the bitches, Barker, was reached and got out safely, but it looked bad for the other terrier, so bad, in fact, that, after a few days, Cyril had given up any hope of reaching her. It was then that Walter Parkin turned up at the scene and told Breay that he knew a chap who may be able to help. Cyril agreed that this chap could come and see what he could do, but still had no hope of seeing his game bitch again. The weather had turned very nasty by this time and snow blizzards plagued the diggers, chilling them to the bone and dampening morale until gloom and pessimism reigned. Things looked bleak indeed.

The outgoing and cheerful Frank Buck soon turned up, along with a few quarrymen, lightening the tense atmosphere and creating a more optimistic one, with Buck immediately commencing operations, setting explosives in certain places and blasting the hard rock until, finally, and after several days, the terrier bitch was freed from what was about to become her grave. She had endured unbelievably freezing and difficult conditions, but was nevertheless in relatively good shape. Buck was impressed. This was a known bad earth and the bitch had worked wonderfully well and had survived conditions that would easily see off less hardy earth dogs. Breay offered Frank money for his efforts, but he refused, asking for a puppy out of the bitch instead. But Cyril was so grateful that he did better than this; he gave Frank the bitch herself and she was Tiger, the grand matriarch of the Buck/Breay strain which later became known as the Patterdale terrier. Nuttall believes the first terrier Breay gave Buck was Tickler, but this was probably after Tiger had become his, for Roger can clearly remember Breay telling him about this rescue and the bitch given to Frank. It was in 1940, when Tiger was mated to Major Burdon's stud dog at the Bedale, that Frank began his contribution to the strain and from then on both parties had almost equal shares in the breeding programme, though it was Breay who was the brains behind improving type and producing both workers and lookers. Buck learnt much about genetics from Breay and thus he, too, often produced better type, as did his son Max, who used Hardisty's famous Turk in order to produce lookers and workers.

Cyril Breay also used white Lakeland blood in order to spice up the working qualities of his strain of earth dog. During the 1940s the Eskdale and Ennerdale Foxhounds were invited to come and hunt the Lunesdale country for a few days and Jack Porter brought with him a white Lakeland bred out of the Eskdale and Ennerdale line (that country was saturated with fox terrier blood from the late nineteenth century onwards and particularly during the 1920s) called Metz. Edmund Porter can remember his father, as well as several of the older followers of the Eskdale and Ennerdale, talking about this terrier and he stated that Metz was 'a 'ell of a dog'. Breay thought so too. Hounds had enjoyed a good hunt across the high fells and eventually ran their fox to ground at a place called Shiningstones, north of Sedbergh, which was notorious for being rather a difficult place. In fact, it was one of those earths from which it had proved impossible to bolt a fox. Porter then released Metz and he quickly disappeared into the rocky stronghold, with much uncertainty being felt by the followers, who were used to failure whenever a fox got in here. However, the baying signalled a find and Metz bolted, not one fox, but three, from that 'impossible' place, one after the other. This impressed Breay, who was present on this occasion, so much that he asked if he could use Metz on his terrier bitches. Jack agreed and Breay did indeed bring this dog into his strain. Breay later told Roger never to be reluctant to use white Lakeland blood, as some of these were cracking workers.

It was because of such a background that Roger Westmoreland took up the Buck/Breay strain of working terrier and he has no regrets. Jimmy, a chocolate dog, was one of Roger's best and he was out of Biddie (Max Buck's Tina and Hardisty's Turk) and Bingo, a dog sired by Breay's famous Bingo and Westmoreland's Squeak. He wasn't a very hard dog, but sensible and useful for bad places. He did much good work for the Coniston and could find in the deep borrans of their hunt country, being capable of killing any fox that refused to bolt, though he had a knack of shifting reluctant foxes and forcing them back out into the open. Roger valued him so much, in fact, that he used him a lot at stud and all of his current stock goes back to Jimmy.

Roger, Frank and Cyril hunted with several packs, including the Zetland, Bedale, West of Yore, Lunesdale, Coniston and even ran their own hounds, the Wensleydale Harriers, at fox and hare under the Mastership of Donald Sinclair who also owned the pack. Also, they shifted foxes and badgers (when it was legal) for local farmers and gamekeepers and took foxes in the Yorkshire Dales under a bounty scheme for a few years. With such options easily available to them, this team of hunters had plenty of work for their terriers and they were out as much as possible. Superb working terriers were the norm with all of this work available to help bring them on and Cyril Breay and Frank Buck became very well known all over the country. Gary Middleton tells an interesting tale that demonstrates just how well known this strain of working Lakeland was in those days.

Gary had a litter of pups from two terriers bred from Breay's dogs and he advertised them for sale in *The Westmoreland Gazette*, at a reasonable price for working stock. He quickly sold all that he wished to sell, keeping a couple back for himself. A couple of weeks later a Scottish farmer from Galloway knocked on his door and asked if any of the pups remained. Gary informed him that a couple were left over, but that he was keeping them for his own use. However, the farmer wouldn't leave Gary alone and eventually he agreed to let him have the pair. The farmer had complained that there were no decent terriers in his locality and that he needed them for fox control. Gary was puzzled how it was he had come to hear of the litter so far away from the Lakes and the chap informed him that a lorry driver had left a copy of the newspaper at a local café and that he had had a look through it, seeing the ad which had no telephone number and deciding to go straight to the given address, he was that desperate to get his hands on Breay stock, which he knew was some of the best in the country.

Black Monty was another of Roger's terriers and he was obtained directly from Cyril Breay. Monty was another superb worker and

Cyril Breay's Rusty was given to Westmoreland and he died in Roger's kennels at Troutbeck.

Roger bred quite a few litters from him before losing him at work. Hounds had run a fox to ground at a large borran in the Kentmere valley and Monty was entered. He found his fox and began baying, but soon went out of earshot, falling silent. Roger never heard or saw his terrier again and one can only assume the poor dog became trapped after killing his fox.

He used a border dog called Jack as outcross blood and this was a method used by both Breay and Buck, as they used quite a bit of border blood in their strains of working terrier, as did Joss Akerigg who bred his stock along similar lines to Buck and Breay. Some of the outcross blood was rather slow to start, but once entered they made superb earth dogs and several worked with hounds. His present terriers are Tyke and Spike, two black terriers that are very good finders, able to shift reluctant foxes, but also capable of killing any that will not bolt.

Roger freely admits that he learnt much from both Buck and Breay, especially regarding which earths were relatively safe and which were not. He doesn't breed a lot of litters, just when he needs youngsters to bring on, though he has a lot of his stock out with friends and hunt servants, lest he suffers losses and his bloodlines become scarce. He enters a terrier when it is ready to go and he is not at all worried if his youngsters are rather slow at starting, for he has found that many slow starters make the best workers once they catch on. He likes a border cross, for these are very often sensible and will not get too badly knocked about. Billy Irving also used border terrier blood in order to produce a strain of crossbreds that he used particularly for badger digging, or if he wanted a fox bolting, for his Lakeland terriers were far too hard for 'Brock' and they allowed few foxes to bolt. As John Cowan said, Irving's Lakelands were 'murderous' at fox and would kill, rather than bolt, such quarry.

Roger isn't keen on over-large terriers and around fourteen inches and a similar weight is his ideal. They must be good finders, for terriers without nose in the fells are useless. The huge borrans and deep peat earths make finding a must and so this quality is rated above all others in the Lakes. He looks after his charges, giving them good food, housing and exercise, for he requires his terriers to work for at least eight seasons, though he will often get ten or more from his stock. As they get older, however, he will give them less work, in order to provide opportunities for bringing on his young entries. Also, he has terriers for different tasks, stating that some are better

Roger's Judy,
by Spike.

at working borrans, while others are better in soil, or peat earths.

Like Mr Breay, Roger is not averse to white Lakelands and he works Polly, the dam to Mike Nicholson's typey Russell dog, Jeff. Roger once had a spaniel/fell cross named Judy which was a superb worker and he used her when he whipped in at the North Yorkshire Otterhounds which were then hunted by Tommy Harrison who moved to the Kendal and District Otterhounds soon after. Judy was a very good bitch on fox, but exceptional at otter.

Roger Westmoreland has a wide-ranging experience with both hounds and terriers and he is as keen today as he was in his youth. He is a farmer by trade and Master of the Coniston Foxhounds. Foxes do not respect quality, however, and the week I visited Roger at his farm, he had suffered attacks on his lambs by a marauding fox. One survived despite quite severe injuries and he was hoping to catch up with the culprit. Before the hunting ban, Roger encouraged youngsters by allowing them to try their young terriers whenever the chance arose. Terrier work is now more limited in England and Wales, but still, in certain situations, terriers can be used to ground and so fox control continues up in the fells, though hunting folk are trying their best to keep within the law. Westmoreland is optimistic that hill packs will eventually become licensed, for the number of lamb-worrying cases is quite high again and farmers and shepherds need to be able to call upon the vital services of their local hunt when suffering such losses. True, two hounds can be used to flush quarry to guns, but this is rather ineffective up in the fells, or in large tracts of forestry, so packs are needed in such circumstances. When introducing legislation that is supposed to tighten up on what some folk see as cruel practices, the law makers could do no better than to use people such as Roger Westmoreland as consultants; people who really know how to carry out effective pest control in the most humane and efficient manner!

Phil Brogden

I journeyed high into the North Pennines, to Brough, in order to interview Phil Brogden who has been following the Lunesdale Foxhounds since he was eight years of age. Walter Parkin was Huntsman then, with John Nicholson as Whipper-in, and Walt still used his strain of terrier that was founded on Albert Benson's Red Ike, a game Lakeland terrier which served at both the Blencathra and Coniston hunts. Phil bought his first terrier for £1.50 from John Burbeck who lives in the Ullswater district, which he thinks

Phil Brogden's Britt.

154

was either Joe Wear, or Anthony Barker bred. This was Rip, a dog terrier who had a very hard coat, grizzle in colour. Colouring on a terrier is not an issue, but he does like the jacket to be wiry and dense, in order to resist the incredibly hostile weather conditions of the Northern Pennine districts. Phil entered Rip at around two years of age and always waits till this time in order to allow the teeth and bones to fully mature. He believes that dogs entered too early will not have a very long working life. In the Wild Boar area above Kirkby Stephen, hounds ran a fox into a big rock spot and John Nicholson asked Phil to try Rip. The terrier entered keenly and began searching the deep rockpile for his as yet unknown foe. He eventually found and bolted his quarry and it was a good start for the young dog.

Rip mated Bill Brightmore's bitch and Phil was given pick of the litter. He chose a red bitch, which he got working, but then sold when he needed some money rather desperately. He sold her through Brightmore and Bill managed to get £100 for the bitch. As Phil said, 'Bill could always manage to find a buyer for a terrier.' This bitch was Tiny and Mike Fernhead was the Whipper-in at the Lunesdale at the time. Tiny bolted several foxes for hounds, before she was eventually sold.

His next dog of note was Britt, a terrier purchased from the north-east and one that is the ancestor of his present stock. Britt was undoubtedly Buck/Breay bred and he proved a wonderful worker, used mainly with the Lunesdale pack. Britt mated Mick Atkinson's bitch, another Buck/Breay bred terrier, and this union produced Phil's superb working bitch, Tanya. She was an incredibly good finder in very deep places and often went to ground in what many would consider impossible places, which later became her undoing. Phil was out exercising Tanya on the fells above Brough, out on Stainmore, when she went to ground at an unlikely looking place and never returned. Nothing was heard, or seen, for the next few days, but one day when Phil approached the earth he heard faint barking some distance away. His Fell and Moorland Working Terrier Club membership had recently run out and he called in the RSPCA and digging operations commenced.

A JCB dug through slate and peat and then a rock chisel was brought in, for huge slabs stood in the way and these had to be broken up if there was going to be a chance of moving them. A few days of digging created a huge hole in the ground, but still no further sound of the bitch could be heard and operations ceased.

However, barking was heard again and the diggers were called back to the scene. They found a natural fault in the rock, a crevice going right into the earth, and decided Tanya must have followed this to her fox. Eventually, after opening up enough ground on which to start a small quarry, they came across a hole that plunged 35 feet into the substrata, with Tanya there, trapped on a ledge below.

Mountain Rescue was then called in and a caver, Carl Maxon, was lowered down on a rope. Tanya was wet and rather bedraggled and Carl put her into a rucksack and she was then lifted out to safety. She had lost quite a bit of weight, but was otherwise okay. The digging had gone on from 7.30 in the morning until the early hours of the next day on some occasions and huge amounts of earth and rock had been torn out of the fellside. But it had all been worthwhile. The local papers, and even television, reported on the event and Phil's bitch became quite a celebrity.

Tanya was four years of age at this time and had done plenty of work for the Lunesdale, bolting foxes for hounds, but also killing any that refused to shift. At a quarry at Garsdale, former home of the late Joss Akerigg, a superb terrierman and fox-hunter, Tanya bolted a fox for the waiting pack, which was then hard pressed, going to ground again in a drain. Paul Whitehead, the present Huntsman of the Lunesdale, called Phil to the drain and Butch, a powerful red dog, was entered. The fox bolted again, but dragged Butch with it, for he was hanging onto its backside, reluctant to let go his hold. However, Reynard broke free and he proved a game fox, for he escaped hounds and got to ground yet again, in rather a noted bad spot, and was finally left for another day. Butch was bred from Britt and Tanya and he has a good harsh jacket which is ideal for the bitterly cold and windswept country he hunts. As a young dog, Butch killed many a fox in just a few minutes and then emerged without a mark on him, or maybe one or two bites. Many may not believe such claims, but my own dog, Ghyll, was also capable of such feats. He rarely got himself knocked about and quickly throttled his fox when the opportunity arose. Middleton's Old Rex, sired by Wilk's Rock, was another terrier that could kill a fox and come out of the encounter unmarked. Butch killed several foxes in this manner, though as he got older he took more punishment. At Hartley Quarry, not far from Brough and Kirkby Stephen, Butch was put to ground at a rock spot where the fox had got itself into a good commanding position and it took all of the dog's

Paul Whitehead with red Ricky and his black stuff.

experience to overcome it. He took quite a mauling that day, but eventually took control of the situation and killed his fox. Folk have been known to question whether or not Butch has actually killed his quarry, when he has emerged soon after with virtually no bites, and Phil is happy for them to try their terriers at such times. Whenever they have, the dog has soon emerged, uninterested in the lifeless corpse below ground.

A later litter between Britt and Tanya resulted in Phil's bitch, Blott, and, like Butch, she too can worry any fox that will not bolt. Paul Whitehead, Phil says, has had some very good terriers over the years and he has kept a noted black strain since he was Huntsman to the Pennine Foxhounds at Holmfirth, bringing them with him when he took over at the Lunesdale. However, he has recently suffered losses of this strain and had been left with youngsters. So he bought in a couple of terriers from Wales. These proved of little use in rock though, and Phil can remember one occasion when one of these terriers was put in a rock earth at Ingleton. The Lakeland from Wales emerged and so Paul asked Phil to try Blott. She entered eagerly and quickly found her fox, worrying it below ground. Phil is sure the terrier has probably done some good work in soil holes back in Wales, but just couldn't work rock with any effect.

On the fells above Dent, Paul had one of his terriers to ground and it was now getting late in the day, so he asked Phil to try his bitch. Blott entered and quickly joined the other terrier. However, darkness crept on and still the terriers had not emerged, so they were blocked in and the diggers returned later. Paul's terrier was waiting at the entrance, but there was no sign of Blott, so they blocked the earth again and returned at first light next morning. They shifted plenty of rock out of that earth and eventually reached a spot where water was trickling out. The rocks were loose here, though, so they began digging at the other side and finally broke through. Blott had killed the fox and had been unable to get out afterwards. Paul's terrier must have been on the other side of the fox and so was able to get out.

One of Paul Whitehead's terriers, a black and tan bitch, was very game indeed and would kill a fox if it wouldn't shift, but she wouldn't look at a fox again until her bites were fully healed, which tells us something of the intelligence of some of these working Lakeland terriers. Phil says that Paul also had a red dog, Ricky, that was very intelligent. He wasn't a hard terrier, but one that was extensively used for bolting foxes to hounds. However, if they wouldn't bolt and Paul wanted the fox accounted for, he could be called out and a harder terrier entered. If the earth was one that could be dug, then Ricky would stay all day. Phil says that he wouldn't enter some earths and one then knew that such a place was very bad indeed and unsuited for terrier work. Also, he wouldn't tackle two foxes. He would stay all day to just one fox, but wouldn't go if two were in. This suggests that he was probably mauled by two foxes when first starting and the trauma remained with him.

Phil likes a fox-killing Lakeland terrier, though he has seen some very good Russells at work and states that short-legged Jack Russells belonging to Toy Winn have bolted many a fox for the Lunesdale that other terriers couldn't shift. Phil only breeds when he needs young stock and he avoids shows. He believes there is too much bickering at shows and that there are far too many non-workers at these venues. The most important quality he looks for in his terriers is the ability to find in deep rock earths. He doesn't really mind if they kill, or bay, as long as they can find, though he stresses

A terrier pops its head through at the Lunesdale foxhounds' kennels.

the need to have terriers capable of killing a fox that won't bolt in some circumstances, particularly if that fox has preyed on farm livestock. He also stresses the need for a hard, dense jacket and prefers his earth dogs to be around thirteen or fourteen inches tall.

Phil Brogden's terriers have a generous sprinkling of Buck/Breay blood in their pedigrees and they are none the worse for that. He has much respect for this strain of terrier and told a tale of Boxer, a red Lakeland dog belonging to Dick Gilpin who was a close friend of Buck and Breay and who kept this strain of terrier, using it for taking predators from the fells around Brough where Gilpin was a keeper. At Midge Hole (so-named because midges used to congregate in swarms here), Swindale, near Brough, Boxer went to ground and very quickly went out of earshot.

The depth of some of these rock holes has to be seen to be believed and even the most vociferous of working terriers cannot be heard after only a few short seconds of entering such places. Boxer simply disappeared and several days later had not returned. Gilpin tramped home with a heavy heart and concluded that his game terrier was lost forever. The dog was special to him, for Dick travelled all over the North Pennines with Breay, especially in the Mallerstang area, bolting foxes and shooting them, often using

Boxer, or Breay's terriers. Gilpin came to terms with his loss and seven days later he opened his back door in order to head onto the fells, carrying out his everyday keeping duties, and there, waiting for his master, was Boxer, in fine fettle, as we say in the north. Boxer had obviously killed his fox and the carcass had blocked his way out, and so, after chomping on the cadaver for sustenance for a week, he had literally eaten himself out of what could have become his grave, for he had actually put on weight, not lost any! Gilpin was delighted, of course, and went on to take many more foxes with this game and valiant terrier. Phil says that Gilpin would walk everywhere in those days, hiking from Brough to Patterdale in order to hunt with the Ullswater Foxhounds.

Phil has taken part in quite a few lambing calls and he can remember one very frustrating episode when hounds were called out on three occasions to the same farm, but each time hounds just couldn't find any scent. Lambs continued to be taken, however, and so, in the end, guns were called in. They shot six foxes before believing they had accounted for the culprit, but, if hounds cannot find scent around the pastures where lambs are being taken, then it is likely that a badger, and not a fox, is the culprit!

Steve Robertson

After talking with Phil Brogden, I headed for Tebay and there met Steve Robertson who makes a living as a freelance shepherd among the upland farms of the fell country. He well knows the damage foxes can do to farmers' livestock and so keeps a very useful team of terriers, which he employs for carrying out fox control. For me, he was a delight to interview, as he has the same sort of attitude displayed by the founder members of The Lakeland Terrier Association. In other words, he believes it is possible to breed typey, good-looking stock that is capable of working the tough hill foxes inhabiting the country he hunts. Indeed, he practises his beliefs and breeds some incredibly typey and game earth dogs.

He began working terriers almost twenty years ago and started with a small black and tan strain of Lakeland that was bred around the Millom district; small, game earth dogs that could literally get anywhere. They were excellent workers, but, because they could get anywhere, Steve ended up losing this strain when they became trapped to ground and couldn't be rescued. He then took up

160

A blonde fox caught by Lunesdale Foxhounds under Walter Parkin in March 1940. Parkin's strain played an important part in the breeding of the Buck/Breay strain.

Brightmore-bred stock from Mark Hallet; terriers that were a mix of Buck/Breay and Middleton bloodlines, bred to be typey, but being wonderfully game dogs and very often hard fox-killing types. Hallet breeds a strain of blacks similar to those of Barry Wild and, believe me, these are extremely game earth dogs and foxes that will not bolt are doomed when such stock is to ground.

One of his best terriers is Sassy, a Middleton bred red bitch that is very hard and she will stay all day until dug out, or the fox perishes. Sassy is game, but she is also sensible and will not let herself get too badly knocked about. It is a fallacy that fell terriers with pedigree Lakeland blood in their veins had no sense when up to fox. Irving bred plenty of superb fox dogs – terriers that could quickly kill a fox, while emerging from the encounter without serious injury. True, many suffered when working badger, simply because they went in for the kill as they did with a fox, but sense was still common in the early pedigree Lakelands and in fell terriers 'spiced-up' with such bloodlines. Gremmy, his black bitch, is another typey terrier that will stay all day and come out of an encounter at fox without too much injury. Sassy is a strong bitch and Steve has bred some good stock from her, both show winning and working terriers. Steve always breeds with work in mind, but he is also keen on showing during the off-season and does very well with his charges. He follows the Lunesdale whenever possible, but carries out fox control mainly for farmers and keepers whom he works for.

Fell, a red dog bred along almost the exact lines as my old dog, Fell (Wendy and Maurice Bell bloodlines), being from Wendy's Fern and Ridley's Tag, is a smart terrier with a superb jacket, though he is first and foremost a worker. He sires good fox dogs too, passing on his quality breeding which eventually goes back to Hardisty's Turk. Like his famous ancestor, he is not a hard dog, but is game to

Steve
Robertson
with Millie.

162

Steve's Tod
and Gremmy.

fox and is a good bolting and digging terrier. Steve has done particularly well with Fell and recently won the Scottish Champion of
Champions with this tidy red male. Like the early LTA members,
Steve will not keep a non-worker, no matter how typey it is, for his
stock must earn their keep working the bleak fell country around
his home.

His thoughts on entering are sensible indeed and he will allow a
youngster to taste a little work at around nine months of age,
increasing their workload as they mature. Much of his black stuff is
begging for work earlier than this, but he holds them back and does
not allow a young terrier to be mauled, as this could easily ruin a
novice for good. He also breeds with good coat in mind, for terriers
pegged down outside an earth waiting for a fox to bolt, or one to be
reached by the diggers, will suffer badly in bad weather if the jacket
isn't harsh and dense enough.

One of the hardest terriers he has worked was Dollar, whose
bloodlines went back to McCoy, a terrier by Dave Roberts' Rip and
one owned by the late Paul Blackledge. Dollar was originally bred
in Nottingham and went north to work for a keeper at Carlisle. He

was just too hard for a keepered estate, however, for bolting dogs are best in such places, where guns await the presence of a fox above ground, and so Steve took him on. He would charge at his fox, not allowing it the chance to bolt, take a hold and kill it incredibly quickly and he had the habit of eating the head of his fox until finally dug out and pulled off his victim. Dollar had a heart attack whilst working a fox and died suddenly, though Steve believes this was as a result of his hysterical eagerness to get to his foe and quickly maul it to death. Steve has bred some good working black Lakelands (he differentiates between Patterdales, those smooths bred mainly from Nuttall stock, and black box-shaped Lakeland types), though he freely admits that he has also owned some that wouldn't work. On the other hand, many were just too hard for what he requires of a worker and they took too much punishment whilst engaging a fox. He likes a terrier that can be worked throughout the season without having to be 'hospitalised' because of severe bites, and so sense is rated highly. He keeps lurchers, so bolting terriers are essential, though he doesn't mind if his stock

Surge, Steve's smart black and tan Lakeland, bred from Sassy and Fell.

Black Lakeland pups bred by Steve Robertson.

will finish those that will not bolt, as long as they go about it sensibly.

Lakeland terriers are generally self-entering, but sometimes they make a start before their master intends. Steve was out exercising his terrier pups on the fells above Tebay when they suddenly shot to ground at an earth where normally there is never a fox. The pups entered with some purpose and began baying soon after. A fox then erupted from the earth and Steve's fawn lurcher was instantly in action, pulling it down and quickly finishing its quarry. The pups then enjoyed tasting the carcass and from then on never looked back.

One of his best was Billy and one day he entered a rock hole on open fell near Tebay, finding and bolting a fox and then going on to find another in the earth, which he promptly finished below ground. Millie is one of his present bitches, bred from Tod and Gremmy, while Surge is from Fell and Sassy. He likes a good coat on his terriers and stated that he had two smooth-coated terriers out during a bad spell of weather and, after standing outside an earth for a while, they had to be put inside Steve's jacket while he got them back to the warmth and shelter of his vehicle.

Steve has quite a number of his terriers with hunts and game-keepers and, though they are generally typey and competitive at shows, they have been thoroughly tested as to working ability and are well suited to hunting the fells of the Lakes country. Steve is also keen on good working lurchers and one of his best, Dolly, was used on the lamp around the Bristol area and was known to take as many as fourteen foxes in one night.

Near Shap, at a big granite earth, Gremmy was entered and quickly found and engaged her fox. She soon killed the first, then switched to another, which was in rather an awkward spot and was far more difficult to overcome. She had entered at 11am and by late afternoon Steve had made little progress when attempting to dig her out. And so power tools were sent for and a powersaw, with a diamond blade attached, was employed to cut through the rock. The going was slow and very difficult, but eventually the bitch was reached and pulled out at 2.30am the next morning. Gremmy will not leave her quarry and always has to be dug out if the fox won't bolt. Steve has had some long digs to this bitch in particular, though he stated that she hasn't been trapped, just reluctant to come off her quarry while it lived. She is also a terrific finder and he has known her find a fox in a big rock earth after others have said there was nothing in. He can totally rely on her and that is a valuable asset when working huge dens in the northern districts. Without finding ability, fox control would be completely ineffective in such places.

A stud dog and brood bitch must be pleasing to the eye and around thirteen inches is Steve's ideal height. He likes a square, powerful head and a dense, harsh jacket, for he has seen smooth Patterdales suffer from the elements during midwinter. He likes his breeding stock to be narrow at the shoulders and to be spannable, for they must negotiate narrow fissures when working borrans and suchlike. They must also have good temperaments and be peaceable with other dogs and especially children, for he is a family man and kids love to play with terriers.

If bitten, Steve treats his charges promptly and diligently, cleaning the wounds thoroughly and giving them a warm, dry bed in which to recover. Also, he cleans the eyes using drops and makes sure he clears them of any irritating debris. If treated thoroughly, he says, scars will heal very well, though he prefers to work sensible terriers that just don't get themselves too badly knocked about in the first place (no matter how sensible a terrier, foxes in certain vantage points can maul even such a terrier that is intent on shifting, or killing, its foe). I found Steve to be of the old school; one who prizes a good working terrier, one that can find in vast places

Walt' Parkin heading for first draw from Hawes in the early 1950s, with Lunesdale pack and Monty, a terrier bred down from Red Ike and Breay and Buck's terriers.

and come out of an encounter with fox relatively unharmed, yet one that can also win well at shows during the summer off-season.

He has in his possession the head and brush of a very light coloured fox that was caught by the Lunesdale Foxhounds at Crosby Ghyll, Crosby Ravensworth, in 1940, when Walt Parkin was hunting hounds. The memory of this old fellwalking Huntsman continues to be revered throughout the fell country, despite the fact that it is decades since Walter hunted hounds.

Maurice Bell

Another who reveres the memory of Walter Parkin, and one who knew him as a close friend and hunted regularly with him, is Maurice Bell, the long-standing Master and Huntsman of the famous Wensleydale Foxhounds which are kennelled near Hawes.

I enjoyed a delightful drive through the Yorkshire Dales one sunny summer evening in order to visit Maurice at his farm, where he and his wife showed me great hospitality and I found him to be a true country gentleman, still passionate about hounds and terriers and hunting the fell country where he has spent a lifetime among the upland communities.

Maurice says that there were fewer foxes when Walter hunted the Lunesdale and he has fond memories of hounds visiting the area for a fortnight, when the pack were kennelled in the market town of Hawes. Maurice freely admits that he learnt much about hunting hounds from watching Walter Parkin at work and stated that he left hounds to get on with their job unaided, only helping out when absolutely necessary. Foxes were hardier in those days and long, hard hunts were the order of the day which often ended in the fox escaping, a catch marking a red letter day, but still, hounds worked harder and distances covered were vast and always on foot. CBs and cars have made hunting the fells less strenuous to some extent and keeping in touch with the pack is certainly easier, but Maurice looks back to the old ways of doing things with great affection and I could tell that he longed for those days to return. Maybe he is selling himself short, however, for Maurice, like Walter, is a very sound Huntsman who follows the old ways of allowing hounds to work independently and without aid and interference and his pack have thus gained a reputation for being able to work out a cold drag for long distances until finally finding their fox, working mostly by themselves from then on until catching, running to ground, or losing their quarry. As a terrierman he has much experience and at one time he did all of the terrier work for the Lunesdale.

His present hunt terrier, a black bitch named Tally, was bred by Mark Naisby in Scotland and she is descended from the old Britt bloodlines, for much of the black terrier blood found in this part of the world goes back to Maurice Bell's famous Britt and such bloodlines are useful indeed. Tally really knows how to handle a fox and she can bolt one that refuses to bolt from less handy terriers. Britt was bred from Frank Buck's Viper and Maurice's Twist; a superb fox dog which saw much service with the Lunesdale. Twist was in turn sired by Hardisty's Turk, out of Lothian's Rip. This line was from terriers that served at the fell packs across decades and they were sound workers.

Maurice was called out to Easby Abbey after a farmer had several lambs slain by a fox and he took Britt along, which had now become his most useful and reliable terrier. Britt had entered extremely keenly to the first badger he saw, staying with it until reached, and from then on had become a legend at fox. As Maurice approached a nearby earth, on the side of what is known as a 'gutter' in North Yorkshire, a sort of gully that runs down the fellside, a vixen was sitting outside, on the edge of a ditch which contained a known soil earth. The fox disappeared below as they approached and Maurice soon had Britt following, informing the gun to stand nearby in a likely place, in readiness of a bolt. However, Britt had grown harder with experience and allowed few foxes to bolt and he soon engaged this one. Maurice was forced to dig to the furious goings on below and after twenty minutes he had recovered Britt, along with the vixen and dog fox he had killed underground (end of lamb worrying!).

Britt was both a finder and a killer of foxes, but he produced a peculiar quirk in some of his pups. One of these was Nick, which Maurice sold to a chap in Scotland who hunted over 7000 acres of land. When a year old, Nick was put into a cairn and he promptly killed the vixen, but he left all of the cubs unharmed. Jim Stewart of Bentham wanted his bitch mated and Maurice had Nick back at his place for a while, so Jim used this dog as a stud, despite the fact that he wouldn't kill cubs, for he finished adult foxes incredibly quickly and usually worked with great relish when to ground.

Maurice has fond memories of hunting with Parkin and Nicholson and he can remember one time when John was late (unusually) for the meet and kept Walter standing around impatiently waiting for his Whipper-in to turn up. He finally came running down the road, minus his hunting uniform and clothed, instead, in his socialising garb, complete with shiny shoes. Walt wasn't too happy and John explained that he had walked a girl home after the previous evening's hunt social and that he had only just made it back in time to catch hounds before they set off. On another occasion, after Paul Whitehead had taken over when 'Nic' retired, a fox was run to ground and a follower turned to John and asked him which earth it had fled to. 'Aah don't know,' said 'Nic' smugly, 'we allus caught 'em afore they got there!'

When Nicholson began courting with Rita Lothian, her father, George, came up with a rather silly and risky idea and he asked Harold Watson to make a very public announcement at the hunt ball. The announcement was made, but 'Nic' didn't quite catch it for one reason or another, but made enquiries as to what had been said. He was rather surprised, and more than a little shocked, to say the least, to learn that he and Rita were soon to be married. Although he wasn't too happy with this little bit of trickery played on him, he did later marry Rita anyway and they were indeed happy together. Maurice tells another story regarding George Lothian, who was rather a character, and his wife whom most feared and dared not cross. George had got steaming drunk one night and Maurice and a friend took him home on a motorbike, with the drunkard well out of it in the sidecar. However, the hour being late, they decided that it was best not to disturb Lothian's wife and instead they dumped him inside the chicken pen. No doubt the heavy beer fumes kept the foxes away that night!

Some of the best Lunesdale terriers Maurice can remember were Rock, Black Meg and Red Meg. Black Meg belonged to John Dixon, a farmer who whipped-in at the Lunesdale for a time, and she was put to a fox that had been run to ground at Mallerstang. She was a very game bitch and tackled the fox hard, despite the fact that it had wedged itself into a very commanding position from where it did much damage to her. So much damage, in fact, that she later died from her injuries, much to her owner's dismay.

Maurice likes a terrier to work its fox hard, as many will not bolt when they get in a good spot, in order to persuade its quarry that it is best to make for open ground. He has owned many such terriers, but he has also seen some that were as good as useless. One such terrier was put to ground at Bellerby camp. A fox had been run in and one of the followers asked if he could use his dog. Maurice agreed and the terrier went in. Nothing was heard and eventually digging commenced. It took a while, but eventually they came across the so-called earth dog – curled up fast asleep! Hounds ran another fox to ground near Maurice's house, inside a long drain, and the same chap asked if he could use the same terrier. Reluctantly, Maurice agreed and the terrier did the exact same thing once more, suffice it to say that this terrier was never again used with hounds!

Maurice is very careful as to the places he will enter a terrier and, if he deems an earth to be too bad a place for one of his earth dogs, then he will not ask others to risk their dogs in such a bad spot either. He also requires a terrier to be sensible and disciplined, being fully broken to all livestock and cats. He requires his terriers to work foxes hard, but with cunning, being capable of bolting, or even killing, a fox, while emerging from the encounter without serious injury. Britt was such a terrier and he was both game and tractable.

Hounds had run a fox to ground on Roman Fell and the fox found itself a good commanding position under a large boulder. One or two hunt terriers were tried and the fox stood its ground, eventually driving them back and refusing to shift. Maurice had Britt on the couples, but 'Nic' wanted the fox bolted and so had asked that he not be used, for Britt allowed few, if any, foxes to bolt. However, Nicholson knew as well as anybody that this fox wasn't going to bolt and so, in the end, he turned to Maurice and asked him to loose his black dog. This was about fox control and a dead fox was better than one left alive simply because it wouldn't bolt. Britt was loosed and he entered eagerly, but with caution, engaging his fox and taking hold of it and eventually drawing it from under that unmovable boulder. As one of the hunt followers grabbed the fox, Britt let go, knowing it was secured, but the chap let go too and the fox quickly shot back into the earth, with Britt following. Again he drew the fox out and again Britt let go of his hold, thinking it was properly secured, but this time the fox bolted, unwilling to face the terrier for a third time.

Maurice has owned some very good white Lakelands and one of his best was Mandy, bred by Kevin Drummond of Broughton-in-Furness. Tanner was another superb worker, as was Ross, both of these belonging to Wendy, Maurice's daughter, who worked terriers with the Wensleydale for several seasons. At Bank Ghyll a fox went to ground and three or four terriers were tried, but all failed to shift it. Ross was then entered and he succeeded in bolting his quarry. Ross was also used by Frank Buck at the West of Yore and Wendy says that he was so fond of Frank that he would often disappear and then turn up at Harmby, the village where Buck lived, having travelled miles through Wensleydale in order to get there.

Finding is rated very highly by Maurice, though he is quick to stress that he trusts his hounds for marking more than he does his terriers. He cites a case of when a fox was run in at Widale and hounds marked the spot eagerly. Three or four terriers were then tried, but failed to find. Dave Kitson eventually turned up and he called Maurice back, who had decided to move hounds on and try for another, as at last a terrier had found the skulking fox. It has to be said, though, that not all packs of hounds are as reliable at marking and a good terrier is invaluable at such times. Hounds can sometimes false mark out of jealousy, or simply because their Huntsman winds them up as they sniff at an earth. As is the case with terriers, a gentle word of encouragement is all that is needed when hounds are checking an earth, otherwise leave them to it and be silent.

Maurice has also had to leave foxes to ground, though this is rare. He can remember one particular day when hounds ran a fox to ground at Snaize Fell and the terriers couldn't shift it, or possibly couldn't quite get up close enough to make much of an impact. Hounds were moved on and another fox quickly found, which was run in at Groove Ghyll. This was also in a bad spot and the terriers couldn't do anything with it, so, again, hounds were moved on to try for another. Unbelievably, another fox was run it at Johnson Rocks and it too could not be shifted. I have had similar days and have sometimes come across foxes that are on a ledge that is just too high for a terrier to get at, or a spot which is too tight for a dog to follow a fox, and one can only move on when this occurs. But to have this happen three times in one day is rather unfortunate!

Maurice is not too put out by the new law in England and Wales that dictates only one terrier can be put to ground at any one time, for this is generally the rule he has followed anyway and he works his terriers with care, always putting their welfare ahead of how many foxes he can catch. He has learnt much from Parkin, Nicholson and others, such as Frank Buck, and tells a tale of how careful Buck was when working his earth dogs. Hounds ran a fox onto an almost inaccessible ledge at Bishopdale and Maurice was about to loose a terrier, which he hoped would bolt it, but Frank told him not to bother, for he had experience of this place and he knew that the terrier would be badly mauled whilst trying to shift its quarry. Some so-called terriermen only think of how many scars there are on an earth dog and would have loosed the terrier anyway, hoping for a face full of bites that would be paraded around shows during the summer months. Maurice took Frank's advice and kept his earth dog on the couples, leaving the fox for another day, for the last thing he wanted was a badly bitten terrier. What a good example for those who wish to work terriers, but with the welfare of the dog uppermost in mind!

One of the best terriers to serve at the Wensleydale was Mist, bred by Wendy, which killed the first eight foxes she entered to. A fox was run to ground on Snaize Fell and Mist was put in, this being a place from where she had already bolted several foxes. However, this particular fox was not for moving and so the terrier bitch tackled it hard and then became trapped. A dig of massive proportions then began and conditions were not too favourable, as it began snowing and snow in the fell country can make life very difficult indeed. A digger was brought in and it dug out a hole that went twenty-five feet into the hillside and was at least thirty feet deep. At last they uncovered the bitch and she was trapped on a ledge alongside the now-dead fox, but was still a little out of reach. So a young lad crawled into the fissure and soon returned with the terrier, which had been to ground for three days by this time, but was in reasonably good shape, despite her ordeal.

Mist was put in a hole at Deepdale Ghyll after hounds had run a fox to ground, but this was no earth in which to put a terrier. Wendy had loaned her to one of the hunt followers and Maurice wasn't yet at the location where hounds were marking keenly. If he had been, he would simply have moved them on to try for another. Sadly, Mist was never heard of, or seen, again. The earth looked innocent enough, but many of these North Yorkshire 'innocent' earths lead to deep fissures, or join with fast-flowing mountain streams that plunge hundreds of feet into the pitch-blackness below and scores of terriers have been lost in such places over the decades. Mist was yet another of that number and the loss was hard-hitting to the Wensleydale pack.

Another terrier to go the same way was Dave Kitson's Tag, a black terrier that was put into an earth after hounds had run a fox into Johnson Rocks. The terrier succeeded in bolting the fox, but was never seen again. What happened is a mystery and one can spend forever speculating, but one can only guess that Tag followed another fox deep into the hillside and became trapped, or maybe a badger was in among the rocks and killed the terrier.

Maurice requires a terrier to be leggy enough to cross rough country, while being small and narrow enough to get to ground in some very tight and difficult places. He cites the case of Sam, a small, short-legged Jack Russell, when giving an example of how short legs can be a hindrance to a dog required to work in the fell country. Hounds were hunting Walden forestry and he and Tony Kirby, the owner of the little Russell, headed out onto the fell top where the heather is deep, making the going difficult to say the least. Some time later they realised Sam had disappeared and his owner was rather worried. However, on returning to the car down in the valley, Sam was discovered lying under his master's vehicle. The going was far too hard for the short-legged terrier and he had decided that enough was enough and had returned to easier ground of his own accord. A leggier terrier will still not have an easy time of it over such bad country, but they will cope far better and I have yet to see a leggy terrier beaten by rough ground!

Maurice enjoys judging terrier shows and he will never make decisions based on who is holding the lead – unlike some! He looks for good coat, which he deems essential, though this is not surprising when one considers the open and exposed country he has hunted all of his life. Colour is of no importance to him and he has had all kinds, including several whites. He likes an old-fash-ioned type of Lakeland and Hardisty's Turk played quite an important part in the make-up of the terriers that have served at the Wensleydale over the years.

He likes Jack Russells too and came by one in rather peculiar fashion. He was hunting at Easby Abbey and there was a chap there with a Russell bitch and three pups, which he said he was going to drown in the river. Maurice isn't one to mince his words and one can imagine his reaction to this, so he ended up with all four dogs and the chap was sent away with a 'flea in his ear'. He kept the bitch and managed to find homes for the pups, with one going to Sylvia Shepherd and one of the others becoming a well-known show champion which won all over the place. The Russell Maurice kept lived with Fury, a typey bitch that did much good work at the hunt and won well at shows. She won the Championship at the famous Horton in Ribblesdale show when it was staged for the very first time all those years ago, when Dennis Barrow was judging. She won the veterans at Lowther when John Cowen was judging and he told Maurice she should have been entered into the main classes, she was still that typey. Fury was a superb worker, however, and she bolted many foxes for hounds. When she grew older, though, Maurice didn't have to go through the pain of leaving an eager terrier at home because of its age, for she simply refused to go out hunting anymore, once in old age. This bitch played an important part in Wendy's breeding programme and three of my terriers are descended from this line – a line that has scores of terriers that have worked with different fell packs in the pedigree and one that includes many good lookers, as well as an unbroken line of sound workers.

Maurice obtained his first terrier via Iveson and he called him

Rock. Rock did plenty of work with the Lunesdale and distinguished himself as a good bolting dog. At that time the Lunesdale pack made an annual trip to Ormskirk where they flushed foxes to waiting guns and Rock bolted several foxes during these trips. Tragically, he got out of his kennel and was knocked down and killed on the road near Maurice's house.

Although the Lunesdale visited the Wensleydale area for a short time each season, much of the country was left untouched and so Laurie Dent, Frank Buck and a few other locals talked to Maurice about starting up a pack of hounds solely to hunt the Dales country and this eventually led to the formation of the now famous Wensleydale Foxhounds – a pack which has the reputation of being capable of working unaided and one that can work out a cold drag for hours at a time, in much the same fashion as the fell packs of old.

Maurice will not keep a quarrelsome terrier and his best are always quiet and well behaved, being able to live with hounds without any problems. Tally, his present terrier, is quiet, but as game as a pebble at fox. Hounds ran a fox to ground twenty yards from the road and one or two terriers were tried, but the fox stubbornly refused to shift and eventually pushed the terriers out of the hole. Tally was then tried and she stuck at her fox, eventually bolting it. She had taken a few bites, which is inevitable in such circumstances, but still, the very next day she was out and about around the farmyard killing any rats she could find. That is truly a mark of a game terrier.

On Mossdale Moor hounds ran a fox to ground at a large peat earth and twenty-eight of the Wensleydale pack managed to get in after it, emerging after some time covered in grime. It is such grime that clings to a terrier to ground in such places and chills them to the bone, for the temperature underground is often near freezing point. Hounds got into yet another hole on Wether Fell, which was full of water and Maurice feared some would drown. When they emerged, water poured out after them and the followers realised they had got them out just in time. The water had built up so much that hounds would have been lost had they been to ground in that place any longer.

Maurice says that Joss Akerigg always bred superb terriers and he once bought two from him, Badger and Blitz, which were out of a litter of five, though he sold them to Frank Buck when they were a year old as they were smooth coated and Maurice much prefers a harsh, dense jacket. Maurice travelled over to Akerigg's home at Garsdale in order to view the litter and pick his puppies, but they weren't yet ready to leave the nest, so Jossie said that he would let Maurice know as soon as they were fit to be picked up. And so Maurice later received a postcard informing him that 't'laal pups are ready'. He went straight over and picked up Badger and Blitz, handing over the ten pounds Joss had asked for them, but he looked a little miffed and stood there scratching his chin. Maurice asked if anything was wrong. 'Aye,' came the reply, 'it's ten pund for t'pups, but ah want t'price o' t'stamp for t'postcard on top o' that', he said, in all seriousness! What else could Maurice do, but relent in the face of such thrift! He also remarked that John Nicholson could also be a little on the thrifty side and he can remember one day when a crowd had gathered at a public house after a day's hunting in the fells and John Dixon, the Lunesdale Whipper-in, asked the Huntsman to 'get yer fags owt'. 'Nic' later pulled him to one side and told him off, sternly warning him to 'Niver ask mi to get mi fags owt agen when we're in company'.

Cyril Breay once gave Maurice a pup out of his top winning and working bitch, Skiffle, and he and Breay took it to a show where a Kennel Club judge was in charge of the terrier showring. He asked for all of the exhibits to be lifted onto a table to be examined and Cyril was most put out, having never seen 'owt like it at a working terrier show'. But things took more of a downward turn when the judge asked 'what are those?', pointing to scars picked up whilst working fox with the Lunesdale pack. 'Those are medals', replied Breay, turning away in disgust.

Maurice can remember Breay's famous Rusty serving at the Lunesdale and he states that he was a very hard dog to fox. Hounds ran a fox to ground inside a drain at a wood and Rusty was entered. This was close to a road, for the fox got out of that earth rather swiftly, knowing Rusty was just too much for it, and ran under ten cars in its bid to escape hounds. He regards Breay as a gentleman and states that Frank Buck had a heart of gold; a sentiment shared by Roger Westmoreland and others who knew this pair well, though Maurice says that Buck and Breay did fall out for a while over something to do with a puppy.

Maurice has much regard for his daughter's breeding programme and states that Wendy has bred some excellent stock. One of hers went to the Farndale and did much of the work for that pack. They also served at the Blencathra when Will Pinkney was

Whipper-in. Maurice was standing with Edmund Porter at a Langdale meet and a chap was boasting about some red terriers he had seen at work with the Blencathra during a meet held on the previous day, and Maurice was proud to turn to him and inform him that those terriers were bred and owned by his daughter, Wendy. Edwin Winder's Danny was also from Wendy's stock and this terrier was not only a top winning terrier, 'winning all over the place', as Maurice put it, but he was also a superb worker.

The line bred down from Britt has also produced very consistent workers and Tally was in action again after hounds had run a fox to ground near the Bell farmstead. They had hunted a drag for ages and had finally unkennelled their quarry, which was eventually 'run in'. For some reason Tally had been left at home and so Maurice sent a hunt follower to the farm in order to pick her up, as there were no other terriers available. Tally entered the earth, found her fox, bayed, tackled it and persuaded it to make for open ground. It bolted and hounds caught it after a good hunt.

Barry Todhunter

The Huntsman of the Blencathra Foxhounds must be considered a serious terrier breeder as he has continued to breed the old Blencathra bloodlines, which he inherited from the great Johnny Richardson, from whom Barry learnt his trade. Johnny inherited the same strain from George 'Geordie' Bell and he in turn from Jim Dalton, who must be considered as one of the founding fathers of the Lakeland terrier, for he was 'polishing' up his old coloured bloodlines using typey fox terrier stock, long before the Egremont breeders began this practice. Nothing could match Dalton stock for both work and looks during the late nineteenth and early twentieth centuries. Like his predecessors, Barry has very definite views concerning Lake District earth dogs and he doesn't mind quite a large and leggy dog, provided it is narrow enough in the chest to get, being spannable and not too powerfully built in the shoulders. He stated that most of the early fell stock was large and powerful, standing at around fifteen inches or so, and photographic evidence certainly backs up what he says. Some of this stock was too large, but most must have been able to get, for all of the fell packs had fifteen inch terriers serving with them in those days.

The very name of Todhunter (meaning 'Foxhunter') strongly

The late Johnny Richardson, huntsman at Blencartha 1949–1988,
Whipped-in to George Bell 1946–49.

suggests that Barry is descended from Scottish pest controllers who
probably settled in the Lakes country because of the often large
bounties being paid for every predator accounted for, and so
hunting is in the blood, so to speak. His father was a keen terrierman and follower of hounds and his grandfather also kept
terriers for fox control on the Leconfield estate where he worked as
a gamekeeper. Barry's first terrier was Rip, a black and tan bitch
bred from the Middleton strain of Lakeland terrier. Barry had
obtained a position as Whipper-in to John Nicholson at the
Lunesdale in 1971 and he needed a terrier or two to take with him.
However, it was at the '71 opening meet of the Blencathra that Rip
first entered to fox. Hounds had run a fox in at Lonscale Crag,
which stands on the southern side of the Blencathra mountain
above the village of Threlkeld, and Robert Todhunter was soon on
the spot, though Johnny Richardson was as yet some way off. When
the Huntsman and Whip are not in the vicinity, one of the regular
followers will use the first available terrier in order to bolt the
quarry and get the hunt moving again, so Robert entered Rip for
the first time. She went like a tiger, found her fox, got stuck in and
bolted it, despite an early reluctance to shift. Hounds then hunted

and eventually caught their fox. Rip never looked back after this and she became a very useful terrier to ground.

Another terrier he took with him to the Lunesdale was Skip, a black and white fell-bred Russell that became another useful terrier at the hunt. Hounds holed a fox at the army ranges at Mal Plackett, near Brough, in lime-rock scar, which had a reputation for being a bad place. Skip was entered and soon found and bolted his fox. Nicholson was impressed and that is saying something, for he had seen it all by this time, yet he still praised the dog, telling Barry that 'he did well'.

Barry also loaned a terrier or two during those two seasons of Whipping-in at the Lunesdale and one of these was Russ, a white Lakeland bred and owned by George Lothian, Nicholson's father-in-law. Teddy was another terrier on loan; a dog bred by Gary Middleton out of his bitch Rags – a real game terrier that was used for both fox and badger digging, and was sired by Rip, a keeper's dog from Shap Fell, which Gary believes was probably bred from Cyril Breay stock. Rip had seen plenty of work at fox and proved a superb stud dog too, for Teddy was the best finder Gary has ever seen at work and he did much grafting for Arthur Wells, before he loaned the dog to Barry. He proved his worth at a bad shake-hole near Malham – a district famed for bad earths and lethal fissures plunging into the limestone – from which he bolted a fox that had been run in by hounds. However, he was to impress even more when hounds ran a fox into a very bad place at Pen-y-ghent. This is another area famed for 'impossible' earths and, fortunately, the old and much respected gamekeeper, George Perfect, was on hand to prevent Barry from slipping his dog into the earth, for 'Nic' wasn't up with hounds and Barry had no knowledge of this place.

George told Barry that this was a 'terrible place' and so he began gathering hounds in order to move them on and try for another, but his plans were 'scuppered' when Teddy slipped his couplings and got into this bad spot. Barry's heart sank, for he feared he would never see the dog again and he wasn't his to lose, but there was nothing else for it but to wait and see what happened. It took almost two hours before very distant baying could be heard and sometime later the baying grew nearer and nearer, until, at last, the fox bolted, with Teddy right on its brush. It was a lovely sunny day and the sight of that fox scurrying off across the beautiful Dales countryside with a bedraggled terrier and several couple of hounds in pursuit was rather exhilarating to say the least. George Perfect, a man who

Barry Todhunter with some of his Russells.

had a wealth of experience with terriers and is a friend of such nota-
bles as Frank Buck, Cyril Breay and Joss Akerigg, was rather
impressed and lavished praise on the terrier for having successfully
worked a fox out of that place. Teddy was an incredibly good
worker and he was returned to Arthur Wells when Barry left the
Lunesdale in order to join the Blencathra in 1973.

Barry took Skip and Rip with him to the Blencathra and he also
obtained a terrier from Harry Bragg who bred small, hardy, red fell
terriers, which had good harsh jackets and were famed for their
work to fox. Tiny was his Bragg-bred terrier and she was a little
cracker at work and was brought into his breeding programme. He
resolved early on to keep a fell bred line and a Russell line and so
he bred from such coloured stock as Rip and Tiny, while obtaining
Russells from Stuart McIver at the Dungannon Hunt, who had
taken over as Huntsman from Harry Carr, a good friend of Johnny
Richardson's and whose strain Johnny brought into his own
Blencathra bloodlines, they were so useful as workers.

A number of years ago a chap came out for a week's hunting with
the Blencathra and he brought with him some smart Jack Russells
free of Lakeland blood (a bit of a rarity these days!), which

impressed Barry very much. The chap was Eddie Chapman and one of his terriers, Fell, was a little too leggy for Eddie and he offered him to the Blencathra Huntsman. Barry was worried about large rock spots of a type the terrier would not be familiar with, but he needn't have bothered himself, for Fell took to working rock like a duck takes to water and he could shift a reluctant fox from any spot, no matter how large. At Carrock, which lies among some of the wildest and most remote of the northern fells, Reynard went to ground in a large borran and Barry tried Fell. He entered eagerly, quickly found his fox and bayed, teased and nipped his quarry, hassling it until it got fed up and fled the scene, bolting out onto the windswept hills and making off over the rough ground with hounds in full cry.

Barry will keep one or two terriers that are capable of killing a lamb-worrying fox, or one that is decimating farm livestock such as chickens, or maybe gamebirds (much of the Blencathra country is keepered), though most of his earth dogs will stand off and bay at their quarry. However, one that lies two feet away is no good to him, for a fox must be convinced that it is best to take its chances above ground and only a terrier that works extremely close to its

Barry Todhunter with his old Blencathra strain Lakelands that go back to Dalton's original strain.

fox, hassling it constantly, though sensibly, can hope to succeed in a country such as that hunted by the fell packs. He has found that the Chapman strain of Jack Russell do work close to their quarry and they have proved superb fox bolting terriers. Stan Mattinson, the one-time Whipper-in and Joint Master of the Blencathra, confirms that these Russells working at the hunt are indeed very good workers. One of the best to serve at the hunt was Mick, a typey Russell which saw much service at fox and one that won Champion Jack Russell at the Great Yorkshire Show. I saw Mick on several occasions and he was a very smart dog indeed, with a superb temperament, being easily kennelled with hounds. Barry rates sense highly and all of his earth dogs, whether coloured, or whites, are sensible to ground. He has also used outcross blood from the Border and College Valley Foxhounds and every few years he will put Chapman blood back into his Russell line.

His coloured fell, or Lakeland, stock all go back to Rip and Tiny, Harry Bragg's bitch, and Johnny's old strain, which included some Dungannon Russell bloodlines. While Barry says that it has been common for fell pack Huntsmen to loan terriers from others, he stresses that he will not do this, for he is frightened of losing dogs that don't belong to him. He is careful where he puts his earth dogs and does his utmost to avoid losses, but the worry is just too much if a terrier belongs to someone else, so he sticks with his home-bred stock and they seem to suit him well.

Another outcross line was from Grip, a terrier owned by Mark Frost, who was Barry's first Whipper-in when he took over as Huntsman after Johnny passed away. Frost was from the Eskdale and Ennerdale country and Barry believes the terrier was descended from Arthur Irving stock, which, in turn, was descended from Willie Irving strain Lakelands. Temperament is important and his stock must have character and plenty of personality, while being friendly, for people are always petting them at meets, or shows. He likes smaller terriers, but a bit of leg is essential, especially for crossing rough country and for working wet drains and peat earths. His bitch, Tiny, from the Bragg strain, wasn't that leggy, but she was nevertheless superb in rock. His stock is so sensible at work that some of his terriers have retired completely unmarked. They undoubtedly took a minor bite or two during their busy careers, but the rough hair will soon cover minor wounds and judges should think about that when considering putting up terriers simply because of the number of scars they carry. Fell terriers work foxes

B. Todhunter's Eddie, named after Eddie Chapman.

out of some of the worst places in the British Isles, yet I have seen several at meets that were unmarked, despite working foxes week in, week out, for many seasons. Others do carry scars, true, especially the fox killers, or those that get stuck into a fox quickly, tackling it hard, but it is stupidity to believe that the most scarred terriers are the best workers.

Barry looks for the same qualities in his stud dogs and brood bitches and they must have a good head, a narrow front, yet with a roomy chest. A bit of length in the back for twisting and turning among rocks is desirable, though he does not stress a harsh jacket as essential, as others do, for he stated that foxes have very soft coats, yet they are out in the most terrible of conditions and easily cope with the elements. A fox has a dense jacket, he says, and that is what he looks for in a terrier. He doesn't mind a soft coat, as long as it is dense. The only thing I can say on this subject is that, when a fox is out in bad weather it is usually on the move, hunting for food. A fox does not have to stand outside an earth, sometimes for hours at a time, in often freezing conditions, during a dig. But he does have a point and I agree about density in a coat. A sparse jacket is lethal and any fell, Lakeland, Jack Russell, or any other type, which has such a thin and soft coat should be given away as a pet, for it will suffer badly, and probably even die, whilst at work in midwinter.

His terriers are twelve to fourteen inches in height and this is his ideal size. One or two may be a little smaller, but he will not use any that are bigger than his fourteen inch maximum. He has seen some good big earth dogs at work, but they struggle to get in some places and so he avoids those on the larger side. When having to dig a fox out, he stresses that a smaller terrier will be right up to its quarry and that one can drop in right on top of the combatants, whilst one may still be two or three feet away from your fox when digging to a larger terrier that cannot quite get up to it.

Johnny Richardson had a large terrier on loan for a time, a big dog named Mike, who was a superb worker, but he struggled to reach his fox in some places and Barry says that you could tell how far off from his quarry he was by the note of his bark. He likes to keep a hunt flowing whenever possible and Barry states that a smaller terrier will reach its fox sooner and thus have it bolted much quicker than will one on the larger side, which may have to dig on in places, or find another route to its foe. However, despite having some terriers that are a little over ten inches, there are places where a terrier cannot get to its fox, whatever its size, and Cat Crags at Caldbeck is one of the worst places for producing poor results whenever a terrier is put in. Both the Blencathra and the Cumberland Foxhounds have run many foxes into this place which stands above the river behind the village school, yet only one fox has been bolted from this fortress earth in the past thirty years. There must be a ledge out of reach of earth dogs somewhere deep inside this rocky lair, to where Reynard can safely retire whenever he is hard pressed above ground. This earth is on the left side of the river, yet a similar rock spot on the opposite side also holds foxes, though they can be bolted from here by any determined terrier. Barry tells tales of many similar dens throughout the Blencathra country and he is still discovering places that have been walled-up, or where an old rusting iron bar juts out from among the rocks in stark warning to not enter a terrier there.

Gary Todhunter, Barry's son, is the terrierman for the Blencathra and terrier work can still be carried out legally, in order to protect game and wild birds on keepered estates throughout the hunt country, and, of course, foxes can still be flushed to guns using a brace of either hounds, or terriers. And so fox control continues in

Joe Bowman being carried to his final resting place (Spring 1940) with Joe Wear, the new Huntsman following, Joe Wilkinson, Wear's Whip is behind.

the Lake District and the fell packs, using a combination of trail-hunting and legal flushing, play an important role in this, as they always have done.

Eddie Pool

After talking to Barry, I headed down into the Ullswater country in order to interview Eddie Pool who has a wealth of experience with both hounds and terriers and whose father and grandfather were important terrier breeders in the Lake District. In fact, John Pool bred some of the early pedigree Lakeland stock that changed the shape of the old fashioned coloured working terriers forever. John inherited his stock from Eddie's grandfather, Anthony, and most of these were blue, rough-haired earth dogs, which displayed quite a bit of Bedlington ancestry. These were incredibly game, but most had such poor coats that they suffered in bad weather, especially after long spells to ground, or after having waited outside an earth in freezing conditions for any length of time. In order to cure this, and in order to improve type after the show craze had spread throughout the country, even into the remotest of Lakeland dales, fox terrier blood was added to the mix. Jim Dalton, together with Glaister and the Carrick brothers, seems to have been the first to do this, but soon after others began using the same methods.

During the first decade of the twentieth century Jonathan Wilkinson, the father of Sid and Joe, travelled into North Yorkshire and returned soon after with Lill, a fox terrier which I believe he bought from the original Wensleydale Foxhounds, probably after they had disbanded in 1907. These may well have originally come from the Carlisle and District Otterhounds where some of the very best looking and working fox terriers were produced during the nineteenth century, though this can be only educated guesswork, for by now facts are impossible to pin down with regard to such lost matters of history. Whatever the breeding, Lill was game and she was used in order to breed quite a few litters of what Alf Johnston called 'half-breds'. The Wilkinson brothers established their strains based on these bloodlines and Bowman's Lill, given to Sid in 1924 when Joe retired as Huntsman, may well have been descended from this line. Certainly, as Eddie confirmed, Bowman kept terriers out of Lill, which saw service at the Ullswater Hunt.

After Jonathan Wilkinson introduced this bitch into the Ullswater country, the general type of the old working terriers changed and coat and conformation improved dramatically. Working ability suffered not at all, for the fox terrier was still a much-used working dog and any that were used to bring into fell strains were tested as to gameness first, as were their offspring. Non-workers were not tolerated and all of the Lakeland terrier breeders who were responsible for establishing the pedigree type were concerned with working ability first and foremost and only those that proved game were bred from.

Eddie's great-grandfather, Jake Pool, also kept Bedlington type fell terriers and his son, Anthony, carried on his breeding programme, so working terriers are in Eddie's blood, so to speak. He has hunted with the Ullswater for the best part of his life and many of his terriers have served with this pack. He was a great friend of Anthony Barker and hunted regularly with the Ullswater when Barker was Huntsman during the war years. Some of the Egton Lakelands have served with the Ullswater Foxhounds throughout the years and he has been most impressed with such stock, for they were usually smaller and much more narrow in the shoulders than the unregistered type and so were often used in deep borrans in order to reach a fox in a particularly tight spot.

Eddie's old strain of terrier was descended from that of Jake, Anthony and John Pool, with infusions of fox terrier blood from Jonathan Wilkinson's bitch, Lill, and they were game workers. They were used for fox hunting and badger digging and often hunted otters, especially around the shores of Ullswater. Indeed, John Pool was known to take terriers with him if he ferried someone across the lake in his boat, in order to hunt otters while he waited for the party to arrive for the return trip. Otters were also hunted by the terriers whilst he was fishing on the lake. They were far more numerous in those days and the Carlisle Otterhounds often came to the shores of Ullswater in order to hunt otter.

Anthony Pool had terriers from Joe Bowman which were out of Lill, brought from Yorkshire by Jonathan Wilkinson, and old fashioned Bedlington-blooded fell terriers, and this line continued until the 1980s when, sadly, Eddie's old bloodlines died out due to a bitch that wouldn't breed. This line had proved game and it also included infusions of Sid Wilkinson strain Lakelands, through his wonderfully game and good looking dog, Rock. Trim was a son of Rock and he could be traced back to Bowman's stock on one side, and on the other side he was descended from Anthony Barker's famous Rock, Joe Wear's Tear 'Em and Fred Barker's old strain which included the well-known 'Chowt-Faced' Rock. Also, Eddie used Chapman's Crab on one of his bitches after seeing him work a fox out of a bad place at Broad Howe.

Eddie knew Jim Fleming as a close friend and he has fond memories of his most famous terrier, Tear 'Em. Fleming was one of the top breeders in the Lakes and he farmed at Grasmere, providing sound working terriers for the Coniston, Ullswater and Eskdale and Ennerdale packs, though he was also a good friend of Billy Irving's at the Melbreak. Exactly how the Fleming strain was bred remains a mystery, though he was close friends with Joe Wear and loaned several terriers to the Ullswater Huntsman. I believe that the old Ullswater lines, which included the dogs of Fred Barker, Mossop Nelson, the Wilkinson and Pool families, and Joe Bowman (much of Bowman's stock was actually on loan from the above breeders), infused with Melbreak terriers, and possibly stock from other fell packs, made up the strain bred by Fleming, though I cannot be sure of this. One thing is certain, however, and that is that Fleming produced some of the best working stock for several decades and many of the fell pack Huntsmen were keen to have his terriers serving at their hunt. It was even rumoured that Fleming bred Red Ike, though Jim Benson would have had something to say about that, for my research leads me to conclude that Benson did indeed breed this dog and my money would be on Irving's Turk being the sire of Ike. The Melbreak terriers were producing the very best red Lakelands at that time and Ike would have easily fitted into a group of Irving bred terriers during the early 1930s. Eddie says that John Pool was also a good friend of Fleming's and that Dalton lines played quite an important part in the Ullswater breeding programme, so maybe Pool bloodlines and Dalton stock also had an influence on Fleming terrier breeding.

Tear 'Em took to Eddie Pool and often wandered from the kennels, turning up at Eddie's house and spending the day with

Eddie with his terriers. L–R Topsy (Bedlington), Gyp an Irish cross fell from Monty Fairish, Tony a son of Trim, Peggy by Tony and drowned in Ullswater Lake while working an otter. Black Meg and Wasp are at Eddie's side. Wasp is the dam of Meg.

him. He was a large terrier who was utterly fearless and was keen to tackle any fox, no matter how good a spot it had got itself into. If a fox was a lamb worrier, or had being taking geese, or chickens, or a fox had been put in late in the day and Wear didn't want it bolting, then he would use Tear 'Em and Eddie says that he went like a tiger, going straight up to his fox, no matter how big the borran, and seizing and quickly killing it with little fuss and seemingly with little effort. But if Wear wanted a fox bolted, then he would never even think of putting Tear 'Em to ground, for he allowed few, if any, to escape. He was so game that he was used to breed several litters during his time at the Ullswater and Anthony Barker rated him so highly that he brought him into his carefully bred terrier family – a strain that included the gamest of the game. Frank Buck and Cyril Breay also used this dog at stud and Eddie can remember them bringing bitches to Tear 'Em, for his fame had spread throughout the fell country during his career in hunt service.

A fox was run to ground in a very bad place at Birkfell and this was known as a sort of earth from where it was very difficult to bolt a fox, so Joe Wear entered Tear 'Em, knowing full well that most terriers would be severely punished by a fox getting itself into a good, commanding position. Not Tear 'Em, though, for he could kill foxes and come out of the encounter relatively unmarked. He had entered to, and quickly killed, the first fox he ever saw and from then on that had been the pattern of his life as a hunt terrier. He went straight to this Birkfell fox, seized hold of it, pulled it off its rock shelf and swiftly killed it in typical fashion.

At another spot, a fox had found itself a good vantage point and was successfully beating back any terrier sent in to try and shift it. Very good terriers can do little with such a fox in a bad rock earth, and so exceptionally good terriers are required at such places. Tear 'Em had proven exceptional at work and Wear, losing patience, now decided to enter Tear 'Em. He had wanted this fox bolted, thus continuing what had been a good hunt, but Reynard was intent on staying exactly where he was and so Wear now decided that he wanted his quarry finished below ground instead. Once again, Tear 'Em went straight to his fox and finished it swiftly and efficiently, returning to his master soon afterwards and being rewarded for his efforts.

Eddie says that Joe was immaculate in everything. His house and, indeed, himself, were always neat and tidy and he spent hours keeping the kennels spotlessly clean. After a hunt, he would make sure that his hounds and terriers were treated, if they were injured in any way, and he would begin by checking the heads and working right down the bodies, looking at paws and other places which may have picked up injuries, however slight. He did this with every hound and terrier after every hunt, no matter how tired he was, then he would feed and bed down his charges before seeing to himself. He was one of the greatest and most respected of Huntsmen and he was also a very good terrierman. He was always careful about where he put a terrier and there were several places where he refused to enter any of his earth dogs, even if others had worked them before him. Bowman and Wilson, for instance, worked Bleaberry Borran, high on the fells above Patterdale, a place where the Egton terriers were often used because they were so narrow, yet Wear would never put a terrier into this notoriously bad place. Quite a number of earths around Brough were avoided by Wear too, because they were that dangerous to an unwary terrier put in to bolt a fox.

One of the best terriers Eddie has seen at the Ullswater was a black and tan dog named Rock, which served at the hunt when Anthony Barker was in charge during the Second World War. Rock was typey, narrow and leggy and was bred from the Egton Lakeland strain, possibly being a son of Egton Rock and belonging to Joe Wilkinson, who went back to farming when the war started, after whipping-in to Joe Wear ever since Braithwaite Wilson had left the Ullswater and had headed south, leaving the Lake District forever. Barker's Rock was a red fell terrier and he was around in the 1950s, so I am certain the black and tan Rock didn't belong to Anthony, but was on loan. The only black and tan Rock of that time was Wilkinson's dog, which became an ancestor of Sid's famous Rock, though Egton Rock must have been getting on a bit when he sired him. Whatever his breeding, Rock was incredibly game.

A fox was run to ground at Gowbarrow and Anthony entered Rock into what was quite a difficult rock earth. Rock partnered a bitch called Whin at this time and, though she was an ugly terrier, she was an exceptional finder and a good bolter of foxes. However, if a fox wouldn't bolt, then Anthony would enter Rock and the quarry would be finished below ground for sure. Rock went to his fox and swiftly killed it, but the drama didn't end there, for Rock then pulled his dead quarry out of the earth for all to see, which was no mean feat, this being a borran earth right out on the fells. Rock was such a good and useful terrier that he was used to carry on Sid Wilkinson's strain, which has influenced Lakeland terrier breeding to a massive degree even in modern times. Probably ninety per cent of fell terriers and white Lakelands today are descended from the dogs of Sid Wilkinson, through Gary Middleton's well-known and much respected strain.

Another terrier from the Egton Lakeland strain was Mick, given to Eddie by Anthony Barker. Eddie kept this dog more as a family pet, but he was quick to stress that the dog was game and worked rat, otter and fox in the Ullswater country, being a particularly good finder in deep borrans. Eddie says that he could get anywhere and Joe Wear would use him in tight places where more bulky terriers struggled to get. He was also a very typey terrier, which one would expect from a pedigree type. Joe Wilkinson preferred the typey terrier and he used quite a bit of the early pedigree stock in order to breed his strain which had a large influence on Sid's breeding programme too, for the Wilkinson family always bred for both looks and working ability.

Eddie worked with Sid Wilkinson's famous Rock on many occasions and he said that he was the gamest terrier in the Ullswater country, and possibly the whole of the Lake District, at that time. He could kill a fox with seemingly little effort, but he was also a very good finder. Combine this with incredibly good looks and one can see why he had such an influence on future unregistered Lakeland terrier breeding. He was *the* most perfect terrier Gary Middleton has ever seen, though, if he was to criticise, he was just a little too large in the shoulders. Eddie was out with Sid Wilkinson and Anthony Barker at Snake Planting and Trim was busy with his quarry, while the diggers progressed towards him, but, before they could reach the spot, Trim began drawing his badger by the snout. He believes he picked up this trait via Wilk's Rock, for Eddie has seen Rock draw quite a number of foxes from earths after he had killed them. Eddie's Trim was sired by Rock, out of Sammy Davis' bitch, Myrt. Sammy was known for having good working terriers and his bloodlines were of the old Ullswater breeding, for Myrt was sired by Anthony Barker's Jim, who was bred down from the black and tan Rock serving at the Ullswater during the war years. Trim's brother went to Scotland and was so game he was used for killing wildcats. A pup off Eddie's Trim went to Dennis Barrow and became a legend, as this was the best terrier he has ever seen at work with hounds, a dog called Tim, for he could bolt foxes from such 'impossible' places as Bleaberry Borran (this is one of the deepest and most dangerous borrans in the whole of the Lake District), without getting himself into trouble.

Eddie remembers the very first terrier that began the Egton strain of Lakeland kennels and Mrs Spence obtained him from a butcher at Penrith named Kitchen. He cannot remember the name of the dog, but he says that it was very typey indeed. My guess is that this terrier was from Dalton's strain of Lakeland that was winning all over the Lake District at that time (1920s), and this was a strain that had a reputation as incredible workers at all kinds of quarry. Dalton had terriers serving at the Blencathra, obviously as he was the Huntsman, but his stock was also serving at the Cockermouth Otterhounds and possibly the Carlisle and District Otterhounds too, so it had been tested to the full and was both good looking and game. Also, Peter Long, one of the keenest of hunting folk, based his strain of pedigree Lakeland on Dalton's terriers and he wouldn't have touched them with a barge pole if they were no good as workers. In turn, Peter Long's terriers had a huge influence on early pedigree Lakeland stock and all of the top breeders obtained dogs via Long. Truly, Dalton played a major role in the breeding of Lakeland terriers, both registered and unregistered stock, and few fell and Lakeland terriers of today will be free of Dalton strain Lakeland blood.

Eddie knew Maldwyn Williams well and he says that the Ullswater Whips' stock was from Joe Armstrong's very useful strain which included plenty of Irving bred pedigree Lakeland in the lines, for Joe was a regular follower of the Melbreak and a close friend of Billy's. Maldwyn had promised Eddie a terrier from this line, but he was lost in a rock earth at Mardale after a fox had been run to ground by hounds. One of the best terriers to serve at the Ullswater was Punch, a powerful terrier that is seen with Joe Wear in the famous 1953 photograph of Fell Huntsmen at Rydal Hound Show. Punch was bred by John Pool out of his bitch, Peggy, by a red dog of Wear's which was probably a son of Tear 'Em.

Another superb worker that saw quite a bit of service with the Ullswater pack was Eddie's bitch, Wasp. She was useful in that she would not even look at a badger and would pass one by in order to get to and bolt her fox, but in her later years she seems to have had a change of heart. Badgers had been unknown in the Ullswater country until the early 1940s when they began settling in the Glencoyne area, but within a few years they were found throughout the district, despite many of them being dug out and despatched. Eddie was out at exercise one evening with Wasp and walked past a rock hole known to house badger, without any fear of her going to ground, for she ignored them. However, she entered the earth, much to his surprise, and began baying hard at her quarry. Eddie couldn't dig her out, so he went home and waited and later on she returned home. From then on she was not reliable in any earth that housed badger, for she would engage this quarry as readily as she would a fox.

Eddie has walked hounds for the Ullswater for many years and one of his best was Mountain. He was so good that the Coniston used him to bring into their breeding programme and one day Eddie got to see his offspring at work, for the Coniston and Ullswater met up at Kirkstone and joined forces, hunting their fox into Martindale where it went to ground. Jimmy Robinson's terrier bolted the fox and the hunt continued, with Eddie being very impressed by Mountain's youngsters, which played an important part in the proceedings.

Stan Mattinson

The morning after a most enjoyable evening with Eddie in the White Lion at Patterdale, I headed back to Threlkeld in order to have a chat with Stan Mattinson who has much experience with hounds and terriers, for he whipped-in to Johnny Richardson for several seasons and also hunted the Coniston for a number of years, being forced to quit because of bad health and then becoming Joint-Master of the Blencathra for a time. He has bred his own line of working terrier for many years and they have proved most useful when serving with hounds. In fact, one of his best, Bodger, served with Anthony Chapman at the Coniston for a few seasons and the Huntsman could not speak too highly of the dog. Stan grew up at Bassenthwaite and was always keen on hunting. Johnny Richardson had a litter on when Stan was a young lad and one of the pups was a 'recklin', meaning runt of the litter in fell parlance. Johnny let him have the pup and he paid £1 for it, though Richardson didn't want to take any money from the boy. The dam was Harry Corr's Jack Russell, Paddy, and the sire was Richardson's well known and extremely game dog, Tinker, who was sired by the famous Tarzan. Stan then bred from this bitch and a border cross at

Johnny Richardson and Stan Mattinson, Huntsman and whip to Blencathra Foxhounds.

Millbeck, which was in all probability from Joe Armstrong Lakelands, for Joe used border crosses quite a bit, as did Billy Irving when he wished to create sensible badger-digging dogs. And this is where Stan's strain originated.

He remarked that Johnny had some superb working terriers during his long and eventful life and two of his best during the 1980s were Jack and Jill, two Russell types bred out of the old Blencathra lines and the terriers bred by Harry Corr of Ireland. This pair were quite small and were used in particularly deep borrans, where they could find foxes and shift them. Whilst Johnny was preparing to take hounds to Keswick carnival, Jill disappeared. She had a habit of wandering onto the lower reaches of the fell and digging into rabbit holes found all over the foot of the Blencathra mountain. My own terriers have got into these self-same places while out at exercise and they can sometimes get in for quite some distance. On this particular day Jill dug in and couldn't get out, so Johnny phoned Stan and asked him to have a look for the bitch whilst he attended the carnival. Gyp, Stan's terrier, marked a hole and so he dug down, eventually uncovering the little bitch, which had got herself stuck fast in the tight passage of the burrow. Johnny was well pleased when he returned, more especially because Jack and Jill were favourites of his wife, Sally. They lived indoors for most of the time and Sally was reluctant to allow Johnny to take them out hunting, lest they got lost, so he had to come up with all sorts of cunning explanations in an effort to take them out, for they were most useful to the pack. If she had seen the size of some of the borrans this pair worked, then Sally would never have allowed them out of her sight, for sure.

During Stan's time at the Blencathra the old system of walking hounds to a farm, or country inn, or any other place they could stay for that week's hunting, was still in use and the hunt servants, hounds and terriers, would walk for miles to the country to be hunted, and back again, once the week was over. It was a hard life and much more strenuous than it is these days, with vehicles available for transportation, though actually hunting out on the fells where vehicles cannot be used is just as laborious as ever it was. On the Monday hounds were walked from kennels to Bassenthwaite, where they usually stayed at the Sun Inn, and they were to hunt Tuesday, Wednesday and Friday, there being no Saturday meets in

Stan Mattinson with his white Lakelands Punch and Judy.

195

those days. On the Tuesday hounds drew along the front of Skiddaw and soon had a fox afoot, hunting it right through Skiddaw forest and out to Carrock. During proceedings Paddy, the terrier obtained from Ireland, broke from Johnny and went off in pursuit of hounds. Hounds returned later, but without the terrier and Johnny and Stan feared the worst, but the little tyke soon caught them up. Wherever Johnny was, Paddy would find him, no matter how long he had been missing for.

Stan worked with Tinker on several occasions and he states that he was a leggy, strong terrier, that could both find foxes and kill them. He worked some of the worst borrans in the Blencathra country and many times Stan and Johnny dug down to find he had finished his quarry, no matter how good a position it had gained before the terrier was entered. Tinker, like his famous sire, was very clever and sensible and would tangle with his foe until he could get in a fatal grip and finish it off, though he also bolted many foxes, probably more than he killed, for terriers that stand back a little and cleverly tease their quarry until they can get to the throat, will usually bolt reluctant foxes in time. It may take twenty minutes, even longer, but bolt they will, when such a terrier is 'at them'.

Stan bred Bodger of the Coniston Hunt by putting a pure border to one of his Richardson-bred stud dogs. Borders are notorious for starting late, but Stan has seen some good ones at work and Bodger, the border cross, was an incredibly good worker and was one of Chapman's best. Another border, Tip, belonging to Harry Slattery at the White Horse Inn, near Threlkeld, was another late starter, but it served the Blencathra well and Stan can remember the day Tip entered. Hounds had run a fox to ground and Tip was loosed from the couples. The terrier wandered around the earth for a time and Johnny rashly concluded that it was no good, probably because he was so used to Lakeland temperament, that made most enter very quickly indeed, but suddenly it entered the earth, quickly found its quarry and succeeded in bolting it – not bad for its first time to ground!

Stan had a border from the North Tyne Foxhounds, which was bred by Ted Thorburn. In those days they had two or three border terriers running with hounds and these were most useful, though they had never before worked such bad places as borrans, or other types of earth to be found in the Lakes country. Stan spent a day at the North Tyne Hunt and hounds finally ran a fox to ground in a drain (known as a 'cundy') after a good, long hunt. Stan and Ted were soon at the spot and they waited for the terriers to arrive, for they often got left behind by hounds, though not for long and they would find them no matter where they were. Up they came and, instead of rushing to the earth and jealously trying to be first to the fox, the terriers stood by Ted's horse and waited for their master to give instructions. One was allowed to go and it shot into the earth, bayed at its fox and bolted it, which was later caught by the determined pack. Terriers are notoriously difficult to control, especially if work is on the agenda, but Ted Thorburn obviously had a special knack of controlling his working border terriers.

Sam was from Ted and he served at the Coniston when Stan was Huntsman, though this dog was roughly one quarter Lakeland bred. Hounds ran a fox into a large earth and it was suspected that a badger may also have been present, but Ted had told him that Sam would ignore 'Brock' and pass him by in order to get to a fox, so Sam was indeed entered into the earth. There had been no sound coming from the den for a long time and suddenly Sam appeared, whipped round and went in again. He must have been chasing his quarry all around that place and had thought it had bolted, but a decided lack of scent around that exit hole told another story and Sam was after it once more, finally pinning it down and barking strongly at the same spot. Reynard wasn't for bolting and so digging commenced. After quite some time the terrier was at last uncovered and the fox now bolted.

Stan was called out on a lambing call in the Langdales and hounds soon took up the drag around the lambing fields where Keith Rowan had lost several of his young stock to a marauding fox. Hounds followed scent up onto the fells, where at last they had their quarry on the run. It gave them a good hunt, but eventually went to ground at Yak Howe borran high on the fellside. This is a huge place and is a real testing ground for any working terrier. Stan had Sam and Misty with him that morning and Misty was put in. She quickly found her fox, but couldn't pin it down and Reynard gave her the run around throughout that vast place for quite some time. Finally, though, she settled at a spot about 100 yards from where she had been entered. Stan now put Sam in too and he went straight to her and the pair killed their quarry in no time at all, though they became trapped in the process.

They were very deep and a hard dig was on the cards, but, as is the case when any terrier is stuck to ground, there were plenty of willing helpers and it took a week of hard graft, toil and buckets of

Johnny Richardson's Jack and Jill, superb finders in deep borrans.

sweat to finally reach the pair of exhausted and bedraggled terriers. They had eaten half their fox and so had kept themselves in good shape, but they were incredibly thirsty. The diggers had shifted tons of rock and had used the clever system of holding larger rocks up using strong timbers placed strategically throughout the borran. The hardworking miners and quarrymen of Cumberland have brought extremely useful skills to fell-hunting, which continue to be used whenever a terrier is trapped to ground in that country.

The Blencathra had a shepherds' meet at the Sun Inn, Bassenthwaite, and hounds quickly had a fox up and running, hunting it to Nutt Ghyll, which is rather a peaty area. Peat can take a toll on terriers and the Blencathra country has more than its fair share of peat earths. A terrier was put in and got stuck into its fox, finally bolting it after quite a struggle underground. The fox was 'clagged up', as Stan put it, with peat and mire and hounds coursed it until it disappeared from view. However, as soon as it came to hunting using their noses, the pack lost their quarry immediately, the peat disguising the scent very effectively. Stan likes to use a leggy terrier in peat, so that it can keep its body as much above the water, or mire, which can be ice-cold in temperature, as possible.

One of the best of Richardson's terriers was Titch, bred from the Tarzan line and, despite its name, one that was a little too large for some of the Blencathra earths, though Johnny used Titch regularly with hounds and he could kill a fox quickly with his massive head. Titch was also very typey and was used by Sid Wilkinson to bring into his own strain of working Lakeland terrier, which was continued by Gary Middleton. As with Jack and Jill, Johnny's wife, Sally loved Titch and the Blencathra Huntsman had to be very careful as to where he would put this dog. Life wouldn't have been worth living if he had lost her beloved 'pet'!

Stan doesn't show his terriers, though he has seen some very good show terriers at work and has been most impressed. He knew Arthur Irving well and stated that he had some very good workers among his pedigree Lakeland stock. He knew Harry Hardisty well too and was most impressed when he saw his famous Turk at work one day when he and Johnny were having a 'busman's holiday', spending their day off with the Melbreak hounds. Hounds were hunting Low Fell and they had run a fox to ground at Red Howe, into a soil-covered borran. Harry put Turk into the earth and they waited for what seemed like a lifetime, without sight or sound of terrier, or quarry, for this place was vast indeed. At last, faint baying could be heard, but the fox was not for bolting and so digging operations commenced. The soil covering the borran was easily removed, but they soon hit large slabs of solid rock and now made little progress, deciding to stand back instead, hoping the fox would bolt. Turk had been to ground and at his quarry for quite some time and he continued to bay at his foe until, finally, Reynard decided to make a bid for open ground. The fox bolted at speed, with Turk right on its brush, and the hunt continued, with Reynard eventually being accounted for. Johnny complimented Harry on having such a good terrier, stating that he was also very good looking, and Stan can remember Hardisty's pride as he informed the Blencathra hunt servants that this was his dog, Turk.

Stan enters a terrier at about eighteen months of age, waiting until he feels they are fully mature, both mentally and physically, before allowing them to face large quarry. He much prefers a rough coat and a leggy terrier, though one that isn't too big. A narrow front is essential for negotiating rock earths in particular and sense is rated highly by the ex-Huntsman. Terriers have to deal with foxes in often-horrendous conditions and one with common sense is vital in the fell country.

Anthony Chapman with Nettle and Myrt, and Rock to the right behind.

Anthony Chapman

Anthony Chapman was the long-serving Huntsman of the Coniston Foxhounds and grandfather to the current Huntsman, Mike Nicholson. 'Chappie', as he was affectionately known, was a great houndsman, but he also played quite an important part in the development of the fell strains, as several of his terriers are found in the pedigrees of modern Lakelands. The very best black and tans came from the Coniston country and these, I believe, were procured from Major Roche of the Ynysfor Hunt during annual tours to the Lake District, for many of the Coniston earth dogs resembled early, unspoilt Welsh terriers. Keith Clement's terriers served at the Coniston and these were top quality black and tans that were both typey and superb at work.

Chapman worked Stan Mattinson's Bodger and he proved a wonderful worker, though he tragically suffocated whilst at work at Skelghyll. Anthony whipped-in to the well known Huntsman and ex-Blencathra Whip, Ernie Parker, who took over from George Chapman when he was forced to retire due to an injury, and Ernie kept and bred some wonderfully game terriers which may well have been from the old Dalton lines. One of his best was Turk, a black terrier which may have been one of the ancestors of the Buck/Breay strain, for Billy Irving believed that the black strain bred by this pair originated partly with Coniston terriers, for several black earth dogs were found around Grasmere and Windermere in those days. George Chapman bred quite a few black terriers during his time at the Coniston and no doubt the strains found in such places were descended from his dogs. Turk was a superb worker and he was put into a borran, along with three other terriers. When four terriers are put to ground, one can be certain that the earth must have been vast and a few would be entered in an attempt to either pin down the quarry, or put enough pressure on it so that it would bolt. Otherwise a fox would give one or two the run around possibly for hours.

After several days to ground, Turk was the only one to emerge and the others were lost without trace. This was in 1935 and the borran was one still worked today, found in the Kentmere valley. A Coniston hunt terrier was mated to Irving's famous Gypsy of Melbreak and this produced Darkie, the dam of Scamp, a Melbreak hunt terrier that was used to breed quality working pedigree stock when mated to Mick of Millar Place. The Coniston hunt terrier was undoubtedly Parker's Turk, for he was probably the best terrier at that hunt during the 1930s and he could finish any fox that refused to bolt.

George Chapman also bred some superb workers and Squib, an ancestor of most pedigree Lakelands, served at the Coniston during his time as Huntman. Another superb worker was Crest. Hounds ran a fox into the notoriously bad earths at Petts Quarries, high on the fells at Kirkstone, and Crest was put in. The terrier killed its fox and became trapped, not emerging for at least a week and managing to get out only after eating part of the fox that was blocking its exit.

Anthony Chapman's Crab was not only a wonderfully game dog, but he was also a looker and he won Rydal before his demise. Anthony had put him to ground on a fox that was proving difficult to account for and whilst he was tackling his foe there was a rush in of soil and stone, which badly injured the dog. He lasted a little while after they got him out, but later died at Anthony's home. It was a very sad ending to a dog that had become a legend in his own lifetime. Gary Middleton was a young lad when Crab was on the scene and he can remember seeing this dog at work whenever he followed the Coniston. Gary was out when hounds hunted a fox all around Bowness and Windermere for quite some time, until it finally made for a drain near Windermere golf course and at last went to ground. It was now late in the day and hounds had enjoyed a long and difficult hunt. Hunting in the fells is about fox control and hounds must account for foxes, or they would lose the support of farmers. And so Anthony decided he did not want the fox bolting, with darkness soon coming on, and he entered Crab into the drain, who quickly killed his fox. Middleton had much respect for 'Chappie', for he often had typey earth dogs that could win well in the showring, but which were excellent at work too.

The late Anthony Chapman was one of the best Huntsmen the Lakes has produced and he is still very much respected. His autobiography (listed in the Bibliography) is a fascinating read and one soon comes to realise that he was an expert with both hounds and terriers, though the methods of Lake District terrierwork do not suit many. Most prefer to have one dog to ground at any one time and the law in England and Wales dictates that this should be so, but fell-hunters often had up to three or four to ground at any one time, though only in the larger borran earths were it is difficult for a lone dog to pin down its quarry.

Chapman was called out on a lambing call and he began drawing the pastures at dawn. Hounds took up a drag and away they went, unkennelling their quarry and then enjoying a long, hard hunt. They pressed their fox so hard that it eventually went to ground at Brock Crag, in a large borran. Tess was entered and quickly found and bolted her quarry, but hounds forced it to ground once more. Jet and Rags were then put in and they worried a large dog fox that had been hunted for five hours. This fox had taken several lambs, but his crimes were now ended most effectively.

Jess was one of the best serving at the Coniston and she was a particularly good finder, though she was owned and bred by Keith Clement, whose stuff was a mixture of Breay/Buck, Joss Akerigg, Arthur Irving and Ynysfor Hunt terrier stock. Clement supplied the Coniston with some excellent workers over the years, during 'Chappie's' reign as Huntsman.

Hounds hunted a fox from Wansfell to Kirkstone and down into Troutbeck Park, going to ground at Park Quarry. Jess was put in and the little bitch successfully bolted her fox, which then returned to Kirkstone and went to ground again at Petts Quarries. Jess was put in again, for she was a reliable bitch that could both find and bolt foxes, even those that had been pressed hard by hounds. Tragically, Jess was never heard or seen again. Many a terrier has come to grief in the stone and shale piles of Petts Quarries.

Edmund Porter

I met Edmund Porter while staying at Eskdale, after I decided to call in on the off-chance of getting to interview him. I found him to be most welcoming and hospitable and we sat outside, in the kennel gardens, during a warm sunny evening and then again the very next morning, with the sun rising over the fells, chatting over hounds, terriers and all things hunting. He pointed out many good spots, as well as bad borran earths, which are in view of his home and I was fascinated as he told me tales of hunting in the Eskdale and Ennerdale country. And one could find nobody better to talk with about hunting in this part of the fell country, for Edmund has been the Huntsman of this pack since the early 1960s, when he took over from Arthur Irving. He is also the Master and owns the pack, lock, stock and barrel, inheriting it from his father, Jack Porter.

One of his best terriers was Turk, a chocolate and tan dog that was a grandson of Hardisty's famous dog. Sid Hardisty actually bred Harry Hardisty's Turk and this dog would probably have gone to the Eskdale and Ennerdale pack, had they not had ample terriers at that time. Instead, Turk went to the Melbreak and there founded

Edmund Porter with one of his best workers, Turk, from Nuttall's Shamrock and Gary Hayes'Jack.

a dynasty of good looking and working stock. It was Sid Hardisty who bred Rags, by Harry's Turk, and this dog mated Edmund's bitch, Meg. From this union came Porter's well known Turk and he was both a looker, winning well even at prestigious shows such as Rydal, despite the fact that Breay's Skiffle, Wilkinson's Rock and Hardisty's Turk were doing the rounds at that time, but he was also a superb worker who could finish any fox that refused to bolt. Edmund's current black and tans, Nip and Ben, can be traced back to Turk, though they are also of the old Eskdale and Ennerdale lines which go back a century and more, all the way to Tommy Dobson's strain of fell terrier. This strain also includes the dogs of Arthur and Willie Irving in its bloodlines, for Willie spent quite a few years, in fact, his childhood and early adulthood, hunting with and whipping-in to the Eskdale and Ennerdale pack and he bred terriers that were used by Willie Porter.

Edmund Porter with Nip, descended from his Turk and old E&E bloodlines.

Turk died after a hunt in the Langdales when he was about seven years of age. He was with hounds for much of the time, checking over the many borrans to be found in this area, and he suddenly fell ill that night. It was too late by then and Edmund believes he was bitten by an adder whilst working among the rocks, for adders will sun themselves at such places. Edmund freely admits that this was a tragic loss, for Turk was the best terrier he ever owned.

Eddie has used Russells from the David Jones strain and they have proved useful indeed, though he now no longer has such terriers at the kennels. His current stock are fell, or Lakeland, terriers, some of the old bloodlines, while others are Nuttall bred. Turk and Tim are two Nuttall-bred terriers, out of Brian's Shamrock, and they are superb at their vocation. Turk is a good finder and bolter of foxes and is particularly good in rock, while Tim is much harder and not quite as useful as his brother. Edmund likes a narrow, leggy terrier and one that can bolt a stubborn fox, and be capable of killing it should it not move. He is of the old

Edmund Porter with Rags (front) and Turk just behind him.

school and believes a fell pack should account for as many foxes as possible during a season and he cannot accept that foxes should be left to ground if they will not bolt. They should be finished below by a game terrier when, and where, possible.

During the 1960s Edmund took part in a dig with Gary Middleton and several of his digging friends when they travelled over to the Egremont area in order to dig a badger sett in a wood there. This was on a steep bank and Edmund can remember the dig being incredibly difficult indeed and the diggers toiled all day long, but eventually accounted for their badger. They all enjoyed refreshments at the Burnmoor Inn afterwards.

Gary Hayes

Gary has hunted with the Eskdale and Ennerdale Hunt for most of his life and he keeps really game terriers of the old type – hard enough to kill a fox, yet sensible enough to avoid more serious injury. His first terrier was Tarn, a white Lakeland bred at Broad Oak by Billy Crow, and sired by Porter's Toby. His second was

Nettle at twelve years of age: a superb bitch.

Nettle, by Barry Todhunter's stud dog out of Roger Westmoreland's bitch. Nettle became the best bitch Gary has ever worked and she started at fourteen months of age, going on to be one of those terriers that had a knack of killing foxes almost casually. During a hot September meet one old hound whimpered at an eight-holed rabbit burrow, with just two holes barely big enough to allow a terrier access. Edmund tried his dog, Rock, but he couldn't quite get, so Nettle, being a shade smaller, was tried and she quickly disappeared. She found her fox and bolted it, but didn't emerge. Gary was forced to dig and then put his young bitch, Myrt, in, which then drew out a dead fox. But still Nettle did not appear, for she had killed her fox and moved on. Gary dug on and soon uncovered a second dead fox, again, with no sign of his bitch. And so he began digging once more, finally uncovering a third dead fox and Nettle alongside it.

Hounds holed a fox at a big, rough spot and Nettle was put in. She found her foe in a stop-end and tackled it hard, while Gary dug down as best he could, though borrans are very difficult places to dig. This proved to be a big dog fox and Nettle had her nose split

Left to right Sam, Jack, Nettle and Jake.

right down it by the fox. Jake was put in to assist her and he promptly killed his quarry. Jake was bred out of Nettle and Roger Westmoreland's working border terrier and he proved incredibly game and very useful on late afternoon foxes that went to ground and needed to be accounted for, or those that had been killing lambs during the early spring months. Jake's sister was more of a border in type and she was very sensible, being a useful fox-bolting terrier. Hounds ran a fox into a large borran in the Langdales and Jake's sister, together with one of Edmund's bitches, was entered. It was a very windy day and no sound could be heard, but a fox bolted soon after, quickly turning and re-entering the earth. That fox, together with the two terriers, were sadly never seen again.

Ben was one of the first terriers Gary had and he was sired by a John Cowen dog. He is now with Gary's father, but he has done some good work with hounds and was a superb finder, though he wasn't a hard dog. He mated Nettle and this produced Jack and Myrtle. And Jack became the sire of Porter's Turk and Tim, when he mated Nuttall's Shamrock. Gary has used Roger Westmoreland's

Mick twice to bring into his own strain and he kept a chocolate dog, Sam, from one of these unions. Sam is a narrow dog and is most useful in tight places.

Gary is very patient when it comes to entering his terriers and he will gladly wait until they are two or even two and a half years of age before allowing them to see a fox, for, as he said, there is no rush. He wishes his stock to be fully mature and always has adult earth dogs that can be used anyway, so he doesn't mind waiting for a youngster to develop properly before putting it to fox. Jake, for instance, was three years of age when he entered and he proved mute, preferring to latch onto his very first fox and kill it quickly, rather than stand back and bay. Hounds marked a borran and Jake and Myrt were put in. Jake latched onto his foe, but Myrt fell into a crack in the rocks and a slab fell over her and trapped her. Jake, typically, quickly killed his fox below, but a two-day dig was on the cards in order to reach the bitch. Pit props were used in order to support the rocks, preventing them from falling in and crushing the rescuers, or the terrier, and Myrt was successfully rescued late the next day. Although mining ended in this part of the world some years ago, knowledge of how to use these props has been passed

Gary and his terriers checking an earth. (Jake going to ground).

down and this has come in most handy whenever a terrier is trapped to ground, particularly in a borran earth.

Many borrans have been walled up during past generations, simply because they were deathtraps to Lakeland terriers and sure lifesavers for foxes, even lamb killers. However, over the years stones can shift and entrances can be opened up due to wind and rain, or other means, and this presents a danger if terriers get in among the rocks. When hunting Muncaster Fell one day, hounds ran a fox into a previously walled-up borran and one of Edmund's terriers, together with another belonging to a lad from Broughton, got in before they could be stopped and the pair became trapped, unsurprisingly. Digging operations commmenced, as a terrier

Gary's bitch, Myrt, rescued after two days to ground.

Gary Hayes' Jack, sire
of Edmund's Turk.

could be heard baying, and one was rescued the next day after the
diggers had got around eight feet into the fortress, shifting tons of
rocks. However, this was a granite earth and proceedings could go
no further. The terrier was well and truly trapped and so, with
heavy hearts, the diggers made a very difficult decision and walled
the place up again. Hunting in the fells can be a harsh business
and the hostile landscape means that many hunts have ended in
tragedy with regard to terriers in particular, though hounds do not
have it easy either and they can fall from crags, or become cragfast
for days on end until rescued. Worse still, hounds can sometimes
squeeze themselves in among the rocks where a fox has gone to
ground and, if they are not found, are there forever, as they cannot
get out by themselves in such circumstances. There are many
'horror' stories concerning hunting in the fell country.

Turk was once trapped in a Langdale borran. They were on a
Friday hunt and hounds had holed their fox by late afternoon. Turk
was put in and he soon engaged his foe, his strong, steady bay
easily audible. Edmund moved on after some time, drawing for
another, as this fox was not for moving. By nightfall, Turk was still

211

to ground and it became obvious that he was now in trouble and couldn't get out. Gary was working that day, but Edmund telephoned that evening and asked for his help. That Saturday morning Edmund, Gary and a couple of other diggers began making inroads into this borran and, thankfully, Turk wasn't too deep. However, this was a wet borran, one with water running through it, so the going was difficult to say the least. Gary crawled into the mass of piled up rocks and listened and he could hear Turk somewhere nearby. He looked up and could see a seam of broken rock, so he began poking about here and suddenly a few stones fell in, with Turk there, just beyond. He had killed his fox and the carcass was probably preventing him from emerging, or maybe a few smaller rocks had fallen into the passage and had hindered his progress.

The Eskdale and Ennerdale pack had hunted a fox all over the Ennerdale area before it finally made to ground at a two-holed dug out rabbit burrow. Gary put his bitch, Myrt, in and she was quickly onto her fox, but it wasn't for bolting and so a dig was on the cards. This was easy going, however, and was light-relief when compared to the borrans and crag earths of the high country. By the time he reached the combatants, Myrt had worried her fox at the stop end.

Gary has accounted for a number of mink with his terriers during the summer off-season and he also enjoys hunting rats along the various waterways within easy reach of his home. He especially encourages his youngsters in such activities, for it teaches them to use their noses and this helps them to find when they enter to fox. He likes his terriers to be of different sizes, in order that at least one will suit whatever earth a fox chooses. Some are narrow and leggy, while others are quite small and stocky, though are all entered to fox and all work well. Most will kill a fox if it will not bolt, though finding and actually being able to get up to a fox are the main essentials in any terrier required to work the harsh Lake District landscape. His bitch, Bramble, is proving an exceptionally good finder and this seems to be the priority among fell-hunting terriermen. He prefers a dense jacket, whether rough or smooth, as some of the earths are wet and peat hags are particularly bad places for chilling a terrier, so good coat is essential.

Paul Stead

My next port of call was to see Paul Stead of the Pennine Foxhounds and he began keeping working terriers after growing up with them, for his father hunted with the above pack and sometimes worked his terriers with them too. Stead senior kept Nixon-bred Jack Russells in the main, though he also worked border terriers which he obtained from Ron Hillcoat, who also worked his borders with the Pennine pack, with Dodger and Donna being two of his best which served at the hunt. Dodger was very well known and he was used extensively to continue the Todgrove strain of border, which Ron became famous for.

During his later teens, at around seventeen years old, Paul wished to have his own working terrier and his dad had a border for sale at £40. However, Paul was only earning £28 a week at the time and so the dog was beyond him. Ron Hillcoat purchased this border and it was soon after this that Paul met up with Barry Wild one day when he was out exercising one of his black terriers. Paul's dad had a chat with Barry when he called round to the house and discovered he had a litter of pups on at the time, so Paul bought a black pup which he named Ross. He was quite a typey dog and proved to be a very good finder, though he was not a hard dog. Most of Barry's stock are hard fox killing types, but Ross proved an exception to this rule. He entered to fox at the age of twelve months, entering a drain by a cobbled road on the moors above Rochdale. This drain is over one hundred yards in length and Paul's dad's terrier marked it, telling them Reynard was at home. Ross went in, scrambled up the drain, found his fox, bayed keenly at it and succeeded in bolting it. He had never seen a live fox before this time, though he had ragged a carcass or two after hounds had secured a catch.

Paul went into amatuer hunt service at twenty years of age, whipping-in to Chris Wood at the Pennine and using Ross whenever opportunity arose, though he wished to find a professional position and placed an ad in *Horse & Hound*. He obtained a couple of interviews, one at the Grafton as Kennelman and one at the Pendle and Craven as Whip. He was successful at the Pendle and Craven and became their Whipper-in for a couple of seasons, having to learn to ride before taking up his post at the hunt. However, he was very keen on terrierwork and was getting very little, except for some freelancing with a local keeper. He missed his days spent with the Pennine and the strict discipline at the hunt didn't really suit him, so he eventually resigned and returned home to the Pennine hills. He, of course, began hunting again with the Pennine pack and became amatuer whip once more and began using his terriers with this hunt.

He generally keeps upwards of six terriers and feels this is necessary in a country made up of many rock earths that would equal some of the borrans of the fell country of Cumbria and North Yorkshire. Terriers must work a fox hard in order to bolt it from a large rock spot after it has been run in by hounds, or it will stay put and refuse to budge. Bites are inevitable in such circumstances and Paul may have four or five being treated at any one time, so a few are needed. Terrier work can still be carried out in much of the Pennine country, as it is keepered and the law allows one terrier to ground where gamebirds and wild birds are reared and preserved for shooting. This law applies in England and Wales only, though foxes must be shot, and not taken with dogs, even in Scotland where terrierwork can still be carried out in the more traditional way.

Paul loves working his terriers with hounds, though he stresses that private digs are also necessary. Why? He stated that hunt

Paul Stead's Tigger, no looker, but a cracking worker.

servants relied on hounds marking and terriers were then used (before the Hunting Act came into force in 2005 in England and Wales) in order to bolt the fox. And so terriers do not get the chance to mark. When out with just the terriers, however, they must use their noses in order to mark and Paul feels that this is a necessary quality in his earth dogs.

Now enjoying hunting with the Pennine again and having given Ross to a keen young follower of the Pennine some time ago, Paul needed a terrier and answered an ad in the *Countryman's Weekly* from a chap in Leeds. He had bred a litter from Parks and Gould bloodlines and Stead bought a black and tan bitch named Gem when she was just eight weeks of age. Once she had matured, she was put to her first fox after hounds had run it to ground in among some rocks on the moors near Chorley. Reynard wasn't for bolting and a one and a half hour dig ensued, with Gem remaining with her quarry throughout, which wasn't at all bad for a first stint at large quarry. She then went on to do plenty of work for the hunt and was sometimes employed for two or three days in the same week, becoming an extremely game and useful bitch. Paul has taken her everywhere with the hunt, using her in Wales, Scotland, Ireland, Devon and anywhere else to where hounds travelled.

Hounds hunted a fox for what seemed like an age and eventually ran it into a huge rockpile at Glossop, close to the Snake Pass at a locality known as Shire Hill. Gem was put in and the fox wasn't for bolting. Paul took a nine-foot reading on the locator and an incredibly difficult dig then began. He needed help from some of the followers and they made progress until they came to a crack in the rock, with the bitch still further on. Gem stuck with her fox and another two and a half hours of digging saw them at last reach her, along with her quarry. The followers were impressed and quite a few ordered a pup when she was mated. The dig had lasted for at least four hours in a most difficult and awkward spot, yet she hadn't flinched, nor given ground.

Paul then bought two black pups from Manchester, from the Paul Blackledge strain, which was descended from McCoy, which in turn was descended from the dogs belonging to Dave Roberts. These he named Bracken and Barney. Bracken was going to ground at just eight months of age and had to be held back, with Paul allowing her to go at around eleven months, for she was a very mature bitch by this time and was literally begging for work. Barney, on the other hand, was eighteen months of age before he became interested in work and finally entered. This teaches all working terrier enthusiasts to be patient and give a dog time, for Barney became a very good fox killing dog, though he had no sense and proved too hard to survive for long. Paul was exercising Barney on the moors near Rochdale when he shot to ground in a drain and promptly killed a fox. Sadly, a badger was also lurking in the drain and Barney turned his attention to 'Brock'. Paul was forced to dig his dog out and quickly got him away from his quarry, rushing him home for treatment, but he later died of his predictable injuries. A badger lurking in a fox earth can be a real danger to any terrier that prefers to close with and kill its foe.

Bracken became a very good bitch, though she grew harder and harder and less sensible as she got older, which can be typical of Lakeland terriers. She entered a rockpile near Hebden Bridge after hounds had marked the spot and was quickly up with her fox. Reynard refused to shift and so digging operations began, but the bitch and her foe dislodged some rocks in the process and she was quite badly injured when the diggers finally extracted her, together with a large vixen. He was forced to rest her for six months and allow the injuries to heal properly. Bracken was glad to be back at work after a long absence and went into yet another rockpile where hounds had run a fox in. However, her wounds opened up again during the proceedings and so Paul decided to give her away. She ended up back with Darren Cashmore, who had originally bred Bracken and Barney, and was used as a brood bitch, with Paul getting a pup back from her, which he has also named Bracken.

His present Bracken is a trifle large in the chest for his liking, but she is good in rock and has a very good nose, being quite sensible too. She is also black and he has a preference for such colouring, though he also likes other colours and has had all kinds. He also likes a good working border terrier too. He had a brindle bitch once, a terrier named Tigger, which he obtained from Derek Webster. She was undershot, cock-eared, bent-legged, had no jacket to speak of and was considerably of poor type, yet she was a superb fox bolting earth dog who did a huge amount of work at the Pennine Hunt, easily shifting two hundred plus foxes for that pack. And, what is more, he could call her out of a bad place that couldn't be dug. She was no fox killer, but she could usually shift a reluctant 'skulker' attempting to keep out of reach of hounds. In fact, she worked that close to her fox that she hardly had any teeth left in her head when she died. A professional terrierman visiting the Pennine for a day's hunting, saw Tigger at work and offered Paul £600 for her, which he refused.

The pack ran a fox into a drain at Hebden Bridge and the frozen snow was by this time slowly melting and running into the lair. Tigger was entered and soon settled on her foe, baying steadily and continuously while the digging commenced. Paul finally reached her after some time and the lack of jacket had taken its toll, for the bitch was suffering from hyperthermia and had to be rushed to the nearest farm. The farmer, however, was used to dealing with frozen lambs during the early months of spring and so he placed her in front of the fire and turned a hairdryer on her. He soon sorted her out, but a good jacket would have avoided the problem in the first place. On another occasion, yet another fox was run to ground at Dovestones at Saddleworth, above the lake. Tigger entered at 12pm on that Saturday and she settled, baying strongly. By 4pm darkness was well and truly setting in and so Paul was forced to

Paul's Tess and Meg with their prize.

block the earth and return the next morning, as the bitch had obviously become trapped. The weather was very bad, with freezing conditions even during the daytime. The dig lasted all the next day and Tigger was finally reached at 7pm, with torchlight being used after dark. Sadly, the poor jacket had taken its toll yet again, but this time his bitch had died from the freezing conditions. It was a tragic loss, for Paul, as well as the Pennine pack, had come to rely on her greatly.

Paul likes variety in his terriers, with some being larger, and others smaller, though he does not keep any above fourteen inches and around eighteen pounds in weight. He prefers a good strong head, though he has had some with small heads that have been useful. He only breeds when he requires youngsters to keep his stock going. He doesn't particularly breed a specific strain, but will breed from any terrier that proves itself useful at work. His young entry will be allowed to rag a carcass or two, before being allowed to enter at around one year of age and he doesn't use the hole-end method of entering, but prefers to allow his entry to find by itself and thus begin work more naturally and without fuss. He believes a fox that has been harrassed is not really suitable for a young terrier and can strike viciously, quickly ruining an impressionable novice.

Gem was entered into a drain that was rather wet, a type of earth that is quite typical in the north, but it took him four hours just to find where she was. He swept the box all over the place before at last getting a signal. She was only eighteen inches deep, under a large slab, and had hold of her fox by the throat. He found her just in time, though, for the water was up to her eyelids and had she been in any longer she would surely have drowned, for the combatants must have been blocking off the water's exit. It is surely a hard life, that of a working terrier.

Paul believes that one should not bother about what others think of your terriers, as long as they fulfil what you require of them. He cites Tigger as a case in point. She would not have suited many terriermen and there are those who condemn earth dogs that can be called out of a den in the middle of a contest with Reynard, but such a terrier is invaluable in the north, where many earths are undiggable, or require such large numbers of diggers and such effort and expense that it just isn't practical. Frank Buck's Tex was another that could be called out of an earth if need be and only a fool would question the abilities of this dog, for he could find anywhere, shift reluctant foxes where others had failed and kill one that wouldn't move.

Paul's terriers are certainly game and fully tested, for the Pennine country is a very difficult and dangerous place for earth dogs. Tigger, before her demise, was in for a bit of stick, but the ridiculers had not counted on her cunning and common sense. A fox had gone into a rockpile on the hills above Sheffield and Tigger was put in. She soon found, despite the jumble of often-large rocks, and began baying, though she soon emerged. Turning round, she went back to her quarry and did the same thing again, with this occurring a few times, much to the dismay of one or two followers who were saying she was no good at her work. But Paul knew that she simply couldn't quite reach her foe and was seeking another route to it. She eventually climbed out a little and then dropped back into the rocks, now finding a way through and quickly bolting her quarry, which then gave hounds a rattling hunt of one and a half hours. There was now silence among the followers!

Paul makes certain that he practices good kennel management, feeding fresh meat every day, cleaning their living quarters and changing the bedding regularly. In winter, especially during cold spells, or after a hunt, he puts warm gravy on their food as a protection from the cold. When wounded, he treats quickly and regularly and they soon heal.

There is a drain in a field close to his back garden and one day, when Derek Webster was over with his lurcher, Rocky, a real grand fox dog, Reynard was found to be at home, so Paul entered his bitch, Tess. She was in there for an age and so Paul popped into the kitchen and made them both a cup of tea, while they waited. But, just as he was climbing over the fence with the hot cups of tea in his hands, he saw Rocky running all over the place and realised the fox had at last bolted. Rocky nailed his quarry before Paul had reached the spot.

John Cowen

I talked with John at the Cockermouth show and he continues to breed a strain of Lakeland that is descended from Harry Hardisty's famous Turk; a terrier John saw at work on many occasions, for he was terrierman to the Melbreak for several seasons, almost two decades in fact. He hunted regularly with Hardisty and is of the opinion that he was the best terrierman he ever saw in the field, though his greatest influence and inspiration was Willie Irving. John admired Irving's ability to breed top winning dogs that could bolt, or kill, foxes in some of the deepest borrans in the Lakes. In fact, Cowen bought dogs from Irving, though he purchased the crossbreds, as he couldn't afford the pedigree stock.

His very first terrier, Scamp, was purchased from Irving and he was one of the fell types which were a mix of Irving pedigree Lakeland and working pedigree border terrier, that was obtained via the Mitchell family who bred borders which served at the Melbreak even before Billy's arrival in 1926. His crossbreds were for bolting foxes and digging badgers, for his Lakelands usually killed

John and Jessie Cowen exhibiting at Cockermouth Show.

Reynard below and to put them at badger was to court disaster, though some of the bitches could be rather more gentle and were better suited to fox bolting and badger digging. Sadly, Scamp was killed on the road near the Cowen farmstead.

John remembers Mick of Millar Place being at the Melbreak during Irving's last few seasons as Huntsman and he says he was murderous at fox, quickly latching onto and killing any that didn't get out of his way, though he suffered very badly, John says, whenever he came across 'Brock' skulking in a rockpile, which sometimes happened, even during Irving's early days at the hunt when some of the other fell packs rarely, if ever, encountered badger. Mick, and his sister, Trim, had a massive impact on both registered and unregistered Lakeland terriers and there are stock

John Cowen and Colin Armstrong at Cockermouth Show.

Harry Hardisty's famous 'Turk', ancestor of most modern working Lakeland terriers.

around today that are of their getting. In fact, some of Cowen's stock, even today, are near replicas of Mick, though without the sharper lines of the pedigree dog, and I am certain this strain will go back to this dog. In fact, I believe Hardisty's Turk could be traced back to Mick, through the dogs of Sid Hardisty.

Although there has been some mystery surrounding the breeding of Turk, John can remember exactly how he is bred. He was out of a black and tan bitch owned by Harry's brother, Sid, a bitch I believe could be traced back to Irving's strain of pedigree Lakeland, for Sid certainly produced typey stock with more than a hint of pedigree blood about it, and was sired by 'Doggy' Robinson's Mike, a terrier possibly descended from Irving's cross-bred strain, for Turk certainly showed a certain trace of border in his make-up and 'Doggy' Robinson, of the West Cumberland Otterhounds, was a pal of Irving's. However he was bred, he was certainly partly from pedigree Lakeland terrier bloodlines, for he was a typey dog who won well at shows, having the box-shape of a Lakeland and a borderish head. He was also a superb worker, though he was no fox killer. John says that Turk was loaned to Harry after he had killed some of Sid's hens, otherwise he would probably have worked at the Eskdale and Ennerdale with whom Sid hunted.

One of the most memorable outings with Turk was when hounds ran a fox to ground at Red Howe, in woodland. Turk was put in, but Reynard was not for bolting and so digging operations commenced. It was quite a hard dig and Turk remained with his quarry until finally reached. When he was uncovered, it was discovered that he was, in fact, not at the fox, but was instead in the middle of four badgers which he was attempting to bottle up into a stop end. Although he struggled to boss his opponents, which is quite understandable, he wouldn't quit and stuck to his task

John Cowen with a black and tan Lakeland from his famous strain.

223

John Cowen with his Lakeland dog, which is being carefully looked over by the judge.

throughout. At fox, he was game and would tackle his foe hard, bolting many reluctant foxes, though he wasn't hard enough to kill and could do nothing with Reynard if he refused to bolt and the place was undiggable. For this reason, Richard Bland, Harry's son-in-law and one-time Whipper-in to Hardisty, taking over as Huntsman at the Melbreak when he retired, didn't rate the dog and never brought him into his strain, for he requires a dog to kill a fox that will not bolt. However, Cowen rated him so highly that he bred all of his future stock from Turk and this famous strain has produced some incredibly good workers, particularly noted for their finding ability and, unlike Turk, their skill at finishing foxes that will not shift from an earth. As with any strain though, even the early pedigree Lakelands, not all come hard and some will stand off and bay at their quarry.

John has used pedigree stud dogs to bring into his strain, but he stresses that back then all of these dogs were worked. Harry Irving's Mac was one such dog and he was from Willie's stuff, descended from his famous Turk and possibly going back to Mick, for some of the Cowen dogs are near replicas of this dog. All of the Irving brothers got their original stock from Willie and all of their strains were infused with his stud dogs from time to time. Mac was a very hard dog and was so game that Cowen used him on his bitches, breeding both lookers and workers from him. Oregill Copper Shield, another terrier that was descended from Irving stud dogs, as well as his bitches (all of the early breeders, including Meagean, who had several puppies from Willie, Alf Johnston, Bob Gibbons, Mrs Spence and Paisley, either bought puppies from Irving, or they used his stud dogs), was also brought into Cowen's strain of working Lakeland and again this produced lookers which were also incredibly useful at work.

Cowen stressed very vociferously that all of the early Lakeland breeders worked their terriers, or had them worked for them if they could not participate themselves, which only confirms what I stated earlier in the book. Many say that they didn't work their charges, keeping their dogs scar free for the show bench, but that is nonsense. Many of the early exhibits were scarred and judges did not hold this against them at that time, even into the 1950s in some cases, except for some of the Kennel Club judges who had already lost touch with the real world of the working terrier. Cowen says that Paisley, Gibbons and even Tom Meagean were very keen badger digging men in those days and Meagean bought two terriers from John for such activities, for he found the crossbreds more suited to tackling 'Brock'. Many of the pedigree Lakelands closed with badger as they did fox and suffered badly, if they survived at all. Others would be used in shallow earths from where they could be dug out quickly, or they were used at the end of digs in order to seize their quarry in readiness of bagging it. But in the main more sensible crossbreds were used by these men, though their Lakelands were all entered to fox and served at one, or more, of the fell packs.

John knew Arthur Irving well and he stated that Art's terriers, although on the biggish side, were very good workers, with some being incredibly hard. Edmund Porter can remember his dog, Robin, serving at the Eskdale and Ennerdale when Art was Huntsman and stated that he was an excellent worker. Robin was descended from Willie's early stuff and he became a legend in his own lifetime, being used by the Wilkinson brothers to bring into their own strain, as well as many others. Cowen dogs went working at the Lochaber Foxhounds when they first began hunting the Highlands of Scotland. Johnny Richardson also borrowed Cowen dogs and they did much good work at the Melbreak for many seasons. John Cowen is an important link between modern

Lakelands and the old strains and, like Middleton and others, believes that one can produce both typey and excellent working stock. Not only does he believe this, but he has proved it, for his strain have proved incredibly game at both fox and, when it was legal, badger too.

Richard Bland

The day after the Cockermouth show I headed for Lorton and on to Millar Place, home of the Melbreak Foxhounds, in order to have a chat with Richard Bland, their long-serving Huntsman who whipped-in to the famous Harry Hardisty for seven seasons before he retired. He is married to Harry's daughter and so she has spent all of her life living at the kennels, which is situated in a most delightful spot. 'Pritch' Bland, a school yard nickname that has stuck, was born into the world of hunting, for his father kept terriers and hunted regularly with the Blencathra Foxhounds and was a close friend of both Dalton and Pepper, being a resident of the much-hunted Borrowdale Valley, where Pepper also lived, in a house close the famous 'Bowderstone'. Indeed, Pepper's prefix was 'Bowderstone', for obvious reasons.

Richard's father, Jack Bland, kept the superb Dalton strain, no doubt infused with Pepper's stock, and they served regularly at the hunt. They were quiet terriers, but were superb workers. Mist and Floss were two of his best and both served with hounds. Floss was stuck in a gryke at Doddick Ghyll, close to the hunt kennels, for a week, eventually getting out by herself, possibly after eating part of the fox that was blocking her exit.

Nuttall speaks very highly of Richard's strain and they all go back to his father's stock, infused with Johnny Richardson's Tarzan bloodlines, for 'Pritch' used this dog on his bitches, so impressed was he with Tarzan's abilities as a worker. 'Pritch' hunted with Johnny Richardson when he was a young lad and says he learnt much from him, continuing to follow the Blencathra until he took up hunt service at the Melbreak. Rock and Tramp, descended from Tarzan, were two of his best at this hunt and Judy was another outstanding worker. A fox was run in at Scor, Ennerdale, in a large rock spot and Judy was entered, in the hopes of bolting their quarry. Reynard was reluctant to shift, however, and so the bitch engaged her foe and quickly killed it, then turning her attention to a second

'Pritch' Blands'
current bitch,
Judy.

fox she found lurking in the same place. Judy killed this one also
and emerged soon after, with few serious bites. She was incredibly
sensible and such sense had been inherited from Richardson's
Tarzan. Tarzan could deal with his foxes without getting badly
mauled and Bland admires such qualities greatly, for he believes
that Lakeland terriers should be capable of killing any fox that will
not bolt.

Paddy was a white Lakeland bred from the same old Blencathra
lines and was a very good worker, though tragedy struck when he
was put in at a bad spot with quite a large drop, in a rock earth at
Thirlmere. Paddy worked his fox, but then simply disappeared.
One can only assume that he fell into a cavern and was possibly
swept away by an underground stream. Rip was another cracking
worker and she was used in some very bad places, for she had a

knack of entering such earths, finding and bolting her quarry and then getting herself out of there with little fuss.

'Pritch' was good friends with Maldwyn Williams and he says that he was a very hard walker and an excellent digger, being a good man to have around whenever a terrier needed to be dug out of an earth. Maldwyn hunted quite a bit with the Melbreak at one time and he too had some good terriers.

Bland believes that hunting with hounds is the most efficient and humane method of controlling foxes and the use of hounds is the only way to deal with a lamb worrier in the fells. He cites a case of a fox that was taking his own lambs from a field that is next to a kennel full of hounds. He loosed the hounds on discovering the remains of lambs and they took up the scent, going straight up the fell above the kennels, unkennelling their foe and killing it after a short run. What better way could there be of tackling such a troublesome predator? He agrees that in some places shooting is necessary, but he knows that some are injured and often go on to die of gangrene, or some other unpleasant illness. Hounds hunted a fox at Loweswater and all wasn't well, for it just didn't go like a healthy fox would and was soon caught. He inspected the carcass and found that Reynard had been recently shot in the leg.

Both 'Pritch' and Harry's daughter, his wife, say that Hardisty relied more on loaned terriers, rather than those he bred and quite a number were from his brother Sid, as well as Joss Hardisty who farmed at Grasmere. Jim Fleming certainly provided Hardisty with terriers and Joss may well have had stock from his neighbour too, though it is difficult to know exactly from where they came. Some of these terriers serving at the Melbreak during Harry's early days in the 1950s were Riff, Jobby, Nip and Peggy. Despite Harry having some very good terriers, Richard stuck with his old bloodlines and they served him well. One of the worst places in the Melbreak country is Brunt Bield, at Burtness Combe, being one of those places that has proved almost impossible to bolt foxes from. Most terriers fail at this fortress earth, though I know that some of Irving's stock certainly found success here, and Judy, Richard's bitch of a few years ago, was one such terrier that could bolt foxes from this place.

Betty and Tess went to ground on a fox at Combe Height, after a long hunt on Carrock Fell. They chased their fox into an old mine and then became trapped for three days, being rescued after Johnny Richardson was lowered into the mine at a depth of 180 feet. Johnny found them with a now-dead fox and Tess had broken her leg. She was suffering with gangrene, but recovered shortly afterwards. Tess belonged to Jack Bland and was on loan at the Blencathra at the time. Richard can trace his strain back to such terriers and he currently has two, a white Lakeland and a black and tan named Judy, which can kill a fox if it will not bolt. Judy is really quite typey and her good black and tan markings betray the fact that she is descended, in part, from good quality early pedigree stock belonging to Dalton and, most likely, Pepper too.

Richard 'Pritch' Bland lives and breathes hunting, hounds and terriers and he is a close link to the old school who believed in hard hunting, hard running hounds and even harder working terriers. Others confirm Bland's abilities as a terrier breeder and his stock, small in scale though it now is, has a fearsome reputation at fox. I found him to be a gentleman, in every sense of the word, and I hope the fells will continue to produce people of such character.

Colin Armstrong

After seeing 'Pritch' at Millar Place, I travelled over to the west coast of Cumbria where I was to see Colin Armstrong after I had enjoyed a brief chat with him at the Cockermouth show during the previous day. Colin was more into rabbiting than anything else at one time, but after a day out with the Blencathra his passion was aroused for a good working Lakeland terrier. He watched quite a few terrier-men handling their charges, but was most impressed with John Cowen and his famous strain. And so it was to Cowen that he looked for his first Lakeland, having previously owned Jack Russells.

Wisp was this first terrier from Cowen stock, bought directly from John, and she proved a worthwhile purchase, though she was a little slow to start. She wouldn't even look at an earth until one day when the Melbreak hounds ran a fox to ground at an old railway bank. She was fourteen months of age by this time and suddenly she went to ground, bayed at her fox and bolted it. She then became more and more useful at her traditional quarry.

Colin bred Tess out of Wisp, after putting her to Cowen's stud dog, and this bitch was often loaned to McCallister in the north-east of England, where she was regularly used in drift mines. McCallister would put her in and then sit down and wait with his lurcher at the ready. It would often take two hours or more for any action to begin, but eventually a fox would bolt and the lurcher would course and usually catch the running fox. It was a good method of fox control in a difficult country.

McCallister was out with Colin one day and the Melbreak pack when hounds split. Colin went after one part, while Harry Hardisty went after the other. Colin found hounds marking a bad place and Wisp was put in. She engaged her quarry while her master dug on as best he could, finally being forced to crawl in among the rock-piles where he could just reach his bitch. It was pitch-black in there and Colin grabbed his dog and passed it out to McCallister, but he cringed and slunk away, reluctant to get hold, for it was the fox Colin had hold of, not his bitch!

Hounds ran yet another fox to ground at yet another bad place and Colin entered Wisp, for she could find in any borran earth. However, when Harry came up he said that no foxes ever bolt from this place and so, this being late in the day, he took hounds back to kennel. Wisp was still to ground, so Colin left Joe Bell and one or two others at the spot, while he assisted Harry. On returning later,

Harry Hardisty and Melbreak Hounds, with Colin Armstrong just behind (early 1970s).

230

Wisp had emerged, but only after bolting her fox. It was too late though, for there were no hounds to do the catching!

A red pup bred by John Cowen once caught Colin's eye and he put his name on it straight away. Hounds had met at the Cowen farmstead and later both fox and hounds came running through the yard. The red pup was loose and, for some reason, hounds killed it. So he bought a red bitch from the same litter instead. She grew into a superb looker and won everywhere, much to the annoyance of Jessie, John's wife, who had also wanted to keep the bitch. There was quite a bit of friction at the Cowen homestead for a while after this and so Colin bred from the bitch and kindly gave her back to Jessie, much to John's relief!

Colin admires a good working border and he has much admiration for the strain bred by Joe Dobinson of the Zetland Hunt in

Colin
Armstrong
with Sandy
('the Worm').

231

particular; the same terrierman who was great friends with Buck, Breay, Akerigg and so on, and whose dogs were used to bring into such breeding programmes, for the Dobinson border terriers have produced superb workers over several generations. Colin purchased a border dog from Dobinson named Bragg. The Zetland hounds ran a fox into a stickpile and Bragg, although only seven and a half months of age, was keen to get started, for Dobinson's strain have a reputation as early starters, one of his breeding being keen to go at just six months, so Joe asked Colin to try him. He went like wildfire and quickly bolted a fox, with hounds going away on it, although Bragg did not follow his quarry out, but remained below. Joe and Colin were then forced to dig down through the awkward tangle of dead branches and by the time they reached Bragg he had killed the second fox. Some achievement, this, for such a young dog.

When out with the Melbreak, hounds chased a fox across a river and it went to ground in a drain out on the pasture, not far from Cockermouth. Bragg went in and sometime later the water running out turned very muddy indeed, with bits of fur beginning to show. And then the tail end of Bragg began emerging and he was soon out, drawing a now-dead fox.

Sandy is one of the best Colin has ever had and she is bred out of an Irish-bred black Lakeland and Edmund Porter's stud dog, Red, bred from Edmund's Ben. Sandy is untypey and is known as 'the worm' because of being capable of getting anywhere. She has a poor coat too and would certainly do badly at shows, yet she is one of the best workers Colin has ever owned. Tess is related to Sandy, out of the same black bitch, but sired by Nip, a dog from Maurice Bell's Britt line. Tess is red and is another very good worker. She is also typey and Colin won at Rydal with her, which is only open to terriers working at one, or more, of the fell packs.

Sandy and Tess went to ground on fox at a keepered spot in Scotland and Colin successfully dug them and their quarry out, but the two bitches returned to ground and found yet another, which they killed below. However, the diggers couldn't reach them and so the pair of earth dogs spent the night below and were got out the next day.

Peggy is another of Armstrong's terriers and she is out of a Cowen bitch and a Tyson dog bred down from his famous Rocky line. Sam is another typey terrier bred down from plenty of pedigree stuff and he is out of Peggy and a Jed Forest Hunt dog

One of Colin's good quality black and tans with obvious Welsh
markings inherited from early Lakeland terriers.

owned by Gillespie. Colin's terriers generally go back to Cowen
stuff in the main, with some Tyson blood thrown in. All are
worked, though Colin is also keen on showing terriers and has
enjoyed much success at exhibiting. Like Cowen, he believes that
smart terriers can also be superb workers and his stock certainly
prove such theories to be correct. Mac is yet another dog of similar
breeding, sired by Sam, and he too is an out and out worker. A fox
was found in a huge drain and Mac engaged and quickly killed

Sam, descended from pedigree stock and a superb worker.

his foe, despite the drain being nearly full of water.

Fudge is another of Armstrong's working Lakelands and he is red in colour, being by a Cowen dog out of a black bitch. Fudge is incredibly hard and never bays, for he simply closes with his quarry and kills, or draws it. In fact, Colin assures me that he has either killed, or drawn, every fox he has been to. The keepers in Scotland have nicknamed him 'the mincer', due to his eagerness to kill his quarry. If the keepers want a fox killed and not bolted, which is most desirable in many instances, then they always ask Colin to put Fudge in. He has also done quite a bit of work with the Melbreak pack and is certain death to any fox that won't bolt. Although ten years of age at the time of writing, he is still working and still killing and drawing foxes, though I suspect that his career will be coming close to its end by the time this book is released. Trim is a daughter of Fudge and she is quite a typey red bitch that looks very much like the type produced by Anthony Barker's famous Rock. She is a superb finder and has been used in deep borrans with hounds, whenever a fox needed bolting from a bad spot.

Mac was loose one day up in Scotland and he put two foxes up in the undergrowth, catching and killing the first and then going after the second. Colin was just in time to see Reynard turn and face Mac as he went after it and his terrier had it and quickly killed it. It was Mac who was to ground when Colin dug a fox that managed to get hold of him by the mouth, clamping both jaws over his nose and mouth and holding them tight shut. By the time Colin uncovered the dog and got the fox off him, he was on his last legs, having almost suffocated.

Colin bought a black and tan Tyson bred dog from a lad in Carlisle who occasionally worked it with the Blencathra Foxhounds, for a mere £100. Having his new purchase with him, Colin then went out with the Melbreak Hunt and they ran a fox in at Whinlatter Pass. A fox was bolted and another was in, which they dug to. Joe Bell asked Colin to try his new dog and he entered well, getting stuck into his fox and finally bolting it, though it turned and went back in. A black bitch was then put in and the fox dug out.

At another spot, a very bad place, Merle, a terrier belonging to John Jackson, was entered at 2pm and engaged his fox, but it wasn't for bolting. A dig commenced and they didn't break through until 7pm, with the fox in an awkward spot from where it could not be reached. In this situation a harder dog is needed and the black and tan was put in. He drew it out and killed it very quickly indeed. Some of Colin's stock enter very early indeed and Nell, his red bitch, went to her first fox at just six months of age. After this she was put to a few young foxes being dug out for keepers, or on lambing calls, and she killed some of them, never looking back from then on.

One August bank holiday Colin won the Championship at Keswick show and then headed off to Joe Dobinson's for a week of

Cyril Tyson's Rocky, sire of good working and looking stock.

hunting with the Zetland. A fox was run in at a railway bank leading to a quarry and Rip, Colin's youngster, a son of the bitch given back to Jessie Cowen, was put in alongside a Jack Russell. After fifteen minutes or so snuffling could be heard and the Russell emerged soon afterwards, but Rip was gone. A little later the fox finally bolted and there was Rip, hanging onto his foe as it dragged him across the ground at speed, before finally shedding its load. Rip was then left with Joe for that season and he bolted fifty-six foxes during that time, while the terrierman went about his earth-stopping duties. Sadly, Rip was later stolen out of Colin's van whilst he was attending a show.

The sire of Wisp, Colin's first terrier, became stuck to ground after a fox had been put in by hounds at Embleton quarry. Reynard wouldn't bolt and Cowen's dog engaged his foe, but fell silent soon after. Colin helped rescue the dog and was lowered over the edge of the quarry on ropes, where he dug into the cliff face. Reluctantly, the terrier was left in overnight and digging operations commenced the next morning. A large crack had appeared above the site of the dig and so operations became far more dangerous. However, the dog and the dead fox were eventually reached and a successful rescue was effected, for which Colin received an award from the Fell and Moorland Working Terrier Club. Colin later dug another fox out of that same quarry and his terrier ripped some of its claws off trying to get right up to its fox, which was in rather a tight spot with unyielding rocks surrounding it.

Red, the dog Colin bought from Edmund Porter, by his dog Ben, killed the first fox it ever saw while out with the Melbreak. Reynard had gone to ground at Karlin Knott, at a large rock earth, after being hard-pushed by hounds, and Red was put in. He bolted one and hounds were away after that, but another was skulking underground and Red turned his attention to this and finished it below. Red had a promising career ahead of him, but, sadly, was badly injured, smashing his leg and hip joint, when he fell at a rock spot. Colin had won Lowther puppy champion with him and he was developing into a superb worker, but with only three legs now in use he was forced to retire the dog and use him at stud.

One of his outcross stud dogs was one belonging to Willie Stevenson of the Ullswater Foxhounds. This terrier was part Bedlington bred and was sired by a terrier from the Langdales that

A good head is desirable on a Lakeland terrier.

ran with cur dogs and sometimes killed foxes around the farm. Willie's terrier killed three foxes in one day's hunting, all having been run to ground by hounds at separate locations, so Colin brought him into his strain. He cannot remember the name of the dog, but was most impressed with his working ability.

Lakeland terriers have been bred to be narrow, and for good reason. The Zetland ran a fox into a quarry face and Joe put his border terrier in, but, being a little broad in the shoulders, he couldn't quite get up to his fox, so Colin was asked to try his red Lakeland bitch. Being rather a typey terrier, Colin had received a bit of stick from some of the followers who had called her a 'show dog', which is said to imply that a dog won't work. However, the bitch entered eagerly and soon found her quarry, being able to reach it due to much narrower shoulders. The fox bolted and the sight was spectacular, for it jumped from twenty feet up in the quarry face, landed on the ground and was away, with hounds soon in pursuit. Hounds ran another fox in that day and the same lads were at the spot, so Joe asked Colin to put his bitch in yet again. She went to her quarry and remained with it while digging operations progressed. The bitch was finally reached and she had finished her fox by the time they had uncovered her. 'Not bad for a show dog', said Joe, within hearing distance of those who had mocked her! Why some believe that typey terriers cannot work is beyond me. It is just as ridiculous as saying that an ugly terrier cannot work.

Colin Armstrong breeds game terriers that are descended from the early pedigree Lakeland stock that was among the gamest in the world. They have the old pedigree characteristics still, such as narrow fronts and the typical box-shape, in the main, though some are also borderish in appearance too. He believes that a Lakeland should be capable of killing a stubborn fox and most of his are, though some are more 'gentle' in nature and will stand off their quarry and bay. He tries not to enter too early and those that go before twelve months of age usually do so by accident, slipping their collar or such like, or maybe getting into an earth he didn't know was there before he could stop it. He now does much of his terrier work in Scotland and Ireland, but he has fond memories of his times spent with the Melbreak Foxhounds.

Gary Middleton

Gary has been breeding, working and exhibiting Lakeland terriers for over half a century now and he has forgotten more about them than most people will ever get to learn, or experience. He is old enough to have enjoyed the glory days when no restrictions were put on terrier work and so his strain, based on the Barker and Wilkinson bloodlines, which include many of the early dogs such as Irving's Turk and the Egton Lakelands, have been fully tested on all large British quarry. He has worked them below ground, but also above too, flushing foxes to guns, or, indeed, lurchers, with his earth dogs. Most are very typey indeed and his wins are too numerous to recount, having won all over the country at all of the big venues such as the Great Yorkshire and Lowther shows (for more information on Middleton's dogs, see *The Middleton Strain of Working Terrier*, Seán Frain, Pennine Publishing, 2006).

Gary was once asked out on a lambing call at Cartmel Fell and the farmer had tried everywhere he could think of, but just couldn't find the fox that was taking his livestock. After chatting with the shepherd and realising that all of the earths had indeed been

Gary Middleton (centre) with Matt (left) and Seamus Erwin and a bitch from his strain, which works Fox and Mink in Ireland with her owner, Matt.

checked, Gary decided to just go and have a look at a burrow from where he had ferreted scores of rabbits over the years. His inkling proved correct, for there, outside the burrow, which led under a large stone wall, was the remains of prey and several smelly scats (fox droppings) – a sure indicator of occupation. His bitch, Tiny, was put in and Gary then dug a vixen and cubs out of that place and the lamb worrying stopped abruptly. The farmer was rather taken aback, however, especially because the earth was only three hundred yards from his farm!

Gary was out with the North Lonsdale Foxhounds when George Ridley was Huntsman and a fox was run into a drain at Gummershow. Cyril Breay was also out that day and his little red bitch, Tig, one of his best, was tried. She entered the drain, scrambled up it for some sixty yards or so and found her fox, which wasn't for bolting. Digging operations commenced and the combatants were reached soon after. This fox had been hunted for quite some time and distance and wasn't for facing hounds again and so Tig had taken quite a mauling that day. However, Reynard now took to his heels and was caught soon afterwards. Gary returned to this drain about two years later and entered his dog, Chip, after he had marked it as occupied. His ranting and raving signalled a find and shortly after a large white badger bolted from the earth and ran to a huge sett nearby, into which it rapidly disappeared.

Gary was asked to flush foxes to guns in the Kentmere valley and he gladly obliged, taking Lucky, one of his best fox-catching lurchers, and Rip, a red dog bred from Wilkinson's Rock, along with him. He started at one end of the valley and was to drive the gorse towards the guns. However, there was a decided lack of foxes until, at last, scent was detected. Lucky marked an earth and Rip was put in. He found his fox and quickly bolted it, with Gary hoping to drive it through the gorse in the direction of the waiting guns. However, things didn't go exactly according to plan, as Lucky quickly caught the fox before it could reach the certain safety of the dense undergrowth. That was the only fox in the Kentmere valley that day and the guns were not amused when Middleton turned up carrying an already dead fox (though the farmers were quite content!).

When Brian Fisher travelled up to Gary's place in order to buy a terrier named Pick, from the Middleton strain, he asked if he could see the dog at work. Gary took him out, despite there being six inches of snow on the ground, and they soon came across fresh fox tracks, which they followed into the Winster valley. The earth was situated on a rough fellside and Pick marked it. He entered eagerly and soon engaged his foe, which he had finished by the time they had dug him out, this being a shallow place. Gary Middleton much prefers fox-killing Lakelands, for he believes these are of the traditional type, though he doesn't mind if his bitches stand off and bay.

Sid Wilkinson with his famous Rock, ancestor of the Middleton strain.

Gary once sold his bitch, Rags, to a keeper at Shap Fell named John Hodgkinson. He was well known for his ability to catch foxes by setting snares on sheep trods and he had upwards of one hundred ferrets, which he fed on the carcasses of the foxes he took, either with terrier and gun, or with snares. One day he was approaching one of his snares and it had successfully caught a fox, which Rags was running towards, struggling through the heather. As she was doing so, a golden eagle dropped from the sky and picked her up, carrying her off to goodness knows where. Thinking quickly, despite the shock, Hodgkinson fired both barrels into the air and the eagle dropped its prize, which landed safely in the heather. She was in a bit of a mess, however, and needed eighteen stitches to put her right. For anyone who finds this hard to believe, it is nevertheless true and the incident was reported in the *Westmorland Gazette*. Gordon Shaw is another keeper who has Middleton-bred earth dogs and Gary was out with him one day, right out on the moors above Shap, when a black, swirling mist suddenly descended on them. They had walked for miles out into the middle of nowhere, among some of the wildest and bleakest country in the north, in order to check a fox earth that sometimes held. However, they were rather disappointed at such a wasted journey, as Reynard wasn't home that day and then the mist came in. Gary, thinking Gordon would know the ground well enough to get them out of there, looked to him for guidance, but he simply shrugged his shoulders and said they would have to wait until the mist lifted, which it did about two hours later!

Gary likes to see a harsh jacket on a Lakeland and he prefers a bit of leg, as well as narrow shoulders and the chest must be spannable. When badger digging was legal he engaged fully in this activity, removing them for farmers and releasing them unharmed elsewhere, and so he preferred a bigger terrier then. Nowadays, however, with even terrier work to fox being limited in England and Wales, he prefers a smaller earth dog of maybe twelve or thirteen inches, though he continues to breed for good type, as well as working ability, which can, he has proved time and time again, go hand in hand. He likes a large head, with strong, punishing jaws and his strain are famous for having 'a 'ead like a brick', as Gary puts it. Wilkinson's Rock was his ideal terrier and Barker's Rock the ultimate working terrier. Wilk's Rock was a son of Barker's famous red dog and so Gary has bred from this line ever since the days when Sid's Rock was standing at stud in the Ullswater country.

His tips regarding breeding are worthy of note. He has his bitch mated on either the thirteenth or fourteenth day after bleeding begins and puts a stud to her only the once, so that he knows the exact date on which she is due, just in case of any complications. A week before she is due to whelp, he puts fresh bedding in her box and this allows her to prepare the nest for the imminent arrival of her puppies. He uses clean straw, though newspaper is just as good, and plenty of it, if a terrier is kennelled outside, is recommended. If the bitch produces enough milk, he will wean at four weeks, though three weeks is acceptable, especially if their mother is drying up. For the first week of weaning Gary's wife, Ruth, liquidises a complete puppy food, but after that they have it as normal. The tails are docked at three days of age and in some countries this must be done by a qualified vet, leaving just over half of the tail on. Dew claws are left on as these help them scale rocks – an essential appendage in fell country in particular. He will avoid breeding from a terrier with a serious fault, in order to breed that fault out of the strain, and, like many of the older generation of fell-hunters, he will only breed from Lakeland dogs capable of finishing a reluctant fox, and his bitches must be game at fox, though they are allowed to be more 'gentle', baying at, rather than closing with, their quarry.

George Norman was out in the hills one day when he came across Gary Middleton and Jimmy Monteith as they were digging on a steep, rough hillside. Gary's well known dog, Rex, was to ground and he had already killed one fox and had then moved onto another, which Gary was now digging towards. Rex was a son of Wilkinson's Rock, out of a red bitch named Trixie, and was *the* hardest terrier Middleton has ever seen at work. They uncovered Rex and a now very dead fox, though George asked about the other still inside. Gary stated that it was dead, but there was some doubt among the group, it has to be said, so another terrier was put in and it began baying. Another dig was started and soon afterwards the other fox was uncovered. It was stone dead, just as Gary had said, and the terrier was baying because the carcass was still warm and the scent strong, but Rex had finished both foxes in fine style and came out of the encounter, typically, without serious injury.

Gary Middleton produces some of the best looking Lakeland terriers in the world and they have a rich heritage of working in the fells, as well as throughout the country and beyond, being found in Ireland, America and Canada. They look well, work well and are, in fact, near replicas of the early Lakeland so beloved by the Lakeland Terrier Association members such as Paisley, Irving, Farrer and Dalton. Indeed, the Paisley brothers lived long enough to see Middleton's strain developing and they even bought terriers from him. Truly, the other LTA founders and members would, I am sure, approve of the strain bred by Gary Middleton of Kendal.

Appendix I
Bibliography

Cassells New Book of the Dog, Published c.1910

Hark For'ard The Life of a Lakeland Huntsman, ed. Anthony Chapman, Helm Press

Hutchinsons Popular & Illustrated Dog Encyclopaedia, Published 1934

The Middleton Strain of Working Terrier Sean Frain, Pennine Publishing, 2006

The Patterdale Terrier, Seán Frain, Swan Hill Press, 2004

The Fell Terrier, D. Brian Plummer, Boydell Press, 1983

Maud Irving with Lakeland terrier pups – among them future workers at the Melbreak.

Appendix II

Family Trees of Celebrated Dogs

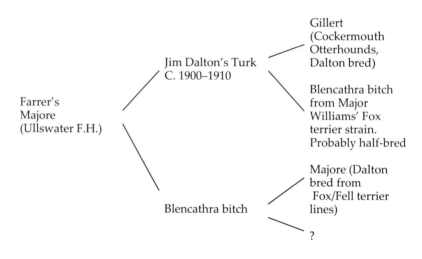

Farrer's Majore (Ullswater F.H.)
  ├─ Jim Dalton's Turk C. 1900–1910
  │   ├─ Gillert (Cockermouth Otterhounds, Dalton bred)
  │   └─ Blencathra bitch from Major Williams' Fox terrier strain. Probably half-bred
  └─ Blencathra bitch
       ├─ Majore (Dalton bred from Fox/Fell terrier lines)
       └─ ?

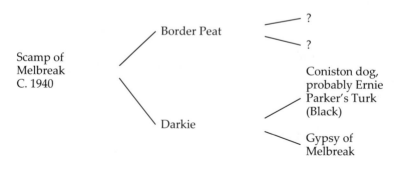

Scamp of Melbreak C. 1940
  ├─ Border Peat
  │   ├─ ?
  │   └─ ?
  └─ Darkie
       ├─ Coniston dog, probably Ernie Parker's Turk (Black)
       └─ Gypsy of Melbreak

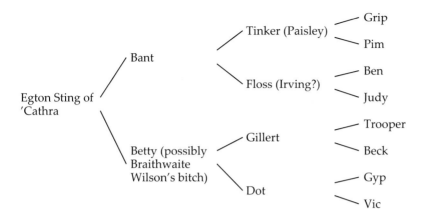

Egton Sting of 'Cathra
- Bant
  - Tinker (Paisley)
    - Grip
    - Pim
  - Floss (Irving?)
    - Ben
    - Judy
- Betty (possibly Braithwaite Wilson's bitch)
  - Gillert
    - Trooper
    - Beck
  - Dot
    - Gyp
    - Vic

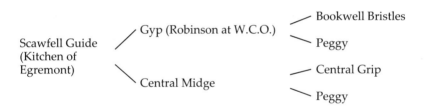

Scawfell Guide (Kitchen of Egremont)
- Gyp (Robinson at W.C.O.)
  - Bookwell Bristles
  - Peggy
- Central Midge
  - Central Grip
  - Peggy

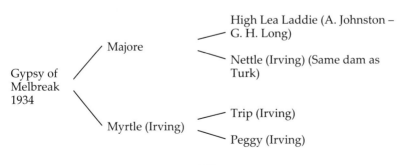

Gypsy of Melbreak 1934
- Majore
  - High Lea Laddie (A. Johnston – G. H. Long)
  - Nettle (Irving) (Same dam as Turk)
- Myrtle (Irving)
  - Trip (Irving)
  - Peggy (Irving)

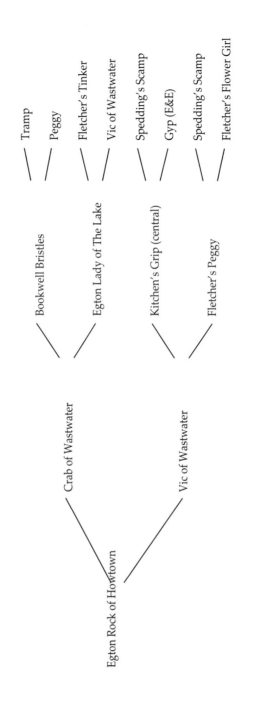

Tramp

Peggy

Fletcher's Tinker

Vic of Wastwater

Spedding's Scamp

Gyp (E&E)

Spedding's Scamp

Fletcher's Flower Girl

Bookwell Bristles

Egton Lady of The Lake

Kitchen's Grip (central)

Fletcher's Peggy

Crab of Wastwater

Vic of Wastwater

Egton Rock of Howtown

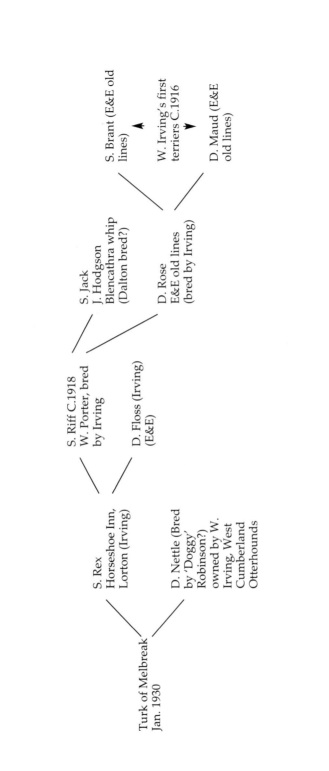

Turk of Melbreak
Jan. 1930

S. Rex
Horseshoe Inn,
Lorton (Irving)

D. Nettle (Bred
by 'Doggy'
Robinson?)
owned by W.
Irving, West
Cumberland
Otterhounds

S. Riff C.1918
W. Porter, bred
by Irving

D. Floss (Irving)
(E&E)

S. Jack
J. Hodgson
Blencathra whip
(Dalton bred?)

D. Rose
E&E old lines
(bred by Irving)

S. Brant (E&E old
lines)

W. Irving's first
terriers C.1916

D. Maud (E&E
old lines)

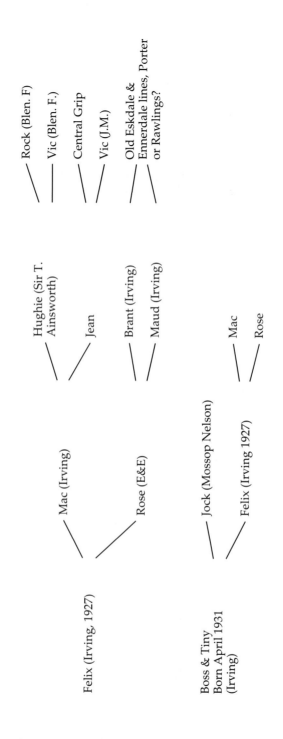

Felix (Irving, 1927)

Mac (Irving)

Rose (E&E)

Hughie (Sir T. Ainsworth)

Jean

Brant (Irving)

Maud (Irving)

Rock (Blen. F)

Vic (Blen. F.)

Central Grip

Vic (J.M.)

Old Eskdale &
Ennerdale lines, Porter
or Rawlings?

Boss & Tiny
Born April 1931
(Irving)

Jock (Mossop Nelson)

Felix (Irving 1927)

Mac

Rose

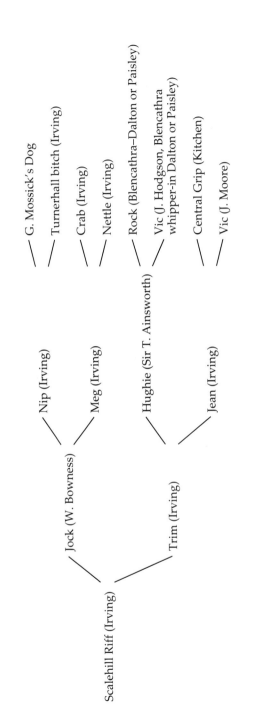

Scalehill Riff (Irving)

Jock (W. Bowness)

Nip (Irving)

G. Mossick's Dog

Turnerhall bitch (Irving)

Meg (Irving)

Crab (Irving)

Nettle (Irving)

Trim (Irving)

Hughie (Sir T. Ainsworth)

Rock (Blencathra–Dalton or Paisley)

Vic (J. Hodgson, Blencathra
whipper-in Dalton or Paisley)

Jean (Irving)

Central Grip (Kitchen)

Vic (J. Moore)

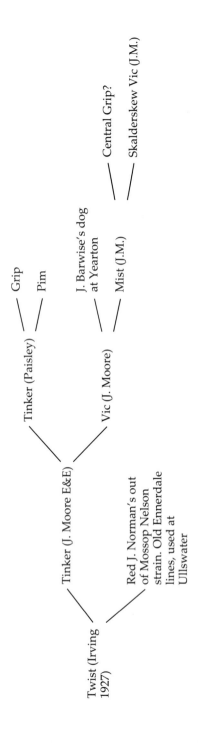

Twist (Irving 1927)

Tinker (J. Moore E&E)

Red J. Norman's out of Mossop Nelson strain. Old Ennerdale lines, used at Ullswater

Tinker (Paisley)

Vic (J. Moore)

Grip

Pim

J. Barwise's dog at Yearton

Mist (J.M.)

Central Grip?

Skalderskew Vic (J.M.)

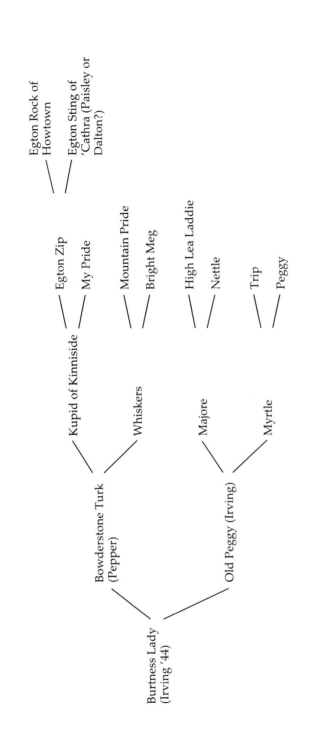

Egton Rock of Howtown

Egton Sting of 'Cathra (Paisley or Dalton?)

Egton Zip

My Pride

Mountain Pride

Bright Meg

High Lea Laddie

Nettle

Trip

Peggy

Kupid of Kinniside

Whiskers

Majore

Myrtle

Bowderstone Turk (Pepper)

Old Peggy (Irving)

Burtness Lady (Irving '44)

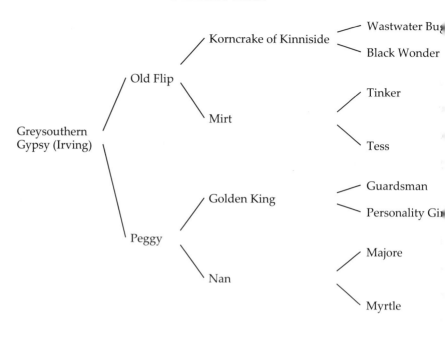

Greysouthern Gypsy (Irving)
- Old Flip
  - Korncrake of Kinniside
    - Wastwater Bu[g]
    - Black Wonder
  - Mirt
    - Tinker
    - Tess
- Peggy
  - Golden King
    - Guardsman
    - Personality Gi[rl]
  - Nan
    - Majore
    - Myrtle

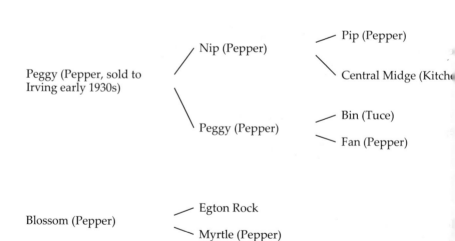

Peggy (Pepper, sold to Irving early 1930s)
- Nip (Pepper)
  - Pip (Pepper)
  - Central Midge (Kitch[en])
- Peggy (Pepper)
  - Bin (Tuce)
  - Fan (Pepper)

Blossom (Pepper)
- Egton Rock
- Myrtle (Pepper)